Commercial Property Conversions

Profit From Turning Old Commercial Property Into Residential Goldmines

Mark Homer & Glenn Delve

Commercial Property Conversions by Mark Homer & Glenn Delve
www.progressiveproperty.co.uk

Design by Luke Bunting
Research by Mark Homer & Glenn Delve
© Copyright 2018 Mark Homer & Glenn Delve

Note for Librarians: A cataloguing record for this book is available from Library and Archives Canada at www.collectionscanada.gc.ca/a-z-index/index-e.html

Printed in Peterborough, Cambridgeshire, UK ISBN: 978-1909846-74-6

Published by Progressive Publishing
Progressive House
Units 8, 9, 10 & 11
Cygnet Park, Forder Way, Hampton Peterborough, PE7 8GX

Email: hello@progressiveproperty.co.uk
Twitter: @robandmark
Facebook: www.facebook.com/ProgressivePropertyInvestment
Instagram: www.instagram.com/progressiveproperty

Contents

PART ONE: THE OVERVIEW

PART TWO: THE 'GO LARGE' COMMERCIAL CONVERSION SYSTEM

PART 3: THE WAY FORWARD

PART ONE: THE OVERVIEW
Chapter 1: Introduction

Glenn's Story

I'm not sure how something so epic could have started from a simple webinar, but it did. Certainly, life had 'set me up' for the webinar, but it was the webinar that took a life that, financially, was crashing spectacularly and about to reach its inevitable sad conclusion, instead sending me down a path that was going to lead to a new business start-up that was described by a seasoned FTSE business leader and coach to senior partners at Deloitte as the most spectacular he had seen in 30 years of business. I had been stuck in a rut, with seemingly no way out of a cash crisis almost entirely of my own making, when a road was revealed that suddenly made such sense.

It was 2013 when Rob Moore of Progressive Property, a company I had previously had a relatively unsuccessful dalliance with, was holding a webinar. I don't even remember what it was called, or why I tuned in. I had subscribed to many webinars in the past and actually attended very few of them, usually letting 'life' get in the way and choosing instead to watch television (vegging out), drink beer or very occasionally dredging up the energy to spend time with my two sons, who back then were about 8 and 10. Something about this webinar must have grabbed me because, as I recall, I did on this occasion at least half listen, with the webinar playing from my laptop whilst I watched TV, at least initially.

It was the content of the webinar that grabbed me – or at least the main headline, which I remember as 'do bigger deals and get paid much more money'. The reason that struck a chord was simple... I needed big money, and fast!

I had been in debt since I was 16. Even at that early age, my financial habits were proving poor. I had a bank account that was already so regularly delinquent that a bank manager called Peter Ridsdale took time out of his busy diary to warn me of the path I was headed down, and the ruin that awaited me. He offered a portent of what was to come, and I ignored him.

Even securing my dream job as fast jet navigator in the Royal Air Force served only to reinforce my poor money habits when, now aged [date I attended Cottesmore], a wise young trainee pilot I flew with occasionally observed on a picture he was signing for me that "insecurity is the key to a bad bank balance."

Despite all the signs pointing to eventual financial ruin, I continued to slightly outspend my income on a consistent basis. The power of compounding was working, but against me. I was one of those people who would consolidate debt onto one card, promising to myself that I would cut up the rest of my cards and never use them again, but always returning to them when I 'needed' to buy something, like an alcoholic returning to the bar. After leaving the military I entered into business, gradually earning greater and greater sums of money, culminating in a senior executive role with the usual associated six-figure income. But I continued to enhance my standard of living, buying things I couldn't afford to with money I didn't have, ever increasing my borrowing. Eventually, I would be made redundant at the age of 47, owing £140K in consumer debt made up of credit cards and a consolidation loan. Suddenly, with no income and a debt burden that cost £3000 per month to service, I had a very real and pressing problem.

Not only did I need money fast, I also needed big money.

When I was made redundant, my initial response was typical of many executives in similar positions: I rang an executive search company. I started looking for another job to replace the income I had just lost. However, I realised that another job would just prolong the agony. I would probably continue to build up debt, borrowing money to pay the servicing costs of the debt I already had whilst still struggling to maintain the standard of living my family had come to expect. I am convinced that had I gone down that route, I would have eventually gone bankrupt, probably when I retired!

But then came the webinar. Something deep down was crying out, barely audible at this stage but nevertheless not something that could be ignored. A nagging sense that there might be something in this. Do bigger deals, get paid a lot more. Bigger deals, paid more. Somehow, it got through to me and something clicked that night. More amazingly, my wife was supportive. Fully aware of our very tenuous existence, she confirmed my suspicion that if I was ever going to pursue my dream of making my way in property, this was the time to try. If it worked out then we would finally be free of the modern form of slavery we call consumer debt. If it didn't, frankly we would be no worse off... if we didn't change something soon, bankruptcy was coming one way or another, better now while we're still young enough to recover.

Do bigger deals... but how? I had the advantage of having overseen a large project in a previous executive role. During that project, I had learnt two crucial truths; those together with the information from Rob's webinar were about to form an alchemy that has proved to be a financial triumph.

In 2004, in an odd set of circumstances, I had arrived at The Rose Bowl (now The Ageas Bowl), home of Hampshire Cricket, as a business consultant.

When I left the RAF, I had wanted to go into business. However, no-one in my family had ever been in business before, so I was given some very wise advice: "get a franchise and find one in a business you are passionate about." I enjoyed playing golf and, accordingly, this seemed a good fit, as there was an exciting golf store franchise called Nevada Bobs Golf Superstores. Initially starting with a store in Cosham, Portsmouth, we did well enough that the franchise operator offered us the failing corporate store in Eastleigh, Hampshire. This was exciting – it was reputed to be the largest golf store in the UK at over 6000 sq. ft.

We rev___ped the store and created 'store in-store' concession areas with the largest manufacturers, such as Callaway, Taylor Made and Ping. We saw turnover increase 250% in 3 years and the store consequently moved into profitability. We became known and attracted attention, although some of it was unwelcome; we had eight burglaries in five years!

Despite this success, we could see the golf retail model changing again, ironically to slightly smaller 'superstores', but in areas of natural footfall, such as golf ranges. We began to look for opportunities to open satellite stores in such locations. So, when The Rose Bowl announced plans for a 60-bay, two-tier golf driving range, I sought them out.

After several discussions, I was appointed as a consultant to the team looking at the opportunity. Ironically, in the months that followed, not only did The Rose Bowl decide that the golf range was not the right use of their land, my own golf business went into receivership following a burglary that, for technical reasons, it appeared our insurance company wouldn't recompense. Going into the winter period with insufficient cash resources to replenish the stock and get through the winter, I had little choice but to call in the administrator.

By this time, though, in a strange twist of fate, The Rose Bowl had identified me as their next Group Managing Director to take them into a bright new future. Thus it was that I ended up at a cricket club knowing nothing about cricket and about to oversee a major project that would teach me the two things that, along with Rob's webinar, would change my life forever – and could change yours. Let's slowly pull back the curtain on those two aspects that are going to be so important to you.

By the time we had finally overcome all the hurdles and achieved planning for the scheme, which had required many tests and surveys, many weeks of work, hundreds of thousands of pounds in costs and having survived two judicial reviews, we found ourselves in the middle of the worst financial crash in living memory in 2008.

Having navigated our way through the planning system to get the consent we needed, we had climbed one mountain, and simply qualified ourselves to climb a bigger one!

I ended up heading a team tasked with building two new spectator stands with hospitality, catering, welfare and seating facilities for about 5000 spectators in each stand, a new 18-hole golf course, and a 175-room, five-star Hilton hotel that provided all the usual facilities associated with the brand, plus a whole lot more: a full spa, a golf clubhouse, conference and banqueting to include the largest room in Hampshire without pillars that could host a banquet for up to [500] guests, and hidden routes for television cabling for all the sports cameras that cover International events. Additionally, all of the rooms facing the pitch were also designed to either become hospitality boxes or some of the myriad of media facilities required, such as a press room for up to 100 journalists, TV studios, radio commentary boxes, camera positions, green room or spectator bars and welfare facilities. The sum of this grand undertaking was £50m, and it was being led by someone with no background in property, construction, design, sport or indeed seemingly any related discipline other than general management.

Furthermore, a humble cricket club, with little funds and no history of making a profit, was trying to build a speculative £50m development, outside of a major metropolis in the middle of a market in meltdown, and with no certainty of outcome with regard to either international cricket or the hotel trade. It wasn't a business plan from heaven... but it was all that we had, and I had to lead the team tasked with delivering the vision. And, in a surprising manner, it formed the foundations for my later foray into turning commercial property into residential goldmines!

The Rose Bowl opened the doors of its new spectator stands in 2011, the hotel opened in [2014], and the golf course welcomed its first members in 2017.

During the course of that amazing achievement, two major ingredients of property development had revealed themselves. Two facts that would ultimately lead to my journey into commercial conversions.

The first secret I discovered was that if you solve an investor's issue, they will fund your development.

In 2008, once we had secured planning for our model test match ground, the banks had scurried for the hills and all our commercial partners' funding streams had dried up. All of our promised funding had disappeared, and after three years of striving to get planning consent for our developments, we were left facing failure.

Your role is to have the vision and communicate it. It is no good to the world if you have a vision for a wonderful conversion but you can't communicate it. If your joint venture (JV) investor doesn't get your vision or they don't believe in it, it is very unlikely they are going to put the money in to the deal, however much they are attracted by the returns.

In the middle of the world's worst financial crisis, we needed £50m. Someone had to be mad enough to put £50m into a cricket ground that had never made a profit, had little money and was being run by someone who had never built a hotel, never built spectator stands and who had never constructed a golf course. But we had such passion and volition around the vision, about the opportunity that the ECB had given us to build the first model test match ground, that in many ways was even better than Lords, that the local authority bought into it. They wanted the trophy asset that we had sold, and they weren't prepared to let it go.

We had created a vision that solved a number of issues for the progressive and innovative Eastleigh Borough Council (EBC). EBC saw an opportunity that would bring jobs and economy to the local area and put the borough on the map, with high-profile international events seen by millions of people around the world. After much negotiation, a solution was found that offered EBC a sound financial return whilst enabling an exciting, high-quality development that put Eastleigh on the global stage.

Everything we had conceived got built. The hotel is a five-star Hilton Hotel with the conference facility, the spa and a restaurant, which is the first in the country for a new concept by Ian Botham, called Beefy's. All the rooms at the front turn into hospitality boxes, except those that are designed as media facilities. Everything we conceived was built, because the local authority had seen the vision.

We solved our investors' issue, and they funded our deal. Lesson 1.

The second secret that was revealed was that all the expertise required to deliver large projects is available for hire!

This second secret revealed itself as we sought to deliver on our promised vision. To bring a £50m vision to fruition required a level and breadth of knowledge that is simply impossible for one person to embody. The professional team was a plethora of highly educated, trained professionals, each of which was an expert in their given field and had probably forgotten more about their subject than I could ever learn. We needed architects, lawyers, surveyors, valuers, designers, brokers, insurers, project managers, quantity surveyors, engineers and trades such as plumbers, electricians, carpenters, ground workers, scaffolders, painters, furniture makers, [add to this list]. But they were ALL available at an hourly or contract rate. My role was simply to hold onto the vision and make decisions based on the information provided by the experts who took us closer to fulfilling the reality of the dream. My days were a collection of meetings with various experts that would lay out different issues, options for solutions and recommendations for proceeding. If one was prepared to listen, accord respect for their knowledge and experience and funnel that in the direction that met our expectations, the result was always going to be spectacular. Furthermore, I can safely say that I actually undertook a tiny fraction of the work needed to design, finance, build and commission the awesome facility now called The Ageas Bowl.

You see, bigger projects come with bigger budgets. If you allow, for instance, 10% for professional fees on a £1m or a £10m or a £50m build, can you see how you have the ability, the facility, to hire whatever professionals you need appropriate to that job. On the £50m project at The Rose Bowl, our legal bills alone were in excess of £2m. I remember when I saw the estimate for what the project manager was going to cost – I thought there must be a typo, I thought he had put an extra 0 on the end. But the professionals are costed into the project, the people that you need are costed in, and the bigger the project is, the more money is available – the amount is roughly 10%. Like most parameters, there will always be exceptions to the rule, but generally it can go down to 7% or up to 13%, depending on the complexity of the project. It is simply built into the cost of the project.

The first thing I learnt was that I didn't need to know anything other than this: could I see the end result? Could I hold it in my head and be absolutely focused on delivering it? Could I make every decision I was asked to make by all the experts, with a view to moving us closer to getting the end result? If the answer for you is yes – if you think you can see a conversion, the end result, in your mind and simply sit in meetings with experts and make decisions that move you gradually towards your end goal – then your world has just opened up. You are perfectly qualified to do commercial conversions and make a lot of money.

It is that simple, and that difficult. Why do I say difficult? Because you have to let go! Simple statistics of human behaviour tell us that many of you reading this book are control freaks; I really feel sorry for you all because you have got the hardest transition to make! I am lucky, I hate detail. It is the most natural thing in the world for me to say "you do it" to someone else when it comes to doing the detailed work on something, but for some of you that is really hard.

So, let me wrap all this up in a little bow for you. Imagine you are not the kind of person that feels able to give a task away immediately; that you like to do it once, learn it and then let someone else do it for you. Just consider for a moment all the skills that are required to deliver a commercial conversion. Before we even start to dig very deep, you need to learn to become an architect, a lawyer (several different disciplines), a surveyor (again, many different disciplines), an engineer (huge number of different disciplines), a planning consultant, a financial broker, a professional project manager, an expert in building systems and building materials – and you haven't even started on site yet! It is impossible. Even if it was possible to learn all those skills, by the time you had finished you would have forgotten everything you learnt at the beginning of your journey and you would have to start again, like the painter on the Forth Road bridge! In your mind, you must understand that you can get everything you need out there – you can hire it in. Everything you need to be able to get your commercial conversion designed, funded and built is waiting for you, and your sole task is to keep the end result in mind.

You are like the conductor of an orchestra: everyone will be playing your symphony. As the developer, you are going to get a raft of people out there who are better able and better qualified than you in their specific areas to help you in your commercial conversion journey. Usually, the conductors of an orchestra is a musician and usually, they can play one or two instruments well – that is how they become a conductor. But do you think the conductor then goes into the orchestra and plays every instrument? No – and neither can you. Don't discount your skills, but don't try and learn everyone else's; you have to move into the role of conductor.

It may be that you are an action taker, or a networker, good at administration, a whizz at spreadsheets, a system guru or maybe you are good at visualising unit layouts in a building. I never thought I would be good at this last skill, but I just happen to be one of those people who can look at a building and know how I can squeeze a lot of apartments in. I never knew I had that particular skill, but the point is, whatever you are good at (and you might be good at stuff that isn't on that list), don't focus on it. Celebrate it and use it, but understand that your role is to become a conductor. You mustn't try and learn every other instrument being played in the orchestra; it doesn't work in an orchestra and it won't work for your commercial conversion journey. Your commercial conversion journey is a simple journey, you are going to play a beautiful symphony. You are the conductor and you are free to use the world of resources out there to deliver it for you.

Understand the music score, see the deal, draw the experts together around you. If you know the score inside out, you know what the symphony should sound like. You are the conductor, and as such, you control the pace and the volume, you manage what happens, you manage the flow of information, you work with the experts to get the best result. You don't dictate to them because they know more than you, but you do conduct them. The conductor conducts the cellist, for example, but probably doesn't know the cello as well as the cellist. The conductor says, "I want you to come in here and I want you to deliver this. How you do it is up to you because I know you know better than me, but I want you to come in here and I want you to play this."

You are the conductor of the orchestra, you are not playing any of the instruments but the resulting symphonic sound is down to you.

Progressive Property (amongst the best educators in property development and investment in the UK) teach that one needs to move up the property pyramid. They suggest one starts with deal packaging or buy-to-let, then progress to buy, refurbish and refinance (BRR), then onto HMOs, then maybe Serviced Accommodation and so on. I am going to be honest, and maybe slightly controversial, here: I fundamentally disagree with that. When I moved into commercial conversions, I had one rental property, I was an accidental landlord having moved out of one house into another and keeping the one I moved out of. I had also been involved with one HMO conversion, but I hadn't really got that right, as my JV investor had to put too much money in and he ended up wanting to sell as he wanted the money back out. If you're reading this thinking, "yes, but I'm not qualified to do this stuff," then great, you are perfectly qualified!

If you can see a vision and you can get your head around out sourcing everything you need, you can convert commercial property and do bigger deals. In my view, it doesn't matter how many buy-to-lets you have bought, how many HMOs you have acquired, or how many small conversions you have done. It doesn't matter if you have never flipped a property, because all the expertise you need is available to you in the market.

This outsourcing of expertise is hugely important and was an epiphany for me. It is why I stand on stages, speaking to people to convince them that they can do so much more than they believe, and why I am confident, without knowing your personal background, that you can use this strategy to add more value, solve more problems and generate bigger profits.

So going back to Rob's webinar, as I sat there listening to the webinar telling me that larger deals paid more money, Rob was unknowingly watering seeds that had lain dormant in my mind, and the resulting growth was a very profitable foray into commercial conversions.

Shortly after hearing the webinar, opportunity came knocking in the form of a government reform called prior approval.

In seeking ways to solve our ever-deepening housing crisis, the government looked to re-purpose the redundant, under-utilised and empty commercial building stock into useful housing. To facilitate this, and perhaps to circumvent an ailing, ponderous and woefully under-resourced planning system, the government introduced an extension of Permitted Development Rights that effectively provided a shortcut for developers to change the use of certain building types into residential accommodation. If my experience of acquiring planning for the development at The Rose Bowl had taught me anything it was that developments requiring planning were fraught with three main risks:

1. No certain outcome,

2. An uncertain timetable that was almost always much longer than envisaged at the outset and

3. Was likely to prove very much costlier than considered likely at the outset.

These were massive risks that could ruin anybody seeking to start out in property development. It required significant upfront expenditure, over a prolonged period, and yet with little certainty of the end result. Prior approval overcame almost all of that risk and is a gift for those wishing to break into property development.

There was just one piece of the jigsaw that was yet to reveal itself: visibility.

I hated networking and I always had. Even as an officer in the Royal Air Force, I had dreaded walking into a room full of people I didn't know. During my business career, I had also been utterly convinced that when I walked into a room, everybody else knew each other and the very last thing they wanted was for me to approach them, much less to actually enter into their conversations! I found strategies to cope (mainly avoidance!) but that was going to prove more difficult if I was going to make my way in property.

Against this backdrop, I was once sat listening to a presentation at the Progressive Property Training Academy that got me thinking. The speaker reminded us that "visibility is credibility," which resonated with my experience of going from being a glorified shopkeeper at Nevada Bobs to being Group MD of the regionally significant Rose Bowl, which had seen me required to do press and media interviews and, in so doing, become quite well known locally. The presenter then offered an opportunity to grab a property platform by becoming a regional host of the newly-launched Progressive Property Network. He had me sold when he announced that for those who hated networking, one of the upsides of being a host was that people would approach us, rather than us needing to approach them!

Building the networking group led to a different kind of visibility too – social media! As part of our host training and induction, we left in no doubt about the hugely significant role social media would need to play in advertising our new groups. As one of those people who had thought that Facebook was for people who didn't have friends, this was a bit of a culture shock for me! But one advantage of us ex-military types is that we are quite good at doing what we are told and following a system. So, I took to Facebook and 'shouted' about the new property networking opportunity in Southampton. I had no idea just how pivotal these efforts to improve my visibility would prove.

The raw elements of my journey into bigger deals had now revealed themselves – there was an amazing planning shortcut mitigating the majority of the risks normally associated with property development. I had learnt I could get anything funded as long as I was solving the investor's issue, and that I could build anything of any size because of the abundance of excellent professional help available. Furthermore, I had a property 'tribe' following me on social media and at our networking event in Southampton. Rob's webinar brought all these together by binding them up with a truth: simply put, doing bigger deals would pay more. And for me, I desperately needed to enter a world that paid more!

T Harv Eker is credited with saying "Value is what determines how much money you'll make. You will be paid in direct proportion to the value you bring to the world according to the market place."

With prior approval providing a planning shortcut to convert larger commercial buildings into smaller residential apartments, funded by investors looking for a relatively scalable but safe way to invest in developments and delivered by experts who are knowledgeable in their fields, I had found a way to do larger deals and add more value.

Then I got lucky too.

There are a number of different building types that have prior approval rights for conversion. Had I been left to my own devices I may have ended up selecting a type that was less easy to scale, but the first building I came across that attracted prior approval was an office.

I knew Eastleigh quite well as I lived close by, and it was also where Eastleigh Borough Council was based, and I had attended many meetings at their offices during the Rose Bowl project. During my time running the networking event, many attendees talked to me about trying to buy properties suitable for conversion to Houses of Multiple Occupation (HMOs) in Eastleigh, how expensive they were and how difficult it was to find suitable properties under the market value.

As I was scouring Rightmove one day, I noticed a commercial tab. The vague notion that I might find something of interest there prompted me to look on this previously undiscovered page. When I noticed a building being sold on Desborough Road in Eastleigh with a suggestion that it might be suitable for conversion "back to residential use", I was intrigued. It was an office that was a mix of two old Victorian semi-detached houses with an additional, more modern, extension. The intriguing part, though, was that at £500K for a 4000 sq ft of building, it was approximately half the value that similar residential properties in that street were fetching, so I arranged a viewing.

Before I viewed, I used some basic analysis data provided by an unofficial mentor of mine to assess the viability of the opportunity. My unofficial mentor had been a property developer for many years and had already assessed another opportunity with me, although that particular building had sold to an owner occupier. But on this occasion, with a viable purchase price rattling in my head, I found when I viewed the building and got chatting with the agent that it appeared I was one of only three people to view the property, only one of whom had gone on to make an offer, which had been very low and refused by the vendor.

Suppressing my excitement, I arranged to meet the agent in his office later that week to go through my offer. In the subsequent meeting, the agent I had met at the property had brought along his boss. I was careful to let the agents lead the meeting, allowing them to be the experts they were, whilst at the same time seeking to establish a degree of credibility of my own. Using my old role at The Rose Bowl and the name of my unofficial mentor, who was well known locally, I provided a base for an offer that was well below the asking price. In the end, I actually showed them my financial model and explained that "unless I had missed something", I could only make it work at £400k. The boss then smiled, looking at his young protégé before looking back at me and announcing that was exactly the figure they had suggested to the vendor!

It became clear that the vendor had pushed for an asking price of £500k, but the agents felt the price was between £400k and £435k. In my desire to get my first deal in the bag, I rapidly left £35k on the table by asking them to wrap up the deal at £435k! The revised offer was accepted. I had probably paid too much but I was on my way!

I had already warmed up an investor to the opportunity of bigger returns from bigger deals using prior approval, and he jumped on board quickly. With his help we performed well, doing exactly what we said we would, when we said we would, and we went on to complete on the purchase of this property in June 2014. In that first month of our larger deal journey, we also completed on the purchase of a bungalow we were going to knock down and build seven new 'down-sizer' homes. (Note: to date (October 2017), we still do not have planning for this site, despite the planning officer confirming before we bought it that this was definitely a development site!)

Amazingly to me, in that first month, I banked two finders' fees and two lots of management charges, which together meant I was paid £36,300 in one month! That was roughly the equivalent of seven months of my old net salary! Having been mired in debt, and up against a payment deadline on my credit cards, this was manna from heaven; I remember phoning my wife and exclaiming in delight and relief, "we are through!" We converted that 4500 sq. ft. Desborough Road office into nine apartments and that first deal went on to pay me in total circa £100k as my 50% share of profit. But that was just the beginning.

Our performance with regards to the purchase of the office in Desborough Road reassured the agents, who clearly then put us on their 'hot buyer' list. We then bought five more properties from the same agent over the following 12 months or so, and by then we were establishing a pipeline and a reputation.

We continued to meet with people, always seeking to solve their problems rather than our own. Business partners, joint venture investors and power team members all suddenly started appearing, attracted to a solution-driven team that was focused on adding value for everybody. It was at this time that I first met the woman who would become my business partner, helping me to accelerate our growth and to take on more projects.

The next few deals we bought were all offices and were conversions to four apartments (we sold this with prior approval but without carrying out the conversion ourselves, and we made circa £90k), six apartments and 12 apartments (both on Romsey Road in Eastleigh, which we would eventually sell with planning, generating a profit approaching seven figures), nine apartments with a profit shared with the investor of circa £350k, and 30 apartments with a profit of circa £730k to be shared 50/50 with a JV partner.

The pipeline of deals we have secured continues to grow, and the scale of the deals is also growing – accordingly, our profit forecasts constantly need rewriting. Annual seven-figure profits within three years of starting a company are mind-blowing to someone like me who has always struggled, but this is the power of the system we use within an opportunity that exists right now and is realised by adding value for others.

My life is now very different. We have a strong and healthy business that takes on between four and six projects per year. We now also run a training programme with Progressive on how to use the very system we use, helping others to discover the freedom and success we have secured. The training business also provides us with a strong monthly cash flow, which we augment with development management fees from our developments. We are adding to our team regularly, always looking out for good talent for our great team, which in turn allows me and my business partner Justine to focus on our principal role of sourcing good deals and networking with investors.

The process by which we assess the deals, redesign the buildings, get them built and then sell the apartments is the subject of the main part of this book. However, even at this early stage I wanted to share my story by means of illustrating the fundamentals of a journey which I sincerely hope lends much hope to would-be developers, even those with little experience.

There is an opportunity right now in the market that provides a relatively safe route into property development.

By adding more value for our investors, adding more value for our end buyers or tenants and doing it on a larger scale, there is a significant opportunity to create huge value and wealth, and one in which you don't have to roll the dice of massive risk.

Mark's Story

Much of Mark's childhood and early business career is well documented, primarily in the book Low Cost High Life. Mark started to get really interested in residential investment property in the early 2000s, initially getting into buying off-plan from developers before the property was built, and later buying new builds abroad in the southern continental United States and Eastern Europe.

Initially believing he was some sort of international investor who could make money while he slept by dipping a finger into property in multiple time zones, he had some hard lessons to learn. Multiple legal and banking environments combined with a completely different set of investment rules for each country being invested in meant that he hadn't got a deep enough understanding of how investments worked.

He was egged on by heady markets and hordes of other market participants (often peddling turd, sorry investments!) instead of going vertical, going knowledge deep, really deep, and working off the back of a refined model then rinsing and repeating; he was playing at a bit of this and a bit of that – complete folly in any business environment. As time progressed, I started to get some salutary lessons about how to value property, how buying off-plan was risky, often didn't work and had many similarities with buying a new car. Contrary to common belief, as with almost anything new, it depreciates the day you buy it – a reality that dawned with time, forcing a significant change in his investment strategy.

After having found and tested a strategy of buying ugly ex-council properties in Peterborough and surrounding towns, refurbishing them to increase their value and obtaining finance based on this increased value, it became clear that rental income as a percentage of the capital value (otherwise known as gross yield) of these properties was much greater. Realising that the income generated for every pound of purchase price was much higher on these properties versus more expensive properties on streets where people often like to buy so they can brag at dinner parties, Mark and his business partner Rob bought more. As the income was high relative to the capital value (yield), this strategy allowed them to borrow the full 75-85% that a bank would offer. After having purchased several hundred of these properties for themselves and investors, many of which have been retained, their letting agency Progressive Lets now manages in excess of 650 tenants.

Believing in a level of financial diversification, Mark has kept one eye on the financial markets, buying into quality companies when they suffer what he sees as fixable short to medium term issues. A keen advocate of spreading investment risk by finding a foil to property, Mark enjoys investing in a mix of equities, bonds and funds in the most tax-efficient way possible, such as through an ISA. Stock markets can be even more fickle than politicians, but the market often looks a year ahead of the real economy, meaning that activity here can be a good gauge of what property is likely to be doing in a year. As it is less liquid, property goes up and down slower than the financial markets, taking longer to react to changes in the economic outlook or mortgage finance in particular. Being at the coalface growing residential property portfolios at a rate of up to ten purchases a month while watching the market crash in slow motion in 2008 compared to the sudden, brutal fall of the stock markets significantly shaped Mark's thinking.

Believing that compounding is the eighth wonder of the world, Mark loves to watch investments compound up whilst delaying gratification. A pound saved today could be several thousand after a few decades of investment returns – such is the power of tax-efficient returns on returns. With overall long-run returns from traditional equity or bond-derived funds that are run by an investment manager historically not performing even as well as a basket of shares in the top 100 companies on the stock exchange, many are questioning the logic of paying their high fees. With the likes of Warren Buffet advocating the use of very low-cost tracker funds such as those offered by Vanguard (the second largest fund manager in the world at the time of writing) for his family to invest his money in when he dies, there seems to be little point paying managers and independent financial advisors (IFAs) their commissions to underperform.

Attempting to time these markets and get in and out when you perceive the market is due for a rise or fall is a mug's game, and it's impossible for the vast majority of people over the long term. Although Mark doesn't always follow his own advice, you should put the money in and leave it, only reconfiguring your investments when your objectives or the structure of an investment changes, rather than trying to time what's likely to happen next.

Interest rates are similarly hard to predict, as the governor of the Bank of England has proved numerous times with his "forward guidance" messages over the past few years. He is surely the best-placed person in the country to predict interest rates, as he sits as the head of the Monetary Policy Committee, which is charged with deciding the UKs central bank base rate. Surprisingly to many, his predictions are frequently wrong. If he can't get it right, what chance does the mainstream press have? As the path of interest rates are frequently influenced by events that are unpredictable by nature, trying to work out where they are going next is like trying to predict the short-term direction of the stock market. It's a mug's game.

As the UK has been stuck in a low inflation, low interest rate environment for more than a decade, many are wondering what structural change in the economy has driven this. Trying to find an answer to this riddle may be explained in part by productivity.

"Productivity isn't everything, but in the long run it is almost everything," said Paul Krugman, the Nobel Prize-winning economist, in 1994. This is as true today as it was at the time, but UK productivity has been in the doldrums since 2007. A measure of economic output for each person working per hour worked, it shows how efficient our labour force is and it should grow over time. As companies invest more in automation, such as with robotics and mechanisation, they become more efficient. Productivity is now no higher than it was in 2008 before the credit crunch hit. Indeed, had productivity continued to increase at the rate it did for the 10 years before the crunch, it would now be 20% higher. The theory as to why it has been held back so much varies from companies investing less in automation due to a less certain financial backdrop, such as that created by continuing economic shocks like Brexit.

Perhaps it is being measured in the wrong way, some believe, and was being driven by high-risk industries with high profits, which were booked early but which suffered big losses later, such as the financial services industry or the offshore oil sector in Aberdeen. Perhaps the digital revolution means that the systems for measuring productivity don't capture some of the activity, or low interest rates have sustained zombie companies, allowing unproductive and irrelevant businesses to continue operating that would have otherwise gone bust years ago.

The Phillips curve says that periods of low unemployment are followed by periods where inflation increases as the slack in the economy is taken up and wages start to rise. As wages rise, the theory is that workers will then spend more on goods and services because they have more disposable income. Since the financial crisis, this relationship has broken down and the model seems to be less relevant. Fathoming this puzzle has become a major talking point for many, such as central banks, which are now looking to use new models that have been adapted to understand the post-2007 crash economic model.

Some believe low rates have been driven more by slack in the labour force, allowing companies to defend themselves against significant wage increases, as there is a steady flow of labour that will accept zero-hour contracts and relatively low increases. If the availability of labour falls, which may be the case when the UK exits the European Union, this position might reverse. Clearly, whatever your view as to why interest rates are so low and have been for so long, the position is likely to be reversed at some point as they rise to the 'new normal', which is around 2 to 3%, according to the governor of the Bank of England.

If we have a period of calm and a time when economic shocks become wider apart than they have been in recent years, the Monetary Policy Committee may get to a position where they feel the economy can handle higher interest rates. When they do go up, mortgage rates are also likely to rise, affecting residential, buy-to-let and commercial purchasers. It could mean that commercial buildings are cheaper, but it might also mean that residential price growth is more subdued. Who knows, predictions here are frequently incorrect, so trying to make them in any precise way doesn't seem like a great idea; most that have tried to do it have been proven to be incorrect with time.

Too many people focus their investment strategy on the opinions of others who have little experience themselves. If you want to be successful, it is imperative to surround yourself with people who are already doing what you want to do, or are in the position you want to be in – and, critically, who got there under their own steam (yes, they could have done it as part of a team, but they should have been central to the process). If they have trodden the path along which you want to travel, they will be the best source of inspiration and real-world knowledge that will get you closest to your goal.

Many people who don't have these relationships rely on those around them and the general news media to make decisions about how to choose, develop and manage their businesses and investments. Most of these people, including many journalists, don't have experience investing in the way they preach. Ignore those who talk and don't do, and take with a very big pinch of salt advice that comes from people who have been put in a position because of the efforts of others, such as parents – unless they themselves have been successfully operating at the coalface for a significant period of time, growing businesses or investments.

Mark was a yield whore – he had found his home with small ex-council properties. But having spent more than a decade of his life viewing literally thousands of them with a view to purchasing, fatigue started to set in – he wanted something new. More than anything, he wanted a way to use time more efficiently to buy larger, more valuable properties, without the yield deterioration you see with as you go up the value chain and buy more expensive residential properties. It was all very well buying a property of £500k that rented for £1500 a month or £18k a year (3.6% gross yield), but why do this when the income return on capital invested was so low? In addition, this meant that leaving £250k in each deal for the next 20 years was seriously hampering the expansion of the portfolio due to the cash being tied up. Banks (and the regulator) are quite rightly fixated on lending against how much income a property produces (while also ensuring they have enough equity in a property that they will get their money back if they need to repossess). Realising the necessity to remain focussed on their strategy has helped with expansion and risk management hugely.

Considering the yield quandary, the alternative to residential is commercial property. Equally high yields can be combined with larger lot sizes, meaning that a £1m commercial purchase could still attract a yield in excess of 8%, and in many cases in excess of 10% while still attracting a good tenant that offers a great covenant. (The credit worthiness of commercial tenants is much more important than with residential, because of the size of investment frequently made to prepare a commercial property for a commercial tenant, and the potential length of void if they fail to pay their rent and get evicted.)

Although Mark and Rob have commercial properties and like the long-term, often stable, nature of the income streams they can create, they have been at pains to make them the central strategy because of the huge disparity in capital growth between commercial and residential property over the past few decades. Over a defined period, the capital growth in commercial building values in London has been 800%; residential property prices have increased 8000% over the same period. While income (and ultimately net yield) is king is the primary consideration when making property purchases, if anything will make serious wealth it's likely to be capital growth. You have no idea when it's going to come or how much you will get, but history shows us that it is virtually guaranteed over the long run in UK residential property.

Commercial can attract increased voids between tenants and huge empty property rates (these can often be 50% of the gross rent of a building, which frequently means you are paying the council £50k per annum for no services for an empty building). There can also be massive value swings during times of recession or structural change in the business environment. These factors have put Mark off loading up and creating a large commercial portfolio. Indeed, commercial buildings (rather than the land they sit on) can suffer a significant deterioration in their value as fixtures and fittings age and the building needs significant sums spending on it, unlike what commonly happens with residential property. Banks can see the issues too. Loan to value maximums on commercial property mortgages commonly top out at 60% versus 75% on residential buildings. This is a good insight into the way the banks view the risk associated with different types of property investment.

Mark talks a lot about leverage. If you are borrowing at 3% and are enjoying net yields in the 8%-plus range, you are making 5% extra just by applying some debt to it. Mark also likes to talk about loan to value rates, and although it's good to use leverage to get as much of the initial investment back as possible, it should be treated with care. It multiplies returns and losses in equal measure; a good investment becomes a great investment with the right leverage applied to it, but a bad investment can become a seriously bad one when leverage is applied, and it can put you in a deep hole with no way out.

Over the long run, it is a good idea to allow capital growth and/or capital repayments to enable the debt down to an average of 50% (or perhaps less) loan to value across your portfolio. At this level, you have room to breathe when the market crashes next (and it will – the timing is impossible to predict). At this level, you are less likely to breach commercial lenders' loan to value covenants should the market fall significantly, which may allow them to come knocking, asking for their money back. If they do, you are also more likely to be able to refinance to another lender without needing to find significant sums to put into the property to get the existing lender to release their charge over your building.

Cognisant that I needed to move up in stages, although buildings are not widgets and progress up the value chain is not a straight line, I have focussed on trying to understand a strategy with sufficient depth before moving up to the next deal size. I still believe this to be the best process with any business. There is no substitute for testing and measuring and seeing results before you move onto the next level to prevent mistakes to be magnified over a large number of units or investments.

Mark's Politics and a Rant

Believing that capitalism is an imperfect system that has been continually bastardised over the years by politicians around the world since its conception, in broad terms it remains the best system humanity has thus far developed. Humans fundamentally need an incentive to work, grow or develop. Systems that go too far in making everyone equal, regardless of the utility they provide, usually end up failing, as too many become fundamentally lazy and inefficient. Not that communism, liberalism and every other -ism hasn't been adapted and bent to look like something else along the way; the point is that they are all versions of an original ideology adapted in a way that politicians want, or think their voters will want.

As a natural Conservative, Mark has in recent years felt a little duped by the UK Conservative Party. The alternatives look even worse. To Mark, Jeremy Corbyn's version of a Socialist Britain looks like a pantomime and would be hilarious if he didn't have much chance of success of being voted in (as he didn't until recently); his rhetoric is enough to concern any sane economist. The notion that we can fix society by borrowing more (Jeremy's colleague and pal Dennis Skinner stated just this), and asking at the Labour Party Conference about Tesco expanding, "do you think they go to a Tesco safe and get the money out? Of course, they don't they go in somebody else's safe" are prime examples of the short-sightedness of this group of people.

This just typifies the reckless claptrap that these people believe, and after lying to the students at Glastonbury about them not having to pay university fees, one would hope that he is starting to wear thin. Ideas from John McDonald that you can just requisition properties, effectively stealing them from private individuals, should worry those at the bottom of the chain as much as it does property owners. A return to the 1970s, with punitive tax rates and irresponsible financial management, will see huge capital flight with many of the biggest taxpayers disappearing to foreign shores.

Such policies have the potential to force the UK into the hands of the International Monetary Fund or similar, as happened in 1976, largely as a result of similar policies peddled by Harrold Wilson's Labour administration. Austerity on steroids followed then, as would again be the case to fix the situation and pay the money back (which they would make us do). Take a look at Greece for an example of the structural changes that are likely to be demanded by such a lender of last resort. Rent control proved to be a disaster in the post-war period too. It leads to a huge deterioration in the quality and availability of properties in the private rented sector, and as the past is the best guide we have to the future, you would expect that doing the same thing all over again and expecting a different result is insanity.

While we don't know if much of this is talk to please his union backers or the reality of how the fine print of these headlines will be implemented, the thinking behind them is bankrupt (in more ways than one!). Hopefully the public will see through Jeremy's smokescreen before it's too late.

Not a great believer that the state is a good allocator of resources, Mark is clearly on the side of keeping taxes low to stimulate investment and the economy. With government managing a yearly budget of around £500bn, which has grown exponentially over the decades, it's pretty obvious that they have a penchant for dreaming up new ways to waste and spend other people's money. Mark does, however, believe that kids should be given a leg up and have the right to a great education, as this is probably the single biggest thing that can push a society to a better place. Infrastructure spending on roads, rail and communications probably pays for itself in increased economic activity, and the NHS helps too many people in such a fundamental way for it to not be free at the point of delivery, but it needs major reform. Frivolous spending by people who don't have commercial real-world experience seems commonplace in the public sector, with many of the people who work in this arena having spent their whole lives protected from reality by the public sector bubble.

Mark believes that people and politics tend to be too fickle in the UK. Opinions should be formed slowly and equal consideration given when views are looking to vary those positions. People voted to come out of the EU one minute and a week later believed they should have voted the other way, clearly not having taken the time to research and consider such an important decision. The Prime Minister is great today, but barely a few weeks after an election the public is saying she should ousted because a set came apart and she had a cold when she delivered a speech at a party conference.

Pivotal decision making based on whims is costly flimflam; the idea of a Chinese-style 30-year roadmap seems a good one. Should the masses be given the choice to vote on complex issues they don't understand? While Mark isn't a disbeliever in democracy, the election of people like Donald Trump is surely an indicator that something is systematically broken in many Western political systems.

Chapter 2: Why Do Commercial Conversions?

Mark – Why Commercial to Residential?

For many years, Mark looked at the size of commercial buildings in the local area, surprised at their low capital values versus residential properties on the same street of an equivalent size (or adjusted on a per foot basis); he thought to himself that there must be mileage in converting these buildings into residential. How was it that the values of these buildings drifted down when residential was rising? Why were so many empty? Surely there was an opportunity for arbitrage here?

Then opportunity struck.

Faced with a growing disparity between housing demand and the supply that builders were able to deliver, the Conservative government of the day, led by David Cameron, had one of those moments when they actually did something that genuinely helped those trying to get onto the housing ladder and the economy at the same time. Unlike their default 'all show and no go' promises, which usually amount to schemes that create headlines but involve tiny drops in the ocean-sized sums relative to the size of the market into which they are injected that have little real effect, these actually have substance.

The stroke of genius was creating incentives to generate the development of brownfield sites to make better use of what had previously been developed but was no longer relevant in its current use, while finding a way to sidestep stodgy local councils and their means of stifling development. As one of the cornerstones of this new strategy, in 2013they introduced permitted development rights to convert B1(a) offices to C3 residential, without the need for the frequently onerous planning permission or cash contributions to the council that usually precedes a conversion.

These new permitted development rights, coupled with the especially depressed values post-recession, meant there was a good, low-risk opening that Mark felt we could take advantage of. After making one of the first (if not the first) applications of this type in Peterborough in 2013, the green light was issued swiftly and the building was converted into just under 25 apartments, which were sold at a healthy profit. Knowing that there was a finite number of buildings in the city that could be converted, Mark knew that there was a window to purchase and convert these. With most agents unaware of the value (or even existence!) of these rights, I didn't volunteer too much information on viewings, keeping critical information flow minimised. Once they worked it out, every agent in town seemed to be telling those viewing the properties how to apply for prior approval on these buildings – or even getting owners of these buildings to make the application themselves, upping the value of the building. This led to streams of people viewing these properties like headless chickens! A series of commercial to residential projects have followed, in which we have performed a mix converting commercial buildings (lots of pubs) into residential which Mark and Rob have sold, along with a number of cluster flat projects, which create much higher yields that they like to keep.

Unfortunately, the government's record subsequently reverted to form, introducing nonsense such as clause 24, which limits the amount of mortgage interest landlords can offset against rental income. A classic example of government promoting ill thought through statute, from which a host of unintended consequences will flow, causing bigger problems later. By responding to the whims of the Daily Mail and The Guardian rather than creating policy that will reward landlords who provide better conditions for tenants with certainty, they have created a mess. In the long run with this policy, which will likely prove to be disastrous, rents are likely to soar and the quality of property in the private rented sector will fall significantly – if the policy is retained or not amended significantly, which with time, seems like a likely scenario.

As well as the low cost of commercial buildings for every foot of space when compared with residential properties, they offer some major benefits when looking at development. Frequently, agents' details show the floor area net of corridors, toilets, plant and other non-office/commercial space, often known as the net internal areas or NIA. Although this is now changing, the gross internal area or GIA is more relevant for conversion. As modern apartment buildings require less plant, smaller corridors and no toilets, and development can often extend to loft or other storage areas, buildings can be a lot bigger than the agents' details show. As commercial buildings are usually valued by floor area, this is a big thing to keep an eye on. Often Mark has bought buildings in the past because of the way an agent has measured the building, increasing or decreasing its size – and therefore value – in the eyes of those competing to buy it. The amount of saleable space that can be generated from the building vs. what the building cost to purchase vs. the area in which it is located per foot is what matters in the end, more than a lot of other noise that flows around the marketplace. Large commercial buildings can frequently have floors built on top of them, depending on the structure of the building, what area the building is in, what is either side of the building and considerations like key views in the local plan, such as those of a Cathedral.

Lots of other commercial building types have seen their relevance diminish. Many nightclubs are sitting empty across the country, such has been the shift away from people using them; this is largely down to the change in licencing laws – people don't have to leave the pubs at 11pm and move onto a club, so demand for them has reduced. Pubs and bars now open later and have variable closing times, so people don't all end up on the street at the same time, and we see a reduction in fighting and anti-social behaviour. The smoking ban hasn't helped clubs or pubs either, as many stay at home so that they can continue to smoke. Restaurant chains have also grown significantly through this period, with private equity groups aggressively rolling out chains such as Pizza Express, Wagamama, Côte Brasserie and Bill's, to name a small selection. With new world choices such as these, people seem to be socialising in different ways. And the excess consumption of alcohol has subsequently reduced, which can't be a bad thing for any of us, not least the NHS.

Care homes would fall into a similar category: many have gone out a of business because of local authorities changing their requirements and rules around who can provide care and the levels to which it must be delivered. A previously booming industry (which it still is for some stronger, more specialised operators), more and more is demanded from care operators without them necessarily having the revenue to support the level of regulation present in the industry. An increasing number of operators have also entered the market offering care in people's homes, which seems to be popular. With so many scandals concerning the deficient – and sometimes criminally deficient – care of old people in some homes, public confidence in these homes has been seriously knocked, causing a number to close.

One project that Mark undertook was the refurbishment and conversion of a failing pub into cluster flats. As an apartment building laid out as one or two-bed flats, it would have been big enough for about six apartments, generating a rental income of around £40k per year. Converted into three cluster flats that total 18 rooms, the building generates a gross rental income of around £90k per year. The resulting value of the building as flats would have been around £600k, but as a co-living type of building with the better income this generates, it was valued at £900k. This illustrates the benefit of creating cluster flats for professionals in some locations. In Glenn's area further south, it would still yield much better than one or two-bed flats, but the yields are generally lower the further south you go.

Many other commercial buildings have seen a premature end to their useful lives come about in recent years too. Many retail spaces have disappeared with the onset of the internet, and while industrial space has let well post-recession due to new operators supplying goods online, many high street operators have suffered. This has meant that the 'uppers' of many of these properties can be converted to residential, as there isn't much use for many of them otherwise.

Architects either make your position much better or worse, depending on whether they are good or not, and depending on whether they are working for you or somebody else. The difference between a well laid out scheme that minimises circulation space and maximises circulation space that the council would be happy with is huge, and can turn a loss into a good profit. Frequently, offices in particular are priced for sale with prior approval already obtained for conversion to residential. This can make the vendor's price aspirations unrealistic and usually increases competition for the building. The irony is that a well laid out scheme that 'sweats' a building that already has prior approval for conversion using permitted development rights is probably not something you want to be pursuing. Much better is when an architect draws a bad, inefficient scheme with large flats that leads to them having a comparatively low sale value per square foot. Even better is when no planning consent has been obtained for development on top of the building or for any extensions that look like they may be possible subject to obtaining full planning permission. As many people looking to purchase schemes like this will end up bidding for them based on the existing layouts, these can be amended later through a subsequent application, thus increasing the gross development value of the project and profit within the scheme.

Commercial buildings often have gas, water and/or electrical supplies, which are over-specified for residential use. It is therefore often the case that services don't need to be significantly upgraded, unlike with new build, where services often need to be put in in their entirety. Traffic movements in residential buildings are usually less than in equivalent-sized commercial buildings, removing issues that councils sometimes try and use to stop a development taking place. Almost all offices will, however, require new windows, upgraded thermal, fire and sound proofing to meet current building regulations, which will have significant cost.

Ground works are often also minimal on commercial buildings. They frequently come with large car parks, roads and landscaped areas to varying standards of finish and maintenance. The reality is that you don't need to spend anywhere near as much on these areas as you would on creating them from scratch for a new build development.

Commercial buildings are also usually designed to take greater loads than residential buildings. In simple terms, most structural engineers will tell you that you can place about 1.5 floors of residential on every floor of commercial. Depending on various factors, including the type of structure or frame and the foundations, this often means that the existing building will support at least one or two extra floors on top, without major changes to the existing structure. This is often where the profit is made on these conversions, and it is frequently an area that is missed by those looking to purchase such buildings.

Glenn – Why Commercial to Residential?

For our developments, it is not accidental that we use a system structure (GO LARGE); it's not just a nice acronym, it is how we work in real life. I first heard about the concept of doing larger deals on a webinar that Rob Moore did years ago, and strangely I don't think he did many of them. In fact, I think he only did a couple, which I found really odd given that it was such a powerful strategy; it really triggered something in my head, and I immediately set about implementing his teaching.

There are a number of reasons that commercial conversions are popular today, but the greatest reason we have found is a planning shortcut that the government has provided. We are going to cover that at length. The system we use is about securing financial freedom without getting tied up in planning; it is about getting involved in larger deals, because the more value one adds, the more problems we solve, the more we get paid. The bigger deal, the more you get paid, it's that simple. But it is not only about doing bigger deals, it's about changing our mind-set, thinking bigger and expanding our vision of what we are capable of.

It is about creating a pipeline and a property business – this is not a hobby. You don't get paid millions of pounds for tinkering. Now this doesn't necessarily need to be a business that soaks up all our time and requires us to work 80 hours a week. However, we do need to be serious about this opportunity and set ourselves up as a business.

This strategy also works whether you want cash flow or a significant cash pot. It is a simple system, but that does not mean that it's easy. As said before, it is much like a diet: it is easy to do and it's just as easy not to do. It is easy to eat the burger every day and it's just as easy not to, but somehow that salad just doesn't look that alluring. Further, this system is simple, but it will only work when you do.

Within the context of simple rather than easy, it is really important to state that it didn't happen for me immediately. The first deal I found, I couldn't get to work. I tried, and tried, and tried. I was chasing that same deal for a few months; in fact, I think we were negotiating for about six or seven months, and yet it didn't come to fruition. I was so focused on it and I re-worked the numbers many times, tweaking the layouts in order to squeeze our offer up. I made regular contact with the vendors, building empathy with them and doing everything I could to get the deal over the line, but I just couldn't get to the amount that the vendor wanted. The vendor had a figure that worked for him, and I couldn't make it work at that figure. It was so frustrating. After many months of trying to do the deal, it seemed so unfair when suddenly the vendor accepted an offer by a third party that had come out of nowhere. But the new buyer was someone who wanted to occupy the office rather than develop it, and consequently their valuation of the building was based on entirely different criteria.

One of my mentors, Rob Moore, has an expression that "you earn or you learn" – this was a learning experience. It seems to me so sad and such a waste that many of us in the property community go from one exciting strategy to another without sticking to one strategy long enough to 'bank' the learning and see the resultant fruits of our labours. So often we spend all our time and energy chasing the shiny penny, eventually giving up in frustration when nothing seems to have worked, when in reality we planted lots of great seeds but never stuck around long enough to cultivate any of them. Notwithstanding that I lost out on that first opportunity, I had learnt so much. I had worked with another of my mentors, who during the process, gave me the first version of what became my deal analyser. We now use a variation of the same analyser to assess every deal we do.

I also learnt not to chase just one deal, but to have a pipeline of deals, so that when one falls over, we are able to simply move onto the next. I learnt that while I could build empathy with vendors, ultimately they may be driven only by the numbers. I learnt that people using different business models will come up with a very different value on a building to me, and that I must only bid what it is worth to me using MY model. But I also learnt that I am tough, because I didn't give up. I kept going. Later, I found another deal and then lost my joint venture partner just as the deal was about to exchange. I could have given up at that point as well, but I didn't. I was in the right community, I found another joint venture partner and the deal went ahead, and suddenly I was up and running.

At this point, going into larger deals had just been a concept, an idea, even a dream. The concept was simple though: we get paid for adding value, and if we undertake larger deals, then we have the opportunity to add a lot more value and thereby generate greater returns for us and our investors. I discovered that we get paid for solving other people's problems. So, if we'd like to be paid a lot of money we need to solve a lot more problems, right? … Or do we?

More problems or larger ones? I sincerely believe that many people out in the property community are spending so much of that most precious of resources, our time, running smaller projects that are a relative waste of their time, efforts and expertise.

Let's take a typical smaller conversion business model, say for instance the purchase of an older semi-detached Victorian house to convert into an HMO. The uplift in value will obviously depend on size and location, but will probably be in the order of tens of thousands rather than hundreds of thousands. To get the conversion done, you may have to deal with the planning department (depending on local rules), find a decent small builder, find materials at the builders' merchants, make daily decisions on finishes, supervise the job, chase the builders when they don't turn up, argue about what was in the original quote, decide how to deal with the inevitable unforeseen issues with the building, discuss or argue about the impact of those issues on costs, chase the broker dealing with the re-finance, supervise cash payments, collect CIS, source replacement items for materials that have gone out of stock… the list goes on and on.

On a larger scheme, you might have very similar issues but on a grander scale, and here is the real 'kicker', you will be dealing with far more professional people and within the context of a proper contract with a great deal more support from a team of real professionals who are near the top of their field. You will be paid much more for solving the same VOLUME of problems, and although the problems may be bigger, it is likely they will be solved by your professional team rather than you. Wouldn't you rather earn more for the same hours invested?

How many problems do we need to solve? Lots, yes. But, if we solve lots of problems for lots of people, the universe is set up so that we get rewarded richly. We are serving the world by solving issues; by carrying out commercial conversions, we serve our investors with better returns on their money, our professional teams with employment, our contractors with work, the bank with lending opportunities, and our buyers or tenants with places to live, and we therefore benefit from a share in the added value in the form of profits.

We will share stories about how we met joint venture partners later on, but I can say that with only one exception, I met them when I was trying to serve other people to solve their problems. I met them when I wasn't looking for them, but when I was living to a value: I was here to solve other people's problems. It wasn't about me, it was about them. When I adopted that approach, suddenly this 47-year-old hitherto financial screw up, who had massive debts and had never made a penny that he had managed to keep, began to attract deals and joint venture partners in an abundance that I could never have dreamt of. I raised over £10m of joint venture finance in just 12 months. Imagine how that amount of money might help you on your property journey!

If we genuinely seek to serve other people, seek to solve their problems, then the world will pay us back. The mind-set has to shift away from ourselves and what we need, to how we can serve other people. If we can grasp that concept and live it out constantly, our lives will change.

Interestingly, we will probably be happier anyway, because if we can move to a place of gratitude for what we already have, that gratitude leads us inevitably to the service of others; many studies have shown those two attributes to be the root cause of happiness! Not only is solving problems a happy way to live, I truly believe that by solving problems within the context of this model that we are going to share with you in this book, you will see your financial circumstances change – and faster than you could ever believe!

Having established why I believe we should all Go Large and do bigger deals, it's nearly time to get in to the system we use. But before we get into the system itself, let's look at what a commercial conversion is.

Chapter 3: What is Commercial Conversion?

Anything that is not a residential property is generally regarded as commercial. It can be an agricultural building, it could be a care home or a nursing home, it could be a pub, it could be a light industrial building, or it could be Glenn's particular favourite – offices. Much of what is referenced in this book will be based around offices because that is Glenn's niche, that is what he has specialised in. He knows far more about the permitted development rules for offices than he does, for instance, about shops or launderettes or casinos, it just happened to be the niche he selected. Mark first specialised in pubs before moving onto other areas but we both believe you should pick a niche, and Glenn's strong recommendation is to use something that permitted development exists for – in particular, the prior approval process, which is an agreed Change of Use under permitted development. But more on picking a niche and using prior approval later.

Whatever approach we take to converting commercial buildings, the basic principle remains the same. Residential values of buildings are usually higher than commercial values. Where that differential is significant enough, we can purchase and convert the building into residential units and generate enough value to create a significant profit or equity margin.

The type of residential unit you create is strongly influenced by your plans to exit the deal, whether by holding for long-term rental return or by selling. What is generally true is that "small ones are more juicy"! Accordingly, conversions will be into apartments more frequently than houses, and in the same vein one-bed apartments more often than two-bed apartments. And again, following it to the inevitable conclusion, the smaller the one-bed apartments are created, the more profitable the scheme is likely to be. We will cover this is more detail in the redesign section of the book.

First though, it is important to look at some guiding principles that are foundational to our commercial conversion journey. Let's start with who this strategy is for, and just as importantly, not for.

Chapter 4: Who is Commercial Conversion for, and Who is it Not for?

Commercial conversion is a strategy for people who want to create a property business that can generate huge profits from a great time vs. return strategy. Many believe it is just for those looking to develop buildings to sell, but Mark has focussed on making it a model that can be used to create a rental portfolio, which can then be scaled into blocks to be held over the long term. Creating passive rental streams that continue regardless of whether you want to work anymore should be a goal for most people. It creates security, frees time and allows you to go off and create new businesses. It can be for those wanting to create a rental portfolio that can be scaled up to create a wall of income that can sustain you for the rest of your life.

Mark came at the strategy by growing up in steps, from houses to pubs to larger offices and bigger buildings, over about 15 years. Its therefore true that he is more of the view that a staged approach is best, working up the lot sizes over a period of time rather than going right in and buying the biggest buildings.

Converting commercial buildings is a serious strategy that requires serious input, time and knowledge. Anybody who believes it is a passive, risk-free strategy or one that you can follow without focussing, doing a 'bit of this and a bit of that', is mistaken. As with any serious business pursuit, it should be treated as something within which you should niche and become a master of. Done right, by someone with the right skills, professional team and experience, the results can be mind-blowing. Casualties certainly exist, however, many of whom have not put the time into learning or experiencing the steps required to refine the strategy.

The most successful operators in this sector often don't do much else. They aren't usually doing new build sites at the same time and most aren't developing commercial sheds for an internet operator. They are focussing on being the best commercial conversion operator in the sector, providing homes for individuals, which means that they become very efficient at making the best of their deals and reducing their risk profiles in the process. This shields them when the market turns (as it inevitably will) and recession follows.

Commercial conversion is not for those who don't want to take risks. Most sorts of scaled property development involve taking and managing risks that many would view as unacceptable. The reality is that it's important to take these risks whilst managing them effectively at the same time. As recession comes, it is a virtual guarantee that sales of property will fall off a cliff like they always have in times of sustained economic contraction in the UK. Plan B needs to exist, which could take the form of renting out apartments when the market turns. This is a favoured strategy of Mark's, as it is very likely that the market will return a few years later.

If you can service your mortgage or development loan payments (which many banks will convert to a long-term investment loan if you rent the units out) with rent from tenants, you will may be able to shield yourself from not meeting your loan repayments, or from the bank calling the debt back in. Situations like this can destabilise developers and often send them into insolvency, especially when other parts of their business hit the rocks at times of recession.

Conversely, developing larger more expensive apartments or houses will usually attract lower rental yields, providing less cash flow and resulting in the bank insisting on more capital, as they will usually support a lower loan as a percentage of the value of the building. In Mark's view, this adds risk to the model over time. The reality is that these bigger houses and apartments are also likely to be hit hardest in the bad times, as fewer people are likely to splash out on them. Therefore they take longer to sell, and actually getting them sold will probably require deeper discounts that will put further financial pressure on the developer, just at a time when other income streams may be drying up due to wide-scale economic collapse.

There is more demand for smaller, lower value apartments, and they will also rent easiest and at the highest yields during a recession. Although people like to generalise by saying that the richest in society aren't affected by recessions and can always afford the best, the reality looks quite different. Small starter homes are probably the safer end of the market.

Given that this strategy relies heavily on focus within the sector and the steady accumulation of skills and experience, Glenn considers that previous property experience is relatively unimportant. He opines that with the right education, support and relentless focus, it is possible to utilise this strategy early, albeit at a smaller scale than one might grow into. He bases this view on his own experience. Armed with the experience of just one Buy To Let (BTL) property being used as a 4 person student multi-let, an HMO conversion carried out in conjunction with a JV partner and his experiences at The Rose Bowl documented elsewhere in this book, he launched full pelt straight into this strategy.

However, his success in the early adoption of this strategy, was based almost entirely on the lessons laid out in the Guiding Principles section later in this book.

Chapter 5: Using Prior Approval or Full Planning

Full Planning

This book seeks to give you a balanced perspective on converting commercial buildings, using either the full planning process or the planning shortcut called prior approval. Glenn almost exclusively uses prior approval as the basis of any deal he does, even if he then goes on to add further value by going through an additional process when the opportunity is worthwhile. Although Mark does use prior approval on occasion, he also regularly and successfully goes through a full planning process. However, a full planning process is not to be undertaken lightly and Mark talks later about how he has been able to make that work for him using very strict criteria for both conversion types, within a tight geographical area where he knows the planning officers approach.

Where both Mark and Glenn agree is that using planning as a means to convert diverse building types into different residential end products combined with taking an uninformed, geographically random approach is likely to lead to a world of pain in the form of frustrated plans, increased costs and excessive delays. One can always choose to do it the hard way if desired or necessary, but we focus on prior approval opportunities because the planning system is largely broken. Although gaining planning consent should be policy driven, with policy being written centrally and, in theory, interpreted in the same way throughout the country, the reality is very different. Planning departments are often under-resourced, lacking in experience and driven by the ethos of the Head of Planning, with their decisions often then overseen by untrained and politically motivated councillors, who can be too frequently driven by concerns about where their next vote is coming from. Mark makes planning work relatively successful for him by using strict criteria to ensure he has a better than average chance of getting the consent he is after, but for new developers the planning system is a risky world to navigate.

Let's be clear: you can go and buy all kinds of commercial buildings, such as nursing homes, care homes, pubs, listed buildings or any other commercial building, which don't benefit from prior approval, and you may get planning to convert them and go on to make money. But when you know there is an easier way, why would you choose to make it difficult for yourself? Both approaches can work, and the good news is that commercial conversions do work, whether you need planning or benefit from prior approval. But it is certainly true that going through a full planning process seems to be the harder path, especially at the beginning.

Our planning system works like our legal system. The government brings out a new planning policy that is lacking in detail. As with the legal system, nobody knows exactly how to interpret the new planning policy until it is tested, in the first instance by the planning departments, then the planning inspectorate through appeals and then occasionally in the courts. Correct interpretation of each policy is thereby determined by the constant testing of the policy in the context of real applications. Each case determined sets a precedent, and accordingly, the interpretation of each policy should in theory become clearer and clearer, although regrettably some cases seems to serve instead to cloud the issue further! As a result, there is always uncertainty. We also need to remember that this process will be interpreted locally, not nationally. Each local authority might take a different view on planning policy, depending on how it fits with their own agenda, such that they interpret it to fit their own circumstance.

In theory, if you abide by the policies of the planning system, with the help of a good planning consultant who knows the policies themselves as well as the local interpretation of those policies, you should end up getting a green light in the form of a consent. It is a great theory. The problem with it is that it's just that: a theory.

The biggest issue of all seems to be how major decisions on planning issues are made. The local authority hires the planning officers, who are usually trained experts in town planning or other such relevant qualifications, and who will know how to interpret the policies. You, or your planning consultant, then work with the officers to produce a scheme that fulfils their policies by liaising and negotiating with the officers, who again are trained in town planning, and have probably been in the role for years. Having worked together, often for months and after many iterations involving the production of many reports, we finally get to a point whereby the planning officers recommend the granting of consent. Then what happens? The final decision is handed to untrained, often politically motivated groups of councillors to have their say. Really? Think about this, let a group of experts make a decision based on policy only to then let untrained politicians overturn that decision? If you wrote that down as the basis for a new way of making planning decisions, I believe it would get laughed out of court!

Imagine yourself in that situation. You have gone through the whole costly and time-consuming process, and you then find yourself standing before a bunch of often politically-motivated, untrained town planning amateurs who overturn the decision, thereby volunteering you for either abortive costs, further months of work, further design costs and/ or additional reports, or possibly even an additional timely and costly planning appeal. And they wonder why more houses are not being built by smaller developers?

Even once you receive your planning consent, you will then often have to enter into a Section 106 Agreement negotiation, although this may sometimes be done in parallel with the application itself. A Section 106 Agreement is a legal agreement whereby the developer is required to pay a contribution towards any number of local needs as laid out in local policy, to include funding towards schools, hospitals, roads, surgeries, green space and much more. It can take many months to negotiate. Furthermore, it is a legal agreement that needs negotiating between sets of lawyers representing both the council and the developer. And who do you think pays all the legal bills, including those of the local authority? **You do!**

When different departments of the local authority argue amongst themselves about what their priorities are, they are arguing with each other on your legal bill. Currently, you may also get a Community Infrastructure Levy (CIL) thrown into the mix. I seem to recall that CIL was brought in to eventually remove the need for a Section 106, and to make negotiations much simpler by coming up with a simple tariff that developers could look at and know very quickly what they were going to have to pay. A worthy goal indeed. Instead, what seems to happen in most areas is that we now have BOTH Section 106 Agreements to negotiate and CIL payments to make too!

A full planning process can take months, and it can cost a considerable amount of money. One example is reports. The local authority will often ask you to come up with different reports to cover various areas of concern. Many of these reports, and the need for them, are completely legitimate and entirely justified. For instance, ensuring that a site hasn't been contaminated in a way rendering it unfit for human habitation would seem essential. However, the problem is that local authorities are so worried about being found liable for making bad decisions that they will often cover their risk by asking developers to come up with what seems like every report conceivable, just in case they come up with something material. Some of these reports appear to be almost completely unnecessary.

Most recently Glenn was asked for a report on exploded bombs in the area of an office he was looking to convert. The office was in the middle of Somerset and the report was going to cost £1400 and delay the planning response by four weeks. The thought occurred to him that being in Somerset they were quite a long way from the southern coastal ports that got bombed in the war, where the risk of unexploded ordnance might seem quite reasonable. According to the unexploded bomb map (yes, there is such a thing) the prospect of finding an unexploded bomb in that part of Somerset was low. According to his consultant, a risk assessment of low is the lowest risk you can get, so why ask for a risk assessment? You might as well just say that unexploded bomb surveys are ALWAYS required.

The problem can be the local authorities deciding what is required in their location. An officer decides it 'might be a good idea' to check for bombs, and the requirement is made with no apparent thought about the costs and time delays to the developer, yet with no consequence whatsoever to the officer, other than the comfort they have of knowing they have successfully covered their backside! Of course, not all officers adopt this approach, and some local authorities are excellent and work well with developers, adopting a pragmatic can-do approach. But if a developer works across different authorities, it is not knowing how each one operates and how the process is likely to be run that creates such uncertainty, doubt and scepticism.

Given all this negativity surrounding the risks of using a full planning process in your development journey, how does Mark Homer make it work for him? He believes you have to be an expert in it – an expert for your chosen conversion type in your selected locality. You need to instruct a really good planning consultant and stay in one area, where you get to know what they prioritise, what they like and what they don't like. And, even if you do that, you need to steel yourself for a lot of hard work and possible extra costs. Of course, that presents a problem because investors don't like unknown timescales. Worse, they are extremely nervous about unknown costs with an unknown outcome. So, even if you want to use planning, you then need to find investors who are comfortable with the associated risks.

Case Study – Planning Nightmares

Glenn was part of a consortium that bought a site near a large commuter town in the south of England. On the site were three barns, two of which were relatively modern and one of which was old but not listed. It also had a little tiny granary and a Grade II Listed farmhouse. We weren't too concerned about the conversion of the granary, given that at best we might have got one very small one-bed flat in there, but that small uplift wasn't significant compared with the rest of the scheme, and we accepted the requirement to get planning for the relatively small farmhouse that would split into 3 small houses.

At some point in the past, the older barn and the farmhouse had been converted into offices, and at that time, it seems to have been decided to turn the site into an office complex, as they had then built two further barn-type structures in sympathy with the older barn. So, in full knowledge that being Grade II listed we would need to apply for planning for the conversion of the farmhouse, we thought we would just go for planning on the relatively small farmhouse and the tiny granary, so we purchased the site as a largely prior approval site with some smaller planning requirements on top.

Then we got a little unlucky. Very shortly after we purchased the site, the government changed the wording of the prior approval rules. Previously, the wording of prior approval policy excluded only Grade II listed buildings themselves. However, they then changed the wording to include all buildings within the curtilage of Grade II listed buildings. The result of this change was that all of the buildings on the site were considered to be in the curtilage of the farmhouse and granary, and as such now required a full planning application. This prompted one of the best emails I have ever seen from an investor. Pragmatic to the core, he emailed the team stating simply that, "a penalty saved is as good as a goal scored". The implication was simple, go save the penalty! That was going to prove rather easier said than done!

We proceeded to enter into the pre-application part of the planning process. The purpose of this part of the process is to get everybody on the same page, both with regard to overall objectives for the site, design, layout and anything of material relevance to the submission of the full application. Conversations often run along the lines of, "well we don't' quite agree with that bit, but if you tweak this then that might be something that we can recommend". 'Pre-app', as it is commonly known, is meant to be a six to eight week process, in which we give them our thoughts, and the local authority responds.

In this instance, with what I must confess I consider to be a particularly poor local authority, we submitted the pre-app on 1 September 2015, which gave the council a target response date of 13 October 2015. Following months with no feedback, and only after threatening legal action, we finally received the first written response seven months later on 12 May 2016. We responded to that by submitting plans in line with their pre-app response on 31 August 2016, which in turn meant that the council's target date for a decision was 17 November 2016. Although they responded quite quickly to that, broadly accepting the scheme on 19 December 2016, we have since then had to argue about minor details and establish the viability of the site through an assessment. We have also had to negotiate a Section 106 agreement and as at 04 December 2017, we still don't have planning consent (or refusal) for this scheme! During this time, we have had four changes of planning officer because they were so under-resourced that they hired in consultants who left or planning officers who went long term sick.

It is very difficult to run a profitable business that is attractive to investors with that degree of uncertainty and risk.

Prior Approval

Contrast that approach (and the case study) with the government-sanctioned planning shortcut that is called prior approval.

Before we start to excite too many of you, we must state that prior approval rules have at the time of writing only been applied in England, and accordingly, Scotland, Wales and Northern Ireland do not benefit from these rights. Furthermore, a limited number of areas in England have secured exemption from prior approval. These are listed in the government prior approval document available via the links provided later in this section.

For those fortunate enough to live or operate in England, prior approval is essentially a pre-determined permission to convert some buildings in specified commercial use classes to residential use, more specifically C3 residential use (essentially for people living together as single household). There are specified conditions to be met for each prior approval class, but as long as those conditions are met, planning approval will be forthcoming. Commonly, the basic conditions of flood, highways, contamination and noise must be checked, with some classes having further tests to be undertaken. Furthermore, prior approval applications are required to be determined within 56 days – just eight weeks – at a fixed cost of only £80, no matter how large the application. Although prior approval applications are generally determined in 56 days, there have been occasions cropping up more recently where the incredibly stretched planning departments are requesting extensions of time, usually small, but generally speaking the timetable is still relatively certain.

Should you find that a building fails one of the tests laid out in the criteria, this does not render prior approval unobtainable. Instead, one merely needs to determine the mitigation required to bring the results of the test back to an acceptable result. For example, if a site was found to be contaminated, then the applicant would simply have to agree with a suitably qualified person what works would be required to bring the site to an acceptably 'uncontaminated' level suitable for residential use. By submitting that remediation plan with the prior approval application, the local authority should then issue the prior approval with a condition requiring the suggested works are carried out, and that evidence is collated thereafter to confirm that in so doing, the land had been rendered acceptably 'clean'.

The list of use classes benefitting from these rights is constantly changing, but at the time of writing, prior approval exists for B1a offices, A1 and A2 retail, B8 storage (soon to finish), B1c light industrial, agricultural buildings, and some sui generis uses, such launderettes, arcades and casinos. It is possible that they will extend this to other use classes, but at present we don't know what they are going to be.

More recently, some local authorities in England have started to apply for Article 4 exemptions from some prior approval rights, usually the prior approval pertaining to the conversion of offices. Accordingly, it's always worth checking the latest status of prior approval in your area with a good planning consultant.

Benefits of Prior Approval

The prior approval has a fixed fee of £80, no matter how big the scheme being applied for. If one is undertaking a larger scheme of say 50-60 apartments under normal planning process, that could cost you tens of thousands of pounds as a planning fee. However, by using prior approval, the fixed fee for any size remains £80.

Prior approval applications should be determined within 56 days.

Prior applications can only be failed in pre-determined circumstances:

- Unresolved issues with any of the four following tests: flooding, highways, contamination and noise from neighbouring commercial premises

- Listed buildings— prior approval does not apply to any listed building,regardless of where it is located or whether it is Grade I or Grade II

- Sites of special scientific interest (SSSI) for some building classes, see Appendix 1

- CA conservation area for some building classes, see Appendix 1

- AONB area of outstanding natural beauty for some building classes, see Appendix 1

We will be covering the benefits of picking a niche and sticking to it later in the book, but this is where they start to become apparent. Each prior approval type has different rules that need to be complied with, so instead of trying to learn all of the rules for each type, it is far simpler to pick just a couple and get to know the rules for those types really well.

By way of example, it doesn't matter if an office is in a conservation area, or an SSSI or even an AONB. To understand this, we need to consider the principle of prior approval. Prior approval is for changing the internal use of the building. You are not allowed to make external changes without an additional planning application, unless it is explicitly allowed within the rules of the prior approval guidelines, as it is, for example, for shops.

Consider what a conservation area is set up to protect: CAs protect the external appearance. In Wiltshire, there is a beautiful old village called Laycock that looks like it's still in the 1700s. It is often used to film period dramas because it looks like it is stuck in time. Now, in theory, if there was an office in the middle of the village in Laycock you could use prior approval. But a shop in the village would be a different story: shops come with a prior approval rule that allows you to make external changes consistent with making them look less like a shop and more like a house. Policy wouldn't want to permit that in a conservation area, because it would then be allowing an uncontrolled change to the external environment. So we strongly recommend that you pick a prior approval type or two, and become an expert on how prior approval is applied to each type.

Prior approval also removes any minimum size requirements, more specifically Nationally Described Space Standards. We will describe the real impact of this in the redesign section of the book, but at this point let's just acknowledge the extra flexibility of the freedom to determine the sizes of the residential units we are seeking to create. A word of caution, even at this early stage: if you are intending to sell the units at any stage, mortgage lenders will not generally lend on any unit of less than 30 m² of internal space.

Prior approval conversions also benefit from being exempt from affordable housing requirements – again, however large the scheme is. This is an extraordinary benefit, particularly as one starts to take on bigger schemes for which, if using a traditional full planning process, local authorities may be looking for very significant contributions. Such contributions could be financial payments or actual units, and can exceed of 35% or more of the development.

Whenever Glenn is considering a new site, he has an email he sends out to the architect, the planning consultant and the conveyancer informing them of the building being considered, giving the price, the location and the address. The planning consultant will then confirm any issues she sees with regard to applying prior approval to that site to include all the tests above, the architect will check the suitability of the building and will start collecting quotes for a measured survey, and the conveyancing solicitor will make checks on the title to the property. One email starts a process that Glenn is barely involved in to ensure that the site works.

With regard to the highways test, given that most commercial buildings will be in or near towns and cities, it is usually possible to demonstrate a sustainable transport plan to include bus routes, trains, parking, either on-site or locally and cycle stores on top of amenities within walking distance. So highways is often a non-issue for many developments, but you need to bear in mind what it might be for your chosen niches. The key issue is being able to provide some sort of sustainable transport plan, and again, your planning consultant should be able to guide you on that very early in the process.

Checking for contamination is usually commenced by getting a desktop survey done. The desktop survey will tell you if there are any likely contamination issues; if there are, then the consultant who undertakes the survey should work with the planning consultant to agree what further reports and/or mitigation are required. As long as that is covered in the prior approval application, it should suffice.

The check for flood risk is also initially a desktop survey. The process is almost exactly the same as for contamination, though mitigation is somewhat different and covered in the redesign section.

By way of summary of the overall benefit of prior approval, it allows us to give greater certainty, for ourselves and our investors, because it is planning permission driven by legislation rather than by committee. Change of Use using prior approval is obtained through a simple process that:

- requires a fixed fee of £80.00

- has to be determined within 56 days

- can only be failed if the building is listed or has a stated issue, of which there are a specified number. The number and nature of the conditions that can be considered by the local authority are different for each prior approval type and set out in the government paper on the government website, the links for which are given later in this section. This is another reason that choosing a niche within which to operate is a good idea, as you will become an expert more quickly in the different conditions that can be applied.

Using prior approval means:

- you know you'll get permission

- you know how long the process will take

- you avoid affordable housing requirements

- there are no minimum size requirements

- there is usually no requirement for Section 106, unless specific issues arise

- you can't be failed for lack of parking in a town centre, as long as you can demonstrate a sustainable transport plan (local amenities, bus routes, trains, bikes etc.)

These are all very important in your pitch to your investor, as they ensure:

- certain outcome

- certain timeline

- no unexpected costs for affordable housing or Section 106 (normally)

- maximum return on investment

- The full government PD Order can be found at: http://www.legislation.gov.uk/uksi/2015/596/contents/made

- There was an update to this document in May 2016, which can be found here: http://www.legislation.go.uk/uksi/2016/332/made

We won't pretend that the prior approval rules you will find at the links above are a right riveting read, as they are, after all, government documents. However, if you pick one or two of the prior approval and become an expert in them, you can make a considerable amount of money. There is gold in that boring text!

Once your planning consultant has completed and submitted your prior approval application and you demonstrate mitigation for any test failures, you should receive your response within 56 days, and your response will be one of only three outcomes:

1. Prior Approval Not Required

2. Prior Approval Required and Granted

3. Prior Approval Required but Not Granted

The first response is the confusing one – prior approval not required. Does that sound like a green light? No, I didn't think so either, but that is the green light. It seems to mean say you don't need approval, but that is the government's way of saying you have got it! Can we use English please? Anyway, that is your green light.

The second response – prior approval required and granted – is a conditional approval. If you found that you needed to provide mitigation for one of the tests (a flooding issue, for example), you then submitted your suggested mitigation for the test failure with your application and the local authority was happy with your mitigation suggestion, they accordingly grant you prior approval. The second response says prior approval is required because you did identify some issues, but they are happy with what you suggested.

Of course, the third one is the one you don't want to get: prior approval is required because you have identified some issues but they are not happy with the mitigation you suggested and it is therefore not granted. You shouldn't ever see this result, as your planning consultant shouldn't let you get to this stage. They should be in dialogue with the local authority and make sure that the mitigation you suggested will be acceptable, and if they want different or further mitigation, it should be negotiated while the application is live. Although you shouldn't see this result, don't panic if you do. It is not the end of the story. You or your planning consultant needs to go and chat with the local authority, and figure out what exactly it is that they want.

If you do not live or operate in England and are now wondering whether this book remains pertinent to you, please be assured that 95% of this book is still of immense value to you. The only difference for you is that you're going to have to work the with the full planning system, which, as we have covered, can be achieved with some confidence if you pick a niche within a given location and get to know the officers and the authority and understand their approach. Of course, a good planning consultant remains essential, if not even more so.

Everything else in this book with regard to conversions, including the use of a power team, outsourcing, assessing deals, getting the redesign done, getting the builders in and exiting the deal, all still applies.

The only advantage you have lost is the use of prior approval, but conversely, the world is your oyster because you are not restricted to certain building types.

Commercial conversions work using prior approval or the full planning process, we are only trying to give you an easier way when we talk about the opportunity of using prior approval. But if you happen to know a really good planning consultant who knows the local rules and is confident that it is not going to be difficult to convert that pub into four or five apartments, and that you are in a perfect location for your serviced accommodation business giving you great cash flow, then you still have a great strategy at hand.

The upside of the clarity on achieving a consent via prior approval, on which we have based our calculations for the development, is certainty for us and the investor. The certainty we enjoy also has the benefit of helping us to secure opportunities by offering unconditionally. Whereas the less confident or uninformed may offer 'subject to planning', our knowledge of the prior approval system allows us to bid with certainty and offer the vendor an unconditional sale. I would strongly suggest that anyone starting out on commercial conversions and needing to use the full planning process for whatever reason considers offering to purchase any building 'subject to planning'.

Every deal Glenn has ever bought has been purchased following an unconditional offer given, entirely based on the confidence of knowing how the prior approval process works. Clearly, a vendor is more likely to sell to someone offering unconditionally. If possible, use your expertise to offer unconditionally, unlike 'Joey' down the road who is not sure, who thinks it "might be alright", but has to put in a conditional offer because of the doubt in his mind.

Common Traps of Prior Approval

It may be useful to understand some common pitfalls of prior approval. Although it is an incredible opportunity, there are traps to be avoided.

Evidencing Correct Lawful Usage

- Prior approval rights only apply if only if the building is in the correct lawful use, for example, an application under Class O couldn't be made if the office is actually an A2, but you could use the A2 use class for that. An office might not just be an office – it might be mixed use and therefore 'sui generis', so doesn't qualify under prior approval rights. If there is no clear primary use, then prior approval rights are not applicable.

- When mixed use, both uses may have a prior approval, but you would have to apply separately for each use.

- Provision of evidence:

  - Dated photographs that demonstrate the use are helpful in proving class

  - Details of previous occupiers – this is very helpful if you can demonstrate what the company's core operation was as this can prove use

  - Copies of licences, leases, selling agents, utility bills, etc. can all demonstrate use class

  - Go through the planning history, you are looking for a previous planning application that states the use – some councils have excellent websites that can assist with evidence

  - Don't underestimate the power of Google – it is possible to pick out all kinds of information using desktop searches about a building

- ° Finding out on what basis business rates have been levied can also be helpful, which can be available on the VOA website

- ° If you think proving the use class is going to be an issue, then gather as much evidence as possible and present it with your prior approval application

Previous Planning Applications or Use or Permitted Development

- Be aware that if there has been a previous planning application on a building that has had conditions applied to it, these conditions may trump the prior approval rights – for example, if permission to use a building as an office has been granted but only for the specific company that applied. There may also be Section 106 conditions on a building that trump prior approval rights.

Restrictions Based on Use Class

- As noted in the above summary, every prior approval class has restrictions and conditions so be clear on what you can and can't do.

- Restrictions on floor space vary by use class and must be checked.

Council Interpretations

- Councils interpret the regulations differently and may try and take account of conditions they aren't entitled to. It is vital that you know your niche prior approval rights. With the understaffing of planning offices and the relative recency of prior approval legislation, planning officers are not always aware of all of the prior approval rights.

Section 106

- With prior approval schemes, councils can't ask for affordable housing but they may still need a Section 106 Agreement for other reasons, such as ecological considerations.

- There may also be a requirement for Section 106 obligations related to prior approval and issues that arise (e.g. transport and traffic impacts) and there may be contributions towards traffic regulation orders, such as yellow lines to prevent overspill of car parking provision.

- The most important thing is to know your area and your niche prior approval rights. Try and keep in touch with your planning officer – they are busy and not always approachable, but if you are able to find out in advance that there is a potential issue you have more of an opportunity to do something about it.

- If you feel that the prior approval rights have not been considered properly, it is perfectly legitimate to ask. Prior approval rights are relatively new, and some planning officers are not that experienced, so they may not be as familiar with prior approval rights as you are.

- Using a planning consultant is always strongly advised. They take away a lot of the pain and can advise you early of any evidence and issues that may arise. You will build up a far better relationship with them and, if they are local, are often from the planning office and know the officers and/or the council well.

Before we move on from prior approval versus planning, we must discuss when you might need both.

There are two main occasions when you might need prior approval AND a planning process. The first of these is when you wish to make changes to the external elevations of buildings that doesn't allow for that within the prior approval rules. By way of example, we often make changes to the outside of offices we are converting to ensure the building looks more residential. The good news with this type of application is that:

1. You have won the 'war' by already having secured prior approval for the conversion. It now means that you and the local authority are now effectively wanting the same things, such as improved street scene, improved amenities for the residents and good provision of bin stores, etc.

2. There is very little cost in submitting these applications.

3. There is no Section 106 or CIL to pay with such applications.

4. They tend to be relatively uncontentious and go through normally in eight weeks.

5. They can often be run in parallel with the prior approval application, ensuring that the development is not delayed.

The other occasion when you may need prior approval and planning is when you think there is an opportunity to extend the building in some way, either up or out.

If you are purchasing a prior approval opportunity with an eye to obtaining planning consent for something additional, remember that the deal must stack up without the extra element. You might take a view that you are going to reduce your normal margin because you strongly believe that there is a really good chance of securing an addition, but we would suggest you never get into a deal that doesn't work without the upside, ever! Take advice from your planning consultant and do not pursue dead ducks. Your planning consultant will understand planning rules better than you are ever likely to; they work in things called policies! We generally work with common sense, but it doesn't usually apply. Planning relies on complying with policy and your planning consultant will know what those policies are, and they will be able to tell you whether those policies are likely to stop you doing what seems like absolute common sense to you.

Chapter 6: Guiding Principles

Our Guiding Principles are:

1. Niching, whether you use prior approval or a full planning process,

2. using other people's money (OPM), and

3. networking.

Niching

As already touched upon in the book, our strong recommendation to you is look in your area, find out what you think is going to provide good deal flow, and pick a niche that you become known for by agents, by your JV partners, by your team and by your planning consultant. In doing so, you will learn faster, you will find deals faster, and you will make more money more quickly, because you are building on continuous learning within a certain area. We meet many people who bring us deals and one week it is this niche, another week it is another niche and the next week another – we know straight away that they are not focused. At the beginning of your journey, you may be trying to work out which one is going to work for you, but once you have settled on a niche, stick with it. FOCUS is required – Follow One Course Until Successful. Find a niche in commercial conversions and focus on it.

Niching can be geographical as well as by property type, and we are going to talk about geography in a little while, looking at how far away you should go from where you live. Many of us are get into property for a better quality of life, do we not? Do we want to be spending hours and hours every day driving to another area that we have chosen to work in? Neither Mark or Glenn are believers in that strategy; we know many education companies think it can work, but we are not of that mind. Furthermore, we don't consider it generally necessary to do, although there are some exceptions.Glenn has already shared his love of prior approval, but sadly this isn't available outside England, as we write. If you live outside of where prior approval is available, you need to consider if it is worth your while crossing the border, so you can do commercial conversions using prior approval.

In considering the benefits of picking a niche, let's go back to the joint venture partner. Imagine these two very different conversations with a prospective investor:

"Hi Mr Joint Venture Partner, I am an expert in commercial conversions, I have done one pub in Basingstoke, I have created an HMO from a small care home in Southampton, er, what did I do next, oh, yes that's right, I then did an office in Winchester... mmm, that didn't go so well, Oh, and I tried to convert a light industrial unit in Huddersfield, yes, I learnt a lot from that one!"

Alternatively:

"Hi, Mr Investor, I am experienced in converting offices to apartments. I currently have 10 large commercial conversion projects in either conveyancing, design or build, and they are all of offices to residential. Eight of them are in the Southampton and Eastleigh Area within 20 minutes of where I live, one is in Farnham because I used to live there and I know the area, and one is in Reading – I am learning a lot from that one."

Who would you invest in? Clearly, the second developer has niched, has specialised by area and by conversion type, is compounding their learning not only about the strategy itself but about specifically office to residential conversions. They will know the local agents, the local contractors, the planners and their approach to conversions, the contributions required by the local authority, and so the list goes on.

By picking and sticking to a niche, each time something is learnt, we are building on our knowledge for that particular area and that particular niche. It massively increases your return and value to your investor because they will look at you and see an expert.

Other People's Money (OPM)

A slightly odd but nonetheless true fact is that Glenn's last car, which he had for 12 years, had the number plate AK03 OPM. Other People's Money! Before he changed that car, one of his investors and joint venture partners who knew him quite well remarked that "AK03 OPM could have stood for active knowledge of 3 other people's money". He knew that the vast majority of Glenn's property journey in commercial conversions had been financed by just three investors! Isn't it funny how life works out sometimes. "Active knowledge of 3 other people's money"!

The first thing we would like to release you from is the thought that you need lots of money from many different sources. You don't need to find a lot of joint venture partners, and indeed, there is a principle here because we would strongly recommend that, if possible, you have only one investor for each deal. We prefer not to blend lots of different people, each lending amounts of say £50k and £100k, to get you to the £500k you need.

Firstly, why not? Well, they all need managing, they will probably all have a different view on risk and they will all have a different view on what is happening in the conversion. Some of them will be high control, some low control, some will expect a daily phone call and others won't mind an email once a month if you have got time. Clearly, if it is blend money to get some momentum going, even to get your first deal under your belt, then go for it because momentum generates momentum. But if you have a choice, always go with just one investor in each deal.

Secondly, and perhaps surprisingly, it is easier to borrow bigger chunks of money than it is to borrow small ones. You may have heard that those with money in our society are getting richer and richer and money is flowing to fewer and fewer people. This is just one of the laws of money, and Rob Moore discusses this in his excellent book, Money. The most pressing issue for those people is that they don't always know how to use it, or haven't got time to use it, or they have got so much money they put some into a pot called 'property investing' and then they want someone like you to go and make it work for them.

Now let's say you are a few years ahead of where you are now and you have banked £5m, so you put £1m in your property investing pot. In fact, why not close your eyes and just imagine what that looks like, what it feels like to know it's there. Now imagine you have got this £1m in your bank account and you want to put your feet up on the back of your yacht in the Caribbean, is this sounding alright to you? Or whatever it is you want to do, maybe it's skiing, driving a fast car, travelling the world, visiting family, whatever you want to do. Are you enjoying this vision of your future? Right, now who fancies dropping that activity that you were so enjoying and now nipping back to the UK to oversee a property development yourself?

Who would instead like a joint venture partner that you have confidence in, that you can give your £1m to, who is going to give you a nice return of 25% annualised over, say, the next 18 months? Does that sound pretty good? Now here is the other option. Would you rather have 20 joint venture partners instead that you have lent £50k each to, requiring you to do due diligence on 20 deals and monitor 20 deals? Or would you rather stick with one really good joint venture partner who is credible, and who you can lend your £1m to in one or perhaps two investments, and know it was all done and dusted? Clearly the second option is more attractive to the majority, and this is why it is easier to borrow large sums of money. Easier to manage and easier to find.

Glenn's life changed when he stopped looking for £50k for an HMO conversion and started looking for £1m for commercial conversions. He wasn't able to raise £10m in 12 months because he found some magic formula, or that he had a wealthy family that he borrowed it from. He simply found deals that were large enough to require bigger investments. Investors are looking for opportunities. We know it's a mind jump for some of you from where you are, because we see it often in the community. But it's true – there are investors out there, and if you bring them deals that solve their issues, normally by providing a good return, it does happen and can happen for you too.

Please do not be like Oliver Twist, though, as this is not an approach to win over a joint venture investor. Looking nervous and ponderous, and glancing up with doleful eyes saying, "Please sir, can I have some more?" is not something any of us are likely to actually do, but it can so often be the approach we subconsciously adopt. Who can relate to having felt a bit like that? Instead, we must consider what we bring. Can you bring at least enough time to oversee a project? Even having read this book, you will have ideas and knowledge that many others will not have. Perhaps you might reinforce this with further in-depth training, and you would then be among the elite. So many people think or dream of doing commercial conversions, but by reading this book you are beginning to really learn how to carry out this amazing strategy. Congratulations, you are educating yourself and investing in yourself, and as a result you bring knowledge and ideas about how to make someone's money work. If you can conceive the deal, have the knowledge of how to do it and the time to carry it out, then you are an investor's best friend, because you are the person who can make their money work for them.

Money is everywhere, too! It is absolutely not scarce. There is SO much money out there. When Glenn started out in commercial conversions in 2013, he had no money; in fact, he had less than no money, as he was in a significant amount of personal debt. He thought money was scarce because it was scarce in his world, and it was definitely scarce in his bank account! When we don't have a lot of money, we are likely to find that in our circle of friends, unsurprisingly, not many of them will have money either. The expression "birds of a feather flock together" explains this beautifully. We are more comfortable with people just like us. When you do have someone in your circle of friends who has got money, it is likely that when you are with them, you get a bit nervous or feel a bit 'unworthy'. Glenn recalls when he was completely broke and he had a friend in his circle who was on the main board of Zurich Bank. He once said to this very successful executive, who was by Glenn's standards at least earning a lot of money, "you are like a mentor to me". Glenn meant it as a compliment, but to his dismay the executive asked him to never call him that again. "We are friends" he said to Glenn, "you are my friend, I am not your mentor". But Glenn had put him on a pedestal because he had money and Glenn didn't feel worthy. Glenn made him a mentor, whereas the executive just wanted to be a pal.

Money is everywhere, though – indeed, there has never been more money in the world. There have never been more millionaires in the UK, and there have never been more billionaires. These people all need to get a return on their money, and many of them are waiting to work with you, or someone just like you who can offer them a relatively safe way to get a return. You just don't know them yet and they don't know about you yet. You don't need as many investors as you think, nor probably as much money as you believe, but we'll come to that in the section on arranging funds.

Again, remember what you bring. After reading this book, you are going to fulfil many investors' criteria. You will have ideas for adding value and solving a problem, you are going to have knowledge from this material, you may have time and you have your skills – these are all gifts to people who have money, but who don't have time to make it work for them.

Once you get going, momentum is amazing. Like pushing the rock up to the top of the hill, it is hard work to get going. Be under no illusion, there will be times when you cannot see where the top of the mountain is, or indeed whether what you can see is a false horizon, just as when you are pushing a massive rock up hill and can't see round it. Eventually, though, you will find the rock is becoming easier to push – deals start to come in and the investors start appearing. You can't quite let up yet but you can see the results and it is beginning to feel easier. You are on the plateau at the top of the hill. Suddenly, once you start getting that rock going down the other side of the hill and it starts roll really fast, sometimes almost too quickly, you will wonder how it could all come so easily and how you ever doubted it!

If you were to ask Glenn's team about how manic his office is, they would tell you about constantly finding new investors, raising many millions of pounds in joint venture finance, securing developments regularly, seeing the developments scaling rapidly and constantly having to revise profit targets upwards. That is momentum, momentum from a start that could have been stopped in its tracks had he given up when his first deal fell through (see Glenn's story on this in the Locating Deals chapter). The he found one investor that led to another investor. The investors told him to bring them more big deals, funded his early journey and then the rest, as they say, for Glenn is history.

Case Study – Serving Others, Not Looking for the Money (by Glenn)

Jon and I met at the Property Investor Show at the Excel in London, on 14 April 2014. It's an important date in my history. I was wearing a garish bright orange Progressive t-shirt. Orange is not my colour, I have to tell you. Why was I wearing a bright orange t-shirt? I was crewing. I was already well on my property journey by then, and I certainly didn't need crew points. I was giving back to Progressive because being a host of PPN had already changed my life. By now I had already bought four or five offices to convert, I had already accessed millions of pounds in JV finance and PPN needed people to staff their stall at the show. Staffing a stall in a bright orange t-shirt is about as far out of my comfort zone as I could get!

The reason I chose to become a PPN host was that I hated networking and I am really nervous about going into a room full of people I don't know. I am one of those people who is convinced that everyone else knows each other and they don't have the slightest interest in talking to me. I am sure I'm not the only one who feels that way. By becoming a PPN host, I had people coming to me for advice. The resultant profile and credibility played a key role in securing joint ventures and the associated funds for my property journey. So, when the call went out for people to crew the stall (even though I couldn't think of anything worse), I decided to show my gratitude by showing up in London and donning the bright orange t-shirt. Our role was to accost people as they wandered past the stall, offering them a report on raising JV finance, which of course meant getting their name and address, which would find its way on to Progressive's ever-growing mailing list.

Let's hear from Jon himself about that day. This interview was held in November 2015.

Q: So Jon, what was your situation when we met? What was it like back then for you?

A: Back then I was just about to take voluntary redundancy from the computer company, I had been in the IT marketing game for about 22 years by that point and there were lots of organisational changes happening. I was fairly comfortable in terms of my career at Dell, I had been there over 10 years and reached a mid to senior management level, managing a global team including a team at the headquarters in the States. I had a decent six-figure salary but I didn't really feel ahead of the game financially, with a big mortgage, etc., and, you know, I was really dependent on the annual bonus to pay for holidays and so on. But I was given an opportunity: with the big changes that were happening at the company, Dell was offering people voluntary redundancy should they want to take it. Because I had been there 10 years I knew I wanted to do something different, and 10 years meant 18 months' money – a decent salary x 18 months would give me enough time to figure out what I wanted to do. By that stage, I knew it was going to be property as I had probably spent the last five years trying to think of business ideas to do something myself and never come up with one. So I realised it was property, but I didn't really know anything more than that.

Q: Ok, so you went to the Property Investor Show.

A: Yes, I went to the Property Investor Show and walked around, talked to lots of people, felt embarrassed because I didn't really know what I was asking. If I am honest, I tried to avoid your gaze as I walked past, probably as I did with everyone, because as you're walking past these people you know they are just there to get your name and phone number and so on so they can hit you afterwards. Anyway, I failed, you caught my eye and we got chatting.

Q: We got chatting, how long did we chat for, can you remember?

A: It probably wasn't very long, no more than five or maximum 10 minutes at the time.

Q: Would you be surprised to know it was about 45 minutes?

A: No it wasn't.

It was, because I got told off by the other people on the stall for spending so long with one person. Jon was talking to me about his situation; it was a lot longer than 5 minutes. What about now? What are we doing now together?

Together we have two joint venture partners where I am the investor, we are working 50/50, we are doing two as a straight 50/50 joint venture. We also are involved in a third one, which is a three-way deal with Glenn, myself and an investor who is a member of my family. Also I am working on one myself with a family member as an investor, so that is where it's at in terms of how I am doing.

I mentioned the six-figure salary – I had 18 months to try and replace that, in fact Mrs Lynch, my wife, gave me nine months to prove that I enjoyed property. That was the most important thing for her, that I was enjoying doing what I was doing, because I was a miserable git doing what I was doing before. But not just that I was enjoying it but more importantly that we could see the money. So, in other words, half way through my 18 months redundancy she wanted me to either start looking for another job, or prove that property could do it. We are now at 18 months. The good news was that after nine months I proved to her I was enjoying it, and we could see the pipeline of salary, I still think a little bit in terms of equivalent salary terms and I think I can see about seven years' salary in the next year.

Q: So, 18 months on you are earning seven times more than you used to earn as a senior person in your company.

A: Yes, that is right, yes.

Q: That is just on existing deals in your pipeline?

A: That is as of today and clearly we are out there trying to get more deals.

Q: So how have you done that, how did you get to that point?

A: In a number of ways: the first one was meeting you, that was the start of it for me. I knew I wanted it to be property but I didn't really have a strategy. I knew that I needed to go and get knowledge, so I went to the Property Investor Show and met you, but also subsequently I went to the PPN Waterloo Networking Event, I think on your recommendation. I then also signed up to the Progressive Property Masterclass, which helped me decide what I did and didn't want to do. I went on commercial conversion courses, I went on the Joint Venture Day course, so I have gone the full hog with Progressive and found it really useful. But probably more important, though, I knew that I needed someone to help me directly, and although we have never really termed it a mentorship, you have acted as a mentor for me, and I latched onto you because you were very credible. If you are going to do a joint venture with somebody and you're thinking about building out projects, I knew it needed to be with someone who was credible. You told the story about The Rose Bowl, and because of that background, I knew you were credible. Also, you were further ahead in your journey in terms of commercial conversion than I was at that time as well, so I wanted to latch onto you, which I did fairly successfully.

Q: So go back to the Excel, did you tell me how much money you had to invest?

A: Not at the point we met at the show. Similarly to what you did with others, you were very gracious with your time and you were interested enough to say you would meet me for a coffee, but only if I drove down to you.

Q: And, you had to drive and…

A: Pay for the coffee.

Q: Now I make a joke of it, what I said to Jon at the time, "look it has been really fascinating talking to you, we have been talking for a while, I really need to go back and start staffing the stall, but if you want to come down and spend some time with me, I am prepared to spend as long as you would like, as long as you're prepared to come to me and buy the coffee". That is actually what I said to you… can you remember what happened at the beginning of the coffee?

A: Well it very nearly didn't happen, I had been in the Costa in Eastleigh for 20 minutes and you hadn't showed up, so I phoned you and I could hear the "ooohhh" and clearly you had forgotten. Actually that's not fair, not remembered, so you said wait there five minutes and sure enough you showed up.

Q: Interesting, I thought I was 10 minutes late; I had forgotten the meeting, sorry. That wasn't a great start – this isn't an exact science, we can get it wrong and it still comes out alright in the end. What happened in the meeting?

A: Well I wasn't stroppy, you knew more than me and therefore I valued your time so I didn't mind, I still bought the coffee. There was one issue that we nearly didn't get past, which was Glenn then went to show me something on his iPad, he opened up his iPad and there was a football game on the screen. That's fine, I play FIFA as well, but it was Aston Villa beating Birmingham City – turns out he's an Aston Villa fan and I'm a Birmingham City fan, so that was nearly the end of a potentially beautiful relationship, but we got past that as well.

Q: How long did we talk for?

A: I would say five minutes, but…

Q: So, we are in the coffee shop for about two and a half hours, and at the end, as I recall, you said something like "I would really like to do commercial conversion, I am pretty sure that is right for me", is that what you remember?

A: Yes, that's right.

Q: So, I would have said something like, "well London has got plenty of opportunity" because you hadn't said anything to me at this point about working with me, can you remember how that last bit went?

A: I am bound to have got it wrong.

Q: Go for it.

A: I think by that stage I'd decided that I would like to work with you, but I don't think we had ever talked about money. From day one, even on the stand, I said I was aware of what I was after, I had time because I had been made redundant, I had access to some funds because I did, but what I did know is I didn't have any knowledge, so that is what I said to you at that point. All the way through our two-and-a-half-hour coffee I don't think we mentioned the funds at any point.

Q: Now I don't know about you, but in my experience up to this point when someone says they have got access to funds that is normally anywhere between £50k and £200k, those kind of numbers, maybe a bit of pension money that has been released. What happened at the end of the meeting was that Jon said "I would really like to do commercial conversion", I said "there are plenty in London that would be great", and he said "well actually, I would like to work with you". I wasn't playing hard to get or anything, but I was very clear by then, as Jon will tell you, my niche and my area is this. So I said to Jon "I only work in Southampton". So Jon said, "well I am quite happy to travel". I said "Jon, commercial conversions take quite a lot of money, do you mind if I ask…?" because he mentioned again that he had access to some funds. And what did you tell me?

A: I said initially £2 million.

Q: And you added something onto that.

A: And more if we need it.

Q: Just give people another two minutes on your circumstances, how did you have that £2m and why did you have more if we needed it? I knew none of this of course at the time.

A: So, other people's money is the answer. It wasn't my money. I described my situation working for the IT company, but one thing I found when I decided to go, in my mind I would say "I am now in property". I started talking to lots of people, and some people were interested but didn't talk about putting any money in. I found out one of my very close family members was not only interested but actually already doing it to an extent, actually to an extent that I didn't know. So when we got talking, it was clear that he had an appetite for property, was already investing in property and wanted to do more. At that point he said if you come across a deal then I will be interested and we will need to set some very clear caveats in terms of expectations of what level of return he was trying to achieve, but that is where it was. We had had a conversation, he would enable a facility for me as long as we got to the right level of return of £2m, but we could look at other opportunities should they hit the gate.

Q: £2m was on mate's rates though wasn't it?

A: £2m was effectively a family loan if you like, yes.

Q: Can you see now what I am saying? I met this guy on a stand where I was wearing an orange t-shirt trying to give back to PPN, grateful to the world for what it had already given me. I got chatting to a guy who said "I need help", I offered help and had no idea we would end up joint venture partners; one meeting later he says at the end he has £2m. Who would like a joint venture partner like that? Can you see now why I have been saying solve other people's problems, serve others and it will come to you. If I had gone around that show looking for a joint venture partner, what are the chances of me bumping into Jon and having a conversation that would have been useful to him, and at the end of which he would have said "by the way I have got £2-million"? And yet isn't that what many of us try in some sort of unacknowledged way?

So, Jon, what have we talked about for the future? I guess what I am asking is, you could easily now do this on your own but what are the conversations we have had?

A: We are now deciding that actually we have learnt a lot and we have the opportunity to just scale, we have agents who are bringing us more deals, even the projects we have bid on and we haven't won we are now starting to build credibility with those agents and those agents are starting to bring us deals. Sourcing them is becoming easier, so we are looking at more deals and therefore we need access to more money. But you know for now equity is a limitation, so we need to go out and find more equity and in order for us to free our time. We also have to systemise what we are doing. I am probably more involved in the execution for my one project, and that is something we need to hand off.

Q: So, Jon is the person I was having a conversation with, and we have said, "Right we have to start using project managers", we have agreed to use project managers on our two deals that we have got, so that we can go out and network for deals and money. So, you might find the idea of finding a £2m joint venture partner almost unimaginable heaven, but can you see how quickly all that happens? You move up another level, and then you move up another level, and then you move up another level. Jon and I met just 18 months ago and we are already reimagining our business; we know now that we need to do bigger deals to hit bigger numbers and therefore we need more money. This is absolutely true, I had a guy ring me up the other day and say "I have got £20m I need to put into a deal outside London, can you help?" And actually, my honest answer is no, I can do it in three deals but I can't do it in one. I don't know of many deals outside London where I can get £20m into one deal. But how had he heard about me?

A: Reputation.

Q: What would your advice be? You are, to many people, exactly what we are looking for: a joint venture partner who is great to work with. I don't mean to make you blush, you had some funds, we have had a good time and we are enjoying it so much that we are going to work together even once you have grown beyond that mentoring position, but how do people find people like you? We sometimes think that investors are some kind of special beings, people we almost shouldn't be in the presence of. You know sometimes I think we elevate a millionaire to a level where we would be uncomfortable knowing them. One of the advantages I had with Jon was that I didn't know, I just talked to him like a normal person. What would you say to people about finding joint venture partners and how to be approachable?

A: You just have to talk about what you're doing, that is the most important thing. You have no idea where this is going to lead you, you won't find out unless you talk to people. You are taking the right step today by getting the knowledge, but network. Network, but not just at property events, do it outside property. Clearly networking for me was that I was at a family event, I started talking about what I wanted to do, that I wanted to be in property, but I had no idea I was going to land that amount of money or access to money. It only comes by having that conversation. The big thing for me was that after 20+ years of being in one world, moving into another, not really knowing what I am doing, I almost didn't want to talk about it through embarrassment. Also, you are worried about your friends and family taking the mickey out of you in case it's not a success. Don't worry about that, just talk about what you are trying to achieve, that is probably the single biggest thing you can do.

Q: One final point, you haven't said who your brother is but would you mind sharing with people how much money your brother has in his property trading account.

A: Again, so I said it was a close family member, it is my brother. I always refer to him as the investor as it makes me feel better about myself. I genuinely didn't know he is a high net worth individual but I knew that he had put money into property over the years. He had been funding his father-in-law, who had been knocking down cottages or bungalows in Bournemouth and then building up two places in their place. I knew he had been doing that for a while, but what I didn't know was that every time he met someone, he was talking to them about what he was doing. So, the guy that built his house in Wimbledon, parents of the friends of his children, developers, he had been putting money in there. So, from 2002 to today, his company has built up I think something like £25m of equity out in property deals. Now they didn't start with anything like that amount, but that is what is out at the moment in various schemes.

Giving back in a show, giving back in a coffee, a £2m joint venture and, as Jon mentioned earlier, we have done a deal with his brother, who has £25m equity in his trading account. We were with his brother at a lunch one day, I can't remember if it was then or another occasion, but he has also said if he gets to the point where he is exposed enough, then he has got a load of mates and he will introduce us to all of them. Who thinks his mates might have a few quid in their back pockets? So, the over-riding theme to this section is, if you are credible, if you serve others, if you are generous and you have a deal, the money will come.

This was a long interview to include in the book, but it contains such a rich collection of points with regard to the use of OPM, how to meet them, how to work with them and what it can lead to that I decided to leave the entire interview in.

There is more than enough money to fund YOUR property journey out there. The scarcity scripts we run in our mind, cultivated in most cases since childhood, are just that – scripts. It is not true that money is scarce just because it has been scarce in our lives to this point. Enjoy the freedom of knowing other people would like to fund the deals you find.

Networking

If you are going to succeed in this strategy, you will need to network, network, network. It's so important we've said it three times. Having taught more than 1,000 people on this subject and seen more than 100 people go through our commercial conversion mentoring programme, it has become clear that the biggest differentiator between those who succeed in this strategy and those who give up before they see the other side of their first deal is networking; it is everything, absolutely everything. It is the difference maker, the accelerator and the turbo charge.

Why do certain people succeed where others fail? The successful person never gives up, is passionate and networks continuously. They are always out, meeting people and meeting them with a purpose that is followed up.

I don't know if you remember from the story of his journey, but Glenn genuinely doesn't like networking. As he mentioned, he would walk into a room and see everyone else talking and be convinced they all knew each other, and that the last thing they wanted was Glenn walking up to say, "Hi!" He used to feel like he was some little kid and that he was the 'not in' person. Sure, it is in our heads, but it felt real to him. For those of you who also suffer this, it is as real to you as it was to Glenn, so what did he do? Networking was so important that he set up a networking meeting! He paid £9k for a Progressive networking franchise just so that he didn't have to go and talk to other people! This is serious, and completely true. However, he then went on to raise £10m in JV finance in the first year, and it was because he was prepared to do whatever it took. What you are going to do to make sure you get over your fear of networking? Why not find a friend who enjoys networking and go with them, because it is often the difference between success and frustration.

We have a particular mentee on our mentoring programme who is a full-time mum. She has a small buy-to-let portfolio, she home schools her four children of various ages, and she has just about every reason for life to get in the way of her success. Do you know what she did better than almost anyone? She made time to network like nobody you have ever seen. She made it work by turning it into something she could look forward to by taking agents out for a coffee, out to the pub for a drink, popping in for a chat (having driven many miles out of her way to be 'in the area'). Despite home schooling, having four children and being tired, she found an approach that was a break from her normal routine and was therefore as good as a rest.

For her, it went into overdrive when she met one particular agent, took him to the pub, and they clicked really well. The agent was hungry and young in his role and delighted to meet a serious buyer who was desperate for deals. He went and found loads of deals for her, she paid him a fee for any deals he brought to her but that he wasn't acting for the vendor on, and she has rapidly become the 'deal sourcing queen' of our mentoring programme. She has networked her way to success. It took her 7 or 8 months but now there is barely a month that goes by that she doesn't get a deal. Some deals she passes on and gets very good money out it, some deals she converts herself.

Network your way to success. The larger the web of contacts you create, the juicier the stuff that flies into your web is going to be. What are we trying to achieve? We want that little black book of amazing contacts, and we want to be visible and known. You might be able to do this without networking if you are a shrinking wallflower and don't want anyone to know what you are doing, but it is going to be a lot more difficult. You need a reputation for being known (for the right things), you need to be staying current in the property and funding markets, and what better way to do that than to network with the people who are in those markets.

The property community is generous, have you found that so far on your property journey? What better way to solve your problems than to be networking and mixing with people who are doing what you are trying to do. They may be six months or a year ahead of you, but you know what, those of us who are in this know that there is more than enough for everybody and we are more than happy to share our knowledge.

We were created as social beings. That is why so often prisoners are punished for misdemeanours by being put into isolation. For prisoners of war, the worst punishment was to be chucked in 'the cooler', what does that say about us all? The prisoners might be on their own for weeks on end in the dark and cold, and it was considered to be such a severe punishment because we are not created to be like that. So, get out into the community. It will be a boost to your morale, and it will help you succeed faster and bigger than you might otherwise do.

When networking, do not be the person in the room who is only there for themselves. Do not be the person who walks into the room to solve just their own problems. Glenn was part of a mentorship programme called VIP, which is run by Progressive. He was on VIP for three years, but he experienced very mixed success during that time. He recalls, *"The first year I did VIP, I achieved absolutely naff all. I attended just four of the 12 monthly events I was entitled to attend, and when I did turn up, I was only interested in myself. I was an arrogant 'executive' who, despite my mentors being people who were already successful in strategies I hadn't yet implemented, I ignored everything they said. I was a 'successful businessman' so what could they teach me? Even on those occasions I was at VIP, I didn't go with the right attitude. I didn't go to help, I didn't go to serve, I didn't go to solve other people's problems. I instead approached it with an attitude that smacked of, 'What can you give me?' and do you know what, it is hardly a surprise that I achieved naff all with an attitude like."*

But we see people like that at every networking meeting. They walk in and 'cruise' the room, saying a cursory hello to people in an effort to discover who in the room might have that £50k they need for their latest project, walking from one person to the next, spending as little time as possible as they 'discard' one person after another in their search for cash. We may be exaggerating to make the point, but only slightly. We need to be genuinely interested in other people and solving their problems, helping them in whatever way we can. Even some words of encouragement can go a long way if someone has had a tough month. The more problems you solve for other people, the more you will be amazed how quickly the world pays you back. Be proactive, identify the good groups and go to them, be interested, talk to people.

Everyone's favourite subject is nearly always themselves. We are each fascinated by our own life. So, if you want to make a massive impact on someone, when you meet them focus on being the world's best listener. Don't be insincere, but show a genuine interest in people. You will learn more than you would believe because people are genuinely interesting and are doing, or have done, some amazing things. The stuff people have overcome can lend us energy and belief. If you have a conversation with someone and listen even 70% of the time, they are likely to go away considering you to be absolutely the nicest person they have met in a long time, and ironically remember you as a great conversationalist! If you give people the option to talk about themselves, they will love you for it. There is no better way to be popular than to give people a 'damn good listening to'. It is a forgotten skill, because our favourite subject is ourselves, and we are desperate to talk about our favourite subject. When networking, keep in mind that we were all given two ears and one mouth – you will do well to use them in that proportion.

Be patient; a strong network can take time to build. Your network should consist of three groups of people: inner circle, established contacts, new contacts and acquaintances. The largest group should be established contacts. The inner circle are people with whom you have very strong connections and you reach out to for advice, and who you can count on to be there when you need them and vice versa. Your network will probably be the source of your 'inner circle' though, so it is very important to focus on strengthening existing relationships and not spend all of your time just making new connections. Your established contacts are people you know well and who know you well. You have helped each other and have a genuine relationship, but without the depth of your inner circle. The new contacts and acquaintances are people you meet at events who introduce themselves, are introduced to you or who you introduce yourself to. At this stage, you are simply getting to know them. As you do so you, will need to decide whether to invest time making them an established contact or whether to keep them at an acquaintance level.

By choosing our mentors, we are bringing them into our inner circle. We need them in our inner circle because they have already done what we are trying to do – they are modelling it. Both Mark and Glenn pay tens of thousands of pounds a year spending as much time as they can with their mentors because the more time they spend with them, the richer they get. Their knowledge rubs off, their influence, their networks and professional team contacts. They have proven that they know what they are doing.

We have all heard that "your net worth is your network" and that we will be the aggregate of the five people we spend most time with. So, we try and make our mentors within the business context the five people we spend the most time with, because they make us wealthier. Who are you going to put in your inner circle? Who can you help on that journey? Our mentors are helping us become very successful, and by spending time with them we create more wealth for ourselves.

Just a last thought, be approachable and smile a lot. It can make a massive difference because we are a lot less scary when we smile.

Case Study – You Never Know Where Networking Will Lead (by Glenn)

My business partnership was born at a networking meeting!

For those of you who wanted to buy a new car, once you had decided on the model and the colour did you see slightly more of them on the road than were there before? All the time. Now do we really think there are more on the road after we had decided on that car or were they there all the time? Of course, **they were there all the time**. So why did we see more of them afterwards? We were tuned in to that picture in our mind.

The Holy Grail Joint Venture is tuning in to exactly what you need to take your property journey to the next level. You need to know who you are and most importantly who you are not and what you are not good at. We all need somebody; if you are brilliant at strategy and big picture thinking, you are likely to need help with detail and process, and conversely, if you are detail and process driven and maybe also quite risk averse, you are going to need someone to help you get over the line on deals, or you may never buy anything.

Personally, I love big-picture thinking and am quick to make decisions, but I rarely stick around long enough to get enough data and evidence to be sure I have made a good decision, rather than just a fast one. I knew that for my new business to thrive, I needed to be working with someone who enjoyed taking on tasks I didn't like, and who brought some process and systems to my 'seat-of-the-pants' approach. The following interview, recorded in November 2015, tells the story of how I met the person who was to become my business partner.

Q: So, Justine, how did we meet?

A: I actually went along to a PPN meeting in Southampton, which Glenn was obviously hosting because he runs the group, and part of that section of the meeting was when you stood up and in one minute said who you were, and why you were there. I got to that point by reading a lot of books and watching a lot of DVDs, and I managed to totally confuse myself, so I stood up at the networking meeting and asked if anyone could help me because I had managed to completely confuse myself and didn't know which way to go in property.

Q: What did I say to you after the meeting?

A: Glenn very kindly offered to meet me for a coffee and talk about where I was financially and what my options were in property, and we would have a quick discussion in Costa Coffee about what the best steps were for me to take to progress my journey.

Q: I didn't know you very well then did I? I had literally heard you stand up and speak for one minute.

A: Exactly, we didn't know each other at all, we had never met.

Q: So, first principle, there was nothing in it for me other than giving back, does that make sense? Somebody in the room stood up and said "I am really confused, I want to make progress in property but I don't know how", and my instinct was just to solve their problem. If you serve the community, it is amazing how often the world pays us back. Hearing some confusion, I thought this is what I am here to do, I am the PPN host so why don't I meet this person for coffee, we can have a chat for a couple of hours and I will see if I can help.

Before we talk about what happened in that meeting, what is the relationship between us now?

A: We are business partners.

Q: We are business partners, how did that happen?

A: Well we met for coffee, had a quick discussion about what finances I had available, what knowledge I had and where I wanted to go, and we quickly came to the conclusion that maybe HMOs was the way forward for me, so we finished up our coffee and Glenn asked me what I do in the real world, outside of property. We had quite an in-depth discussion about my history in business and what my strengths were and we kind of went from there.

Q: Kind of went from there, so what are your strengths?

A: My background is in business, I have built a few businesses and sold them, I franchised another business, so my strengths you could say are systemising businesses, putting them through a format, putting them into a manual so anyone can pick up that manual and run that business, and that is exactly what Glenn needed at that time.

Q: A detail person, processes, systems, do you get the idea that I might have needed some of that? I knew that somewhere along the line I needed to get someone on board who could cover my weaknesses. I knew what I couldn't do, and I was looking for someone to do that. Now I didn't know Justine at all from standing up and talking about property, but when we started talking about her background, a light bulb went on in my head. I wasn't quite gauche enough to say would you come and work with me, can you remember what I said?

A: You said there are lots of people in property who need someone just like you, and you should hang out with groups of people who are doing what you fancy doing in property.

Q: Justine had £50k available and one of her questions was how do I stretch this? I actually said to Justine at the end of the meeting, "Justine I don't think your cash equity is your real equity, I think your real equity is who you are and your business experience, and I think if you leverage that equity in the property marketplace, you will make much faster progress", and that is what led to the conversation about going off and having chats with people. Now, in fact what did you say?

A: Can I come and work for you please?

After just one meeting, Justine said "well actually I would quite like to work with you".

Two years later, as we write this book, Justine and Glenn have become firm friends and 50/50 business partners in all they do. Their partnership has accelerated the journey for both of them, built on complimentary skills and behaviours and allowed them to scale much more quickly than either of them could have on their own. Their partnership is truly synergetic; it has transformed their work, lives and profitability, and it all came from networking! Rob and Mark also met at a networking event. Their own journey is very similar to that of Glenn and Justine. They too have become friends, enjoying a synergetic partnership that is hugely profitable, enjoyable and releasing, allowing each of them to deploy their own strengths. Two amazing business partnerships forged from chance meetings at networking events illustrates what amazing opportunities can be found through effective networking.

To repeat, networking is about giving as well as what you will get out of it. Other people know whether you are genuinely interested in helping them and getting to know them, or instead you are only motivated by what you can get out of them. As mentioned above, focus on how you can help others and you never know how or when it will pay you back. If you don't have experience yet, you have other skills, and we can all support, encourage and become people 'in the know' who can introduce people to others in our network who may be able to help them.

Of course, you want to get something positive for yourself out of your networking efforts, but it's important to take an approach that will benefit others. In the long term, helping others always benefits us because we all like to help people who have helped us. Remember this is about digital networking as well as face-to-face – be active in your social media groups and offer help and support wherever you can. As a start, why not identify three people, either in your current network, or people you would like to get to know, and come up with one way that you could help each of them within the next week? If you are new to networking, you will need to take action in order to build your network. Once you start, you will find that your profile will grow and people will begin to come to you. Start by identifying local property networking groups and prioritise attending them regularly.

Our experience is that property people have an abundance mentality and are keen to see others do well. When you go to a networking group, you can expect people to be welcoming and friendly. If you are brave enough to attend on your own, you will quickly find that standing near a group will lead to an introduction, or perhaps the organiser of the event will introduce you to a friendly crowd. Going with people you know is an obvious solution to the 'first date' nerves. You don't need to have a reason to be there, other than an interest in property. To start, identify property networking events near you that you can attend.

Networking is easy once we get hold of the idea that people normally like to talk about themselves and their business interests or lives. Show a genuine interest in others and be curious about what they are doing, how they decided to start their business or what property model they started with, how long they have been networking at that event, what courses have they done, which would they recommend. Obviously you don't want to make it like the Spanish Inquisition, but curiosity is invaluable in getting to know people and will pay dividends later – especially if you follow one of the other principles of being organised about your network.

You will need to be patient and not expect overnight results, instant offers of JV finance or deals, or free advice! Impatience demonstrates desperation, which is never a good look. Focus on building strong relationships and giving away your time, expertise, advice, encouragement, support – whatever you have to offer. Make sure you follow up with every person you network with. Try to make your follow up as personal as possible, remaining professional and not being too 'chummy'.

As we have been emphasising, the value of your network will be found in the quality of the relationships you form, rather than the number. This can be measured by how well you know the people in your network, how relevant they are to the work you do and the level of influence each of you has.

We need a mix of people in our networks and, although it always feels encouraging and as though we are more likely to achieve greater things if we know industry leaders, the reality is that they already have their inner circles and established contacts. Most industry leaders are very busy, as they have built successful businesses that require time and attention (even when they are highly leveraged!) so when they add to those groups, they will be likely to look at peers rather than new starters. This isn't because they are 'too big for their boots'. Industry leaders are likely to be friendly when you meet them and even offer you help and advice at the time, but they have to be strategic about how they use their time. You may also find that their advice is beyond where you are and can be overwhelming. It is often better to seek advice and help from people who are much closer to you in terms of your property experience. You don't need to completely forget about networking with industry leaders, but make that a much smaller part of your networking efforts at first. Your focused efforts should be on power team contacts, those that may be able to assist you either finding JV finance or providing it, and those who can support and help you with their experience and advice from a position about 12 months ahead of you.

Consider now, who do you have in your network already (in terms of categories)? Where do you need to develop your network? Focus on meeting and being introduced to those people and developing relationships with them.

Don't forget to smile and make it easy for people to talk to you. This sounds obvious, but when we are a little nervous about networking we can forget that others are too. We can also be too eager to dominate the conversation and tell people about us and what we need – hold back, show an interest and curiosity in others first. They will do the same for you, and if they don't, that will help you to decide which part of your networking circle they may stay on!

It's really easy to overlook the importance of networking and think that you have a million other more important things to do. However, its importance can be measured by the amount of information we have put about it in this book. There are few activities that will yield better results in the long term than building up a strong network of quality connections.

The time you take in your networking will be in two main areas: finding and attending networking events and meetings, and your follow-up activity from anyone you meet. It is the second of these where the real relationship building will happen, so be sure to follow up with people and book those coffees. It is when you meet people for coffee that you get an idea of how to serve and help them. You also get to know what is important to them and can then build on your early rapport into a working relationship.

Why not grab your diary now and schedule networking activities, including time on social media? Make it an appointment for 30 minutes a day so you don't sit on Facebook all day though! Also, schedule follow-up time after a networking event; this should not just be emails, phone people – the personal touch makes a lot of difference – and book those coffees!

To add value to your network and for it to add value to you, you need to organise it in some way.

Information that is helpful to note:

- Name and any contact details (obviously)

- Where and when you met them

- Personal details they shared, like family members, where they like to go on holiday, hobbies etc.

- What social media groups are they part of

- Any needs they expressed, even if you don't know anyone who can help right now

- How they fit into your network – this may change over time but what is your feeling right now?

- Categorise them – key influencer, expert, friendly (choose categories that work for you)

- How are you going to follow up?

To keep track of all this information, set up a spreadsheet of all the people you consider to be a part of your network. On a regular basis (weekly, fortnightly), go through the spreadsheet and connect with these people by leaving comments on their social media posts, sharing their posts or direct contact. When you go to the event where you met them, look out for them and use the information from your spreadsheet to make the reconnection more personal. Did they get the help they needed with x? How is that deal coming on? Did your daughter do well in her music exam? Etc....

The initial part of your networking efforts will be to help you find a deal, analyse it and find the money to fund it. Be on the lookout for all potential members of your future power team, but, in particular, to begin with your network should be varied and inclusive and have the following objectives:

Contacts – the most obvious benefit of networking is to meet potential power team members (more of this in the next section), investors and deal sourcers, and identify opportunities for partnerships, joint ventures or new areas of expansion for your business.

Visibility – with business relationships 'once seen, never forgotten' is almost never true. You need to meet and communicate with people on a regular basis to raise your personal profile and keep you front and centre in the minds of the right people. This is a people business, so it is vital that people know what you do and what you are looking for too. If you are a giver as well as a taker, you will almost certainly see the rewards of visibility in networking.

Reputation – you can use networking as an opportunity to become known as someone that is friendly, open, easy to communicate with and 'in the know'. This makes you an invaluable resource as well as a person people will want to do business with. Be known as someone that is interested in other people, not just themselves. Be amazing at solving other people's problems and see how quickly people gravitate towards you and begin to solve your issues without you even having to ask!

Staying Current – in an ever-changing business climate, especially in property, it is important to keep up with overall trends in your industry. Attending seminars and networking with your peers and business associates on a regular basis will help you stay current.

Problem Solving – in addition to the potential of increasing your contacts and opportunities you can often find solutions to your own business problems or needs by networking. This is particularly true in the early days, when you are trying to find out how much things cost in order to analyse your deals as accurately as possible.

Sharing Knowledge and Experience – networking is ideal for expanding your knowledge by taking advantage of the viewpoints and prior experience of others.

Confidence and Morale – most business people are optimistic and positive, particularly in the property world. Regularly associating with such people can be a great morale boost, especially in the difficult early phases of starting something new. If you are not naturally outgoing, regularly meeting new people can also boost your confidence and on a personal basis you may form new friendships with like-minded people.

PART TWO: THE 'GO LARGE' COMMERCIAL CONVERSION SYSTEM

Chapter 7: GO – Get Outsourcing

Earlier in the book, Glenn mentioned how he had somehow ended up in a role that required overseeing a £50m development comprising of a five-star hotel, two new spectators stands and an 18-hole golf course. He had no clue, no background, no idea. If he had known what he was getting into when he accepted the role, he says he may never have done it! Maybe you feel that way about getting involved in commercial conversions?

The good news is you can pull it off! How? Well, every conversion comes with a professional fee budget and there is a world of experts out there who are not as smart as you. You are probably reading this because you don't want to trade your time for money anymore. Here's the great news: there is a world of experts who set their lives up to trade their time and expertise for your money. Oh sorry, it's not your money because it is your investor's money, or is it the development finance company's money? Even better then, they are going to trade their time for somebody else's money but to your benefit. That is outsourcing, that is what Glenn learnt at The Rose Bowl and that is our gift to you in this book.

This is the secret that we consider gives everybody the opportunity to use this strategy to change their financial circumstances forever. There are professionals out there who know more than you could ever learn in one lifetime. Don't try and learn their jobs, don't try and be better at it than them. Simply hire the best experts and never quibble with their bills, because if they are the best they won't need to rip you off and if they are the best they will make you more than they cost. Don't go with the cheap option – it's a bit like builders, you never go with the most expensive builder because there is always a builder who says I don't really need the work so I will put a stupid fee in and if they are stupid enough to accept it at least I am making an absolute mint. Then the builder at the other end promises you the earth, but he is going to deliver nothing except a very big headache, because he is so desperate for the work that he puts in a really low cost. So use the same rule by never going for the cheapest and never going for the most expensive. However, you do want to be nearer the more expensive end because good people charge for their services. Now look, if you want an average development with average profit then go and hire slightly better than average people. If you want to be known for being excellent at what you do and you want excellent results thereby making excellent money, then hire excellent people who are going to help you be excellent.

Your team for commercial conversions will get quite broad in time, but not at the beginning. At the beginning, we like to keep things simple and we need just five key members of our power team:

1.   Commercial property agent

2.   Planning consultant

3.   Architect

4.   Commercial property solicitor

5.   Commercial finance broker

Your commercial property agent is easy to find. At the beginning of your commercial conversion journey, you will achieve most by finding and connecting with the dominant local commercial agent(s). There is often one local agent, not usually more than two at most, with just one or two offices each that seem to deal with 70-80% of the smaller commercial property in the area. You can locate them by the prevalence of their 'For Sale' or 'To Let' signs, either virtually or on the real streets. Later in the book, we mention a website by Property Estates Gazette. If you search on that website for commercial properties in your area, and change the search criteria to look for the smaller properties (say under 10,000 sq ft), you will notice that one or two agents dominate the search results. Alternatively, you could simply jump in your car, on your bike or even walk the streets to look at the physical boards on show. The agents that are most prevalent in advertising the smaller properties are the commercial agents that you need in your early power team. They are the ones that will have 80% of the appropriate smaller properties for your early deals and building rapport and relationship with them is vital.

Your second team member is a planning consultant. You might be tempted to dispense with a specialised planning consultant and instead use the services of an architect, or possibly even do it yourself. Please resist that temptation. Even though we both niche and know the permitted development and planning rules really well, we both use a planning consultant. Glenn has been fortunate enough to meet a lady called Ruth and she has made him a lot of money. Notice the choice of language. She has made Glenn a lot of money, and she certainly doesn't work for free!

As a small example, Glenn had a development in which he had converted an office into eight apartments using prior approval, but there was a carport there too. He had applied to convert the carport into another unit, and the planning officer contacted him saying he was going to refuse permission. Glenn wouldn't have known how to change that planning officers mind. His planning consultant made a phone call to that planning officer explaining her interpretation of the permitted development rules, and by the end of the day the planning officer was apologising for having to ask for an extension of time so that he could write an approval. Two days later Glenn got consent for the conversion of that carport. The carport cost him around £30k to £40k to convert, he had already bought the land as we had bought the whole building and he sold the completed unit for £125k! Even after selling agent's fees, that is a really nice profit of around £80k that he would have left on the table had he not been prepared to pay a £2k bill to his planning consultant. If you were offered the opportunity today to swap £2,000 for £80,000, you would be up for that! Do not skimp on your planning consultant – a good one will make you money rather than cost you money.

The next member of your five-person power team is the architect. You may think architects, WOW, it takes years and years of work to become an architect. Given all training, you may think that all architects are incredible, but sadly, some of them are commercially clueless. Particularly if you are doing permitted development, the poor ones are not practically-minded and they are even less commercially-minded. They may know how to put a building together and how to do some clever technical drawings, but trust us, that doesn't mean they are necessarily the people you want. You will need an architect who has done permitted developments before, if that is the strategy you are going to follow; you need to see evidence of what they have done on those prior projects, and you need to speak to their previous clients. You do not want to learn the hard way that you have got the wrong architect – that is not a pain barrier you need or want to go through.

Next, you need a commercial property solicitor, who you should find through word of mouth. Networking meetings are a good source of this kind of information, particularly if you are attending one in which people are already undertaking commercial conversions. Commercial property solicitors are very different from their residential conveyancing colleagues, so don't presume you can use the same person you may have used for residential transactions. They don't have to be local, so it is more important to find a good one.

Finally, you will need a good corporate finance broker, but more about them when we discuss funding the deal later in the book.

At first, finding five excellent people in different disciplines who you are going to rely on heavily could seem quite daunting. Here, though, is how it works: you will be looking for what you need next. Let's say you find an absolutely fantastic planning consultant. Do you think fantastic planning consultants work with really awful architects? Are they going to recommend someone really terrible to you? No, because they won't want to work with them and they won't want their reputation tarnished by them. The really great thing about this is you don't have to find five people for your power team, you only really have to find one or two, and then you ask them who else they would recommend. Build your power team by networking, and when you find someone brilliant, ask them for recommendations and go from there.

Before we go on to the rest of the GO Large six-step system, a quick word on due diligence. Do your due diligence! This could easily be another core principle of commercial conversions, except that it is really a core principle of all business, in whatever sector. But it is amazing how often this step seems to be overlooked.

It doesn't matter how good any system is or whether you think you know people. You will have seen them on Facebook, and wow, yes they seem to be everywhere and look, they seem to be doing amazing stuff, so they must be alright, mustn't they? Whomever you joint venture with, whomever you give money to, whomever you give your trust to, whomever you give your time to, please ,please do your due diligence, and don't skimp on it. Unfortunately, like many profitable sectors, the property world is full of really fantastic people, but also a load of sharks too! It is full of people who are telling you that they know everything. Go on Facebook and there are people everywhere shouting that they know about commercial conversions and offering mentorships and training. Well, before you go and work with them and before you part with your money, before you go and join their programme, do find out how many conversions they have done, find out what their results were, speak to their investors, speak to the people who have worked with them and do yourself a favour by checking them out thoroughly. And that goes for everybody, if you get a recommendation of a planning consultant, speak to their clients. If you have come across trainers or professionals who won't give you contact details for people they have worked with, run a mile. However good their reputation is, the good people will always give you that kind of information because they have nothing to hide and everything to gain from you speaking to other satisfied clients. Commercial conversions is a great strategy and it can transform your finances, but there are people out there who are not all they seem.

Chapter 8: Locate Deals

The commercial agents are the largest source of commercial buildings; most companies will think of them first when looking to put a property on for sale, and many companies that own buildings they no longer need will use existing relationships with agents at a national level to sell the properties for them. This is usually good news, as commercial agents that are miles away are often not able to conduct viewings very frequently, and many of them are stodgy and hard to get hold of at the best of times. Unlike residential agents, who are generally better at marketing properties, the commercial agents are usually staffed by better qualified people, often with RICS after their names. Able to give better advice, these people, who frequently come from a surveying background, are though generally less responsive. With many businesses continuing to trade from premises once they are advertised, lots of commercial agents need to market commercial buildings 'without' marketing them.

I hear you ask, what this is supposed to mean?! The reality is that many of these buildings don't have a 'For Sale' board placed on the front of them, as the seller is often concerned that it will put the punters off if it is a pub, or worry the tenants if it is a building that is let out. Companies often don't want staff in their offices to know that the building is for sale, as it might lead to them leaving before the company is ready, as the company may be moving away or closing in the longer term. Herein lies an opportunity: the more poorly marketed properties you can find, the higher the likelihood of you finding a deal for the right price.

Both Glenn and Mark have frequently instructed agents to act when sourcing commercial buildings. They sometimes have their own contacts who can provide early notice of buildings coming up for sale. Yes, you end up paying the agents a fee, but we have found that they can find ways of negotiating the price of the property down and provide insights you may not ordinarily get. Starting to pay agents commission is also a good way to get them to focus on your requirements, and it will make them more likely to contact you and recommend you in the future to vendors they are acting for as a good buyer who performs and completes on deals.

Many poorly advertised properties exist in the pub or leisure sector. Pub sites, such as the *Morning Advertiser*, Daltons and Christie can be good. Often the publican doesn't even know the properties are in there, as it is the pub chain that is selling them without their knowledge. Many won't want to attract the interest of the Campaign for Real Ale (CAMRA) or local people who may put pressure on local counsellors to try and stop the local pub being closed or converted into another use. These groups may also try and apply for asset of community value status (ACV), which may slow your conversion down. You may then need to prove through the planning process that the pub is not commercially viable (which many aren't) in order to persuade the local council to grant you planning permission.

Commercial properties listed with residential agents or shown on Rightmove can be another good source. As residential agents are not usually experienced in selling or valuing these types of property, they will often not have the right buyers or suggest that purchases are attempted with unsuitable mortgage brokers or solicitors. As the conveyancing process in the UK is complicated and truncated, there a whole host of issues that can either significantly delay or mean a sale becomes abortive. This can make the property look unappealing to buyers and drive the price lower in the process. It is a universal rule that you want to be buying property from the worst marketers as you are likely to get pay lower prices.

Auctions can be another source of commercial properties ripe for conversion. Although a sometimes expensive route to purchasing buildings, especially near the top of the economic cycle, properties at auction are at least ready for sale, with the auctioneer having done most of the preparation work in terms of legal pack, etc. This means that properties are ready to exchange once the hammer goes down. The potential downside here is that you need the full 10% deposit available on the day of the auction and you will usually need the full balance 28 days later. This makes obtaining finance very difficult, as even bridging lenders (despite what they say) often aren't ready to supply funds within this period, meaning that lots of people end up losing their deposit. Later in this chapter, we cover other ways in which auctions can be a good source of property.

A superb site for finding properties for sale in auctions is Essential Information Group (EIG). It is so good because it collates all properties for sale nationally at all of the different auction houses. You can set up an automatic search so that it only displays commercial or residential properties in the areas where you are looking for properties. There is no better, more time efficient way to find commercial properties coming up at auction houses in the UK than EIG, and its owner David Sandeman is a pretty good bloke too.

The reality of purchasing big buildings like this is that they require vendors' board approval and often involve multiple levels of management to frank the transaction. This takes time, and can leave the deal open to competitors putting higher bids in. To de-risk the deal, Mark sometimes likes to put the prior approval or planning application in (if required) so he can at least get into discussions with the council prior to exchange, which should give visibility on how they are likely to deal with the application, how many units and their sizes. Mark once had a deal take 12 months to actually get exchanged, as the vendor had to have the deal approved by so many levels of people to make a decision and commit. This is common with big entities; often the right hand doesn't know what the left hand is doing.

Another great way to find buildings like this is through word of mouth. Paying commissions to local participants who have contact with local public bodies, businesses or individuals who are looking to offload such properties is a great way to create deals. Builders, workmen, letting and managing agents and surveyors also bring deals. Why wouldn't they want to earn commission by passing deals to you?

Mark likes driving around looking for deals. Frequently buildings look abandoned, or the chap who runs the local corner shop (often a goldmine of local information) knows that a business is on its way out or that a building owner needs to make a sale. Getting on the HM Land Registry site and doing a search for an owner's details is a good way to get their address, so that a letter can be prepared offering to purchase the building. It's a great idea in these scenarios to be as flexible as possible, offering to purchase in a timeframe that suits them, perhaps exchanging now with a completion some time later. Perhaps confidentiality is the most important thing to them; if so, you can easily offer this, so no board or online information will appear about the sale. If you can do a deal whereby you are able to obtain planning permission or prior approval (if an office) during this extended period, all the better, as this will speed up the process and perhaps reduce the risk of the deal for you.

Some have systems that write en masse to the owners of large buildings by taking publically available data and using it to create a mailing campaign. It's more difficult to make this process work as well as we got leaflets to work when targeting residential properties. As building owners don't live in commercial buildings, and are often not based there, you are often not targeting the right individuals. In addition, there tend to be less concentrated clusters of the buildings you would want to purchase on commercial land, with so many different planning use classes and types of commercial building, you will end up with a lot of wastage.

Later in this section on locating deals, we will be covering how to find and assess possible deals and how the use of our Ready Reckoner can help save you a huge amount of time in filtering those deals that come before you. Then we will cover viewing the property and the kind of things you are looking for when visiting sites. If you decide to go to offer, then your offer must position you as an expert and somebody the agent wants to deal with, so we give some tips for that too. Should you be successful with your offer, then conveyancing and completing the deal is also covered.

Richard Koch wrote a book called **The 80/20 Principle**, which amongst other things outlines simply that we should target 80% results from 20% of our work. If we only achieved 20% results from 80% of our work, then we would be setting ourselves up for a lot of work and probably unsatisfying results. If we adopt the 80/20 principle, then we can improve exponentially by identifying the 80% of our efforts that are rendering such minimal output and reinvent them. By re-inventing our ineffectual work in this way, we make ourselves much more effective at achieving ever-improving results.

With regard to finding a property to convert, it means that while there lots of ways to finding a deal, some of them are more effective and a better use of our time. By adopting this approach, we can aim to get 80% of our results from just 20% of our effort. Given that strikes rate of securing a deal can be as little as 1 in 100 looked at, becoming ever more focused on ways of finding deals with less effort would seem eminently sensible, if not vital. Ideally, we want deals coming to us. So, to get 80% of our deals from just 20% of our efforts, as well as doing all the things we have already covered, we also need to set up alerts on the right websites and try and get the right people coming to us with the right deals.

Let's look at getting the right websites working for us.

There are lots of websites that might help you on your journey, but for distilling them down to the most likely to yield results, we can suggest the following: Property Estate Gazette, Fleurets, Christie and Rightmove (commercial tab) and don't forget the EIG site we have already mentioned. The actual addresses are shown in Appendix 2.

Some of the websites are not updated regularly, so when you first go and look through the pages, you may see many opportunities that, on further investigation, prove to be under offer or sold already. However, this should not deter you, as the real intention is to set up alerts for deals as they become available. Although the pages can often be out of date, the alerts tend to be 'live' and offer real opportunities for us to pursue. If anything comes through on an alert, it is live and has probably just gone to market. Ideally, if we are building good relationships with agents then we would hear about these deals even before the alerts go out, but live alerts are the next best thing and can get us started.

On each site, it is possible to set up alerts with various levels of tailoring to our needs. On Property Estates Gazette, for example, we can identify the niche we have selected, such as agricultural buildings, and then apply further filters by area, size and price. This is an excellent way of ensuring that any opportunities that come into our inbox are certainly worthy of our time and, as we will discover later in this section, using the Ready Reckoner can keep that invested time to a minimum – possibly as little as 15-20 seconds to decide whether it is an opportunity worth pursuing. You may not have discovered it, but there is also a commercial tab on Rightmove that you can set up an alert on; it's actually where Glenn found his first commercial office to convert. Fleurets and Christie advertise businesses for sale. But of course, some businesses are worth less than the property they occupy, and this can be a somewhat surprising source of deals for some. Pubs, for example, are going out of business at a worryingly high rate, and you may find a building that can be converted (with planning consent) that is available at an artificially low price. These websites are excellent sources of leads, and we will come on to how to filter those leads shortly.

However appealing it may be to automate our deal search, ultimately people still do business with people, and it is likely that our best source of the that precious commodity, a cracking deal, is going to come from having very good relationships with agents. If you become the go-to person, or at least one of the go-to people for your particular niche in your area, your agent may bring you deals even before they have drafted the brochure. As we mentioned in the networking section, building a profitable relationship of trust with an agent can take time, so be patient and invest in that relationship.

Experience tends to indicate that one of the best ways to start building this relationship is to meet the agent on a viewing. Go and see an opportunity that is within your niche by building type and geography, even if you consider it over-priced and unlikely to work for you. Use the meeting on-site to build rapport and to very gently establish your credibility. Let them be the expert, let them talk and don't contradict them, but also use your questioning to show that you know what you are doing.

You have got to kiss a few frogs and don't be afraid to offer low. As covered in the Get Outsourcing section, we would recommend identifying the agent or agents that are most likely to have the kind of deals you want to buy. This is part of your 80/20 working principle. At the beginning of your journey, this is likely to be the largest independent local commercial agent in your area. At the lower end of the commercial chain, most of the properties being sold will be sold by independent agents selling the smaller units that are perfect for us when starting out in commercial conversions. Shops, smaller offices, smaller agricultural holdings, small light industrial units, care homes, etc. will all be sold by the one or two agents that tend to dominate a localised area. They are your key target agents to start with. You are unlikely to find the perfect first conversion with the likes of Savills, CPRE, GVA Grimley or Knight Frank. You will need to gradually work your way up the food chain to this type of agent – those who are very used to dealing with large portfolios and very large opportunities. The deals you are looking for are much more likely to be sold by an independent, and that is where you start mining for gold.

Our most successful mentees will use the alert system, but they also use their networks. Many of them have got one or two agents that are effectively deal sourcing for them, so this is a little tip for you: when you are first starting out, go around and meet all the local agents. Some of them you might not connect with particularly well; this is life. Sometimes you just don't connect with individuals. What you are looking for though is that agent who is in a geographical area you are looking for and who you suddenly just get that connection with. With which agent is there that spark, an empathy and affinity? Work that person – they are the person to bring into your inner circle. However, you don't want to be limited to one agent's worth of supply, as while one agent may dominate in an area, no agent gets to sell every deal. You would do well to suggest to any agent that you have a good rapport with that you will also pay them a success fee for any deal they bring you from another agent. Very mutually beneficial partnerships can be founded when you find someone you like and connect with, and get them working for you to find deals in the wider marketplace.

For those of you who are wondering about the ethics of it, if the agent is instructed by the client then the agent may not accept a success fee because it could be seen as a conflict of interest. Their job is to get the best price for their client and it may be perceived that they gave you a deal because you paid them a fee, and that they are selling it under value just because they want their additional fee from you. Be careful you don't upset agents by inferring that this is what you are suggesting. What you should be suggesting, however, is that a well-connected agent that knows you and takes you seriously (the sourcing agent) goes around their agent contacts and asks whether any of them have any opportunities they are looking to sell, which meet the specific criteria you are seeking. If the sourcing agent receives something back of interest, they then send the opportunity on to you. Should you proceed on a purchase of that opportunity, the sourcing agent receives a fee from you and the selling agent acting for the vendor gets his fee from his selling client. Accordingly, there is no conflict of interest, as both agents are representing different clients and the selling agent is still incentivised to achieve the best value for their client. The sourcing agent, on the other hand, simply wants to facilitate a deal that might otherwise not get done if the opportunity was being marketed outside your normal network. A classic win-win deal.

Getting to know your agents in this way, finding the ones you really connect with and getting them working for you, is another great way of applying the 80/20 principle. 20% of your work will be getting 80% results, because you have multiple agents scouring the market for deals for you.

Another source of deals can be estate agents, although this doesn't fall within the 80/20 rule. Most estate agents don't sell a lot of commercial property, but they might sell one or two. If they do pick up the odd commercial property to sell, it can be good news for us. They are usually much less experienced in valuing commercial property and you might pick up a bargain. They would usually be dealing with smaller lot sizes that would be suitable for our earlier conversions too, so it's always worth a quick look on the websites, or in the windows as you are passing.

When you first start dealing with agents, be careful about wanting to please them, to be their friend, to be too friendly. Yes we want to build rapport and try to be likeable so they will offer us deals, but be careful not to go about it in the wrong way! Being desperate to gain traction with the agents, we can be tempted to say yes to everything; 'please, show me everything'! Have any of you ever done that? What is that communicating though? Desperation is one thing. Not knowing anything, and a complete lack of focus is another, and yet another poor message from that approach is a chronic lack of confidence. If you are the agent, how seriously are you now taking this desperado who has just walked through your door?!

If you adopt the desperate approach outlined above, if they give you the time of day at all, then they are most likely to send you all the deals they haven't been able to sell to anyone else! Because they know you are a newbie, they know that you might overpay for something that they haven't been able to shift, probably because it was a vendor-led price. If a vendor has ignored the agent's advice and tried to sell something way above value, and the poor agent hasn't been able to shift it on the open market, they may just reach for it right now. All the developers that have looked at it, but know what they are doing have rejected the deal. Then you walk in, saying "I will look at anything" and you're wondering if you are about to make their day! Shudder if you hear something like "I just happen to have got this little beauty for you". Isn't it amazing when you go and see a new agent and they come out with something saying they might just have the exact thing for you, when what they really mean is I might just have something that you are silly enough to buy?

How different is it, do you think, when we go to the same agent and say, "Really pleased to meet you and excited to start working with you. I am established in the area and you might have heard my name, or heard the name of some of my joint venture partners, or the contractors I work with? I specialise in shop conversions and I really only want something in the Southampton area. I might go up to one hour away, but that is really as far as I want to go as I have my power team really close to me, and they manage my projects". Doesn't that sound a little different?

The few agents Glenn uses for the majority of his projects don't send him anything other than offices. One agent that was the main source of his early deals tried to tempt Glenn a couple of times at the beginning with new build opportunities which he politely declined to even consider, and every now and again they test him with something outside his area of expertise. Most of the time in this sort of circumstance we should simply respond by saying something like 'this isn't one for us, thank you very much'. If there is an opportunity in our niche, we want to be on the must-call list, we want to see those opportunities before they even hit the market and this is more likely if the agent knows what we are focused on and specialise in. We want the agent calling us when they are still drafting the details, before it hits the internet listings. As soon as they are instructed to sell a property, the agent might phone three or four people he knows it would be absolutely perfect for. Who would like to be on that call list?

We are on early call lists because the agent is clear about what we want, clear that we know what we are doing and if he brings us an opportunity within our niche that is big enough and at the right price in the right location for conversion, he knows that we will buy it. Human nature drives us all to get as high a return for as little input as possible, agents included. So, if the agent has got a few people who they know they can put onto something and maybe have sold that building even before the details have been published, does that sound like a good deal for them? This is a benefit of niching, as we covered earlier in the book.

We are banging this drum because we know even then some of you will still think, yes but I could still do a little bit of this over here, oh and that looks like such a nice deal I can't possibly let it go! Who has heard themselves saying that? It is particularly prevalent when you are desperate for your first deal! You choose a niche with the best of intentions, you are ready to take on the world, totally focused on one particular building type and then suddenly a different building type pops up and you think, oh yes, it would be nice to get my first deal done, maybe I will have a quick look! Be honest with yourselves, who has been there? We all have. Don't do it. Niching pays.

Niching also applies to our commercial conversion goldmine areas. Many of us will have heard the expression of a goldmine area, perhaps with regard buy-to-let property, or HMOs? Goldmine areas for those strategies can be as small as a few streets in a certain town. But the goldmine area for commercial conversions would be much broader than that. We would suggest that you find a decent sized conurbation within one hour by car. However you intend to travel, whether by car, train, bus or indeed walking or cycling, as long as you can get there in one hour , the developments should be manageable. Find a good sized conurbation within a one-hour travel time and become a specialist in that area. It is easy to view properties if they are within one hour, you can develop your knowledge, you can develop your Ready Reckoner (more of that later) and you can develop your reputation... and reputation is huge.

Case Study – Locating My First Commercial Conversion (by Glenn)

In the area in which I first started commercial conversions, the agent was called Primmer Olds. On the Rightmove commercial tab, they were advertising an office for £499k plus VAT. To the uninitiated, one might look at a price of £499,000 plus VAT to equate to £600k. I knew I didn't have to pay the VAT, so immediately I knew the building was no more than £500k. I called and arranged a viewing. They hadn't heard of me and so in retrospect it wasn't surprising that they sent the junior surveyor out to mee me. I was deferential and asked the agent how long it had been on the market and how many people had been to view it before me. The agent said only two people had been to see it and they had yet to receive an offer. I continued to engage the agent in polite conversation, eliciting as much information as I could but also offering little glimpses of credibility, such as my past experience at The Rose Bowl and the fact that I would have to run the numbers through 'my model'. Even the knowledge that I had a model sets me apart from the tyre kickers that waste so much of many agents' time. When the viewing was finished, I made it clear that I had decided to submit an offer. Again, this was a deliberate and premeditated decision designed to demonstrate that I was serious. What that offer might look like was not discussed.

After less than 24 hours, I called the agent and asked if I could come and present my offer. When I arrived, I knew I had made a good impression because the junior surveyor was now accompanied by his senior partner. Here is how the conversation went. I told them I wanted make an offer but that I was struggling to meet the brochure price. I offered them a chance to review my model to see if they could see where perhaps my assumptions were wrong. I turned my laptop screen towards them, showing them a PDF screenshot of the 'model'. I said, "Look, I really want to buy this building, I really want to start doing office conversions and this could be my first office conversion". This was the first deal I had bought from the agent, so I was building rapport and trust. I continued, "Now, if you can show me where I have got my numbers wrong, I would be really interested to know because I am not an expert in these things and I know you have been around a lot longer than I have. At the moment though, according to my numbers I can't make this building stack up at any more than £400k". Now clearly had I put a bit of fat in there as I was new and I didn't want to cut myself to the bone. Actually, I had put the GDV in at £1.1m and we ended up selling it for £1.3m, but it built rapport with the agent, made him the expert and de-positioned me.

The agent turned to his colleague and smiled, then looked back at me and responded, "Well in truth Glenn, at £400k you are nearer our figure than the vendor is!" Amazing! In the ensuing conversation it transpired that the agent had told the vendor that the building was worth £400k to £435k, and I had come in bang on their numbers! In doing so, I had shown humility but also that I knew what I was doing. I then demonstrated how much I still had to learn by offering immediately to do the deal at £435k if they could get the vendor to agree. I probably left at least £20K on the table but I was underway. I did a deal with the agent, which made the agent look good because he had been right all along, and he got the maximum value the agent had said it could go for. I got a good deal because it was well below the £100 per sq. ft. I had targeted as a workable number in my area, and I had now built a relationship with the agent.

You don't always have to show everything you know to the agent, but equally, don't go in there full of blah. Use that technique to de-position yourself a bit, show them your model and ask them to show you where your numbers are wrong. Then offer low! You never know what they will say, so don't be afraid to offer low.

Finding property can also be about momentum. Try and get people working for you, build relationships and become a hot buyer. We are looking for that momentum and reputation of being a hot buyer. The instant you are seen as a hot buyer by an agent, you have got momentum. You will be offered deals early, the agents will come to you and cash follows them too! Once you have got credibility, the cash follows deals and people who know people might also know people. Your first joint venture partner might run out of money, but they know you, you are credible, they know people with money so they start introducing them to you and you get a momentum of deals and money, deals and money, deals and money.

Suddenly, you will be desperate to sort your systems out, gear up financially and get ready to go to the next level. You could soon be going so fast that you just need to pause so that you can gear up for it. Momentum is real, but a lot of it comes from being a hot buyer and creating the systems and networks that find properties that come to you. Becoming a hot buyer is one of those systems because the agents will come to you with deals. Build credibility, do what you say you are going to do, deliver on it, and your agent will quickly add you to their hot buyer list. If you say you are going to buy something, then try everything possible in your power to make sure you do it. As your reputation grows, so will your network of agents, bringing you bigger and bigger deals over a wider area.

As we mentioned earlier, another possible source of deals is auctions. Whilst you can buy commercial property at auction, with the amount of due diligence required, and given the complexity of raising funds on empty commercial property, we would not recommend starting your journey by buying commercial property for conversion at auction. However, offering on an auction listed property prior to the auction, or picking up commercial property that didn't sell in the auction with an offer afterwards, can be excellent ways of sourcing a deal.

Deal sourcers can also be quite useful in finding deals, although we would urge caution. Some sourcers are simply developers that end up with so many deals because their sourcing system and networks are so good, that they simply can't develop them all. As a result, they may package them up and pass them on. Be wary about the GDVs on any deals that sourcers bring you. It is in their interest to make it look really fabulous and make the profit margins look wonderful because they may have stuck in £100k, £200k, £300k, possibly even more on top of what they paid for the building to get to the amount they are going to flip the building onto you for.

There is another type of sourcer who is less worthy of an uplift and who is trying to make a quick buck whilst adding no real value. This type of sourcer may see you get planning or prior approval on a building, and then contact you in some way saying they have got someone looking for just that kind of building. In reality, they will just elicit the details of the opportunity and then go out to their networks in an effort to try and flip it on. They didn't really have anyone who was genuinely interested, and were only endeavouring to insert themselves as middlemen into your deal, and to take a cut of the value you have added. Sourcers can be a source of deals, but tread with caution.

Locating deals (and arranging funds, as described later) are, in the early days, the two most intense phases of your role as a developer. Earlier in the book, we used the analogy of a conductor to describe our role, but now we are going to change that word. The word henceforth is developer – you are to be the developer. You are not a builder, you are not an architect, you are not any of those things. They make up the orchestra; you are the developer.

When you are starting out, in your early days as a developer, you are still going to be relatively actively involved in the later stages of our system, namely the redesign, getting it built and arranging the exit. What you should find, though, over a period of time of maybe two or three years, is that your deals scale up in size, you may have built a bit of a team around you, though not as big as you might think, and much of the later stages are now being carried out by your team. At that point, these two roles of deal sourcing and finding equity should almost entirely fill your time. For Glenn and his business partner Justine, they now find that 75% of their activity is finding funds and deals. The other 25% of their time is running their team.

Glenn and Justine (together Ocea group) are heading gradually towards a four-day work week, and while they are not quite there yet, they are making progress. Having built a significant multi-million pound profit business in just three years, it has taken some work, and of course it was their choice to go that large in such a short period of time. Most of you will not choose to be quite so manic in your approach! Whatever size business you would like eventually, though, you will need to decide how badly you want to break through. This system is amazing, but it still only works when you do! You may need to work hard initially to get this strategy rolling. Networking two or three times a week can be pretty exhausting; often out in the evening, meeting agents, arranging viewings at short notice, it can be pretty intense at the beginning. As the saying goes, for a while you may have to work like most people won't, so that in the future you can live like most people can't!

As Glenn and Justine move forward though, around 75% of their four days a week should be just working on deals and finance, and most of that will be networking. Now here is the good news: when you get to that point, you can make much of that networking great fun. How do you like spending your leisure time? You may have heard Rob Moore talking about merging your passion and your profession, your vocation with your vacation? Wouldn't it be wonderful to use this strategy to get you to the point at which 75% of your work time could be spent doing what you love doing, with agents and investors? Whatever it is you enjoy – horseracing, fast cars, travelling, music, fine dining, sailing, whatever – find a way of doing it whilst networking with people you need to meet. One of the things Justine and Glenn do is network with the movers and shakers in the industry at Formula One in Monaco. Is that an essential part of our business plan? Yes! Of course! (In case HMRC are reading!)

We can, of course, choose where we network, but consider it seriously, do you think there might be a bit of money hanging around in Monaco during the Grand Prix? As it happens, Justine and Glenn love Formula 1, so they simply arrange various meetings with others in the industry during that week, meeting some of their investors and colleagues, and of course, meeting new people too. So, you can make work a lot of fun too. In the early days, your fun may be in the business itself, looking at buildings, meeting new people, etc., but have a mind to where you want to be in a few years and set yourself up accordingly.

As Stephen Covey said in his bestselling book The 7 Habits of Highly Effective People, "start with the end in mind". Start to build a business that you want and that works for you, because your primary role when you are established is going to be finding deals and money, and if you choose to scale your business, you are going to have to find bigger deals and bigger money and they often hang about in lovely locations! That's how important these two phases are. You should get to the point at which everything else is being done by everyone else and all you are doing is managing the people carrying out the other tasks. However, you will generally always be looking for money and deals.

In the early days, therefore, as you search for your first deal, that is where your energy should go. There is always a way in, and it is always based around networking for money and deals. Let's imagine you are going to buy a white VW Golf – decent car why wouldn't you? Having decided on a white VW Golf, do you suddenly see a lot on the road? Yes, more than you ever saw before. Were they always there? Yes. So why do you suddenly see more of them? Because of course you are looking for them, you have attuned your brain to look out for them.

The law of attraction may have an element of truth in it, IF it is followed up with action. If you sit in your room, adopting the lotus position, closing your eyes and gently humming as you 'imagine' your VW Golf into being, you might have a very long wait. Some people who talk about law of attraction seem to propose doing it like that! However, where the law of attraction seems to have some credence is in each of us being very clear about what we want, then allowing our minds to find the best way of attracting that desire. Used in that way, the brain is an incredibly powerful tool, and absolutely creates and supports the environment for the law of attraction to work for us.

When Glenn was getting into property, he had some pretty dark days and sat broke, no money in the bank, putting training courses on credit cards and wondering how the hell he was going to pay for it all. Many of us have been or are on that hard road. Glenn recalls that, 'when I was on that hard road and was having a particularly tough time, someone challenged me to put my goals into pictures rather than just words. Typically, I had always wanted a nice car and had a particular penchant for a Porsche 911. So, when I wrote down my goals in a vision document, I went online and I looked for a picture of a Porsche. It occurred to me, though, that the picture was effectively like me looking at someone else's Porsche, rather than owning my own. With a bit of a brainwave, I decided to look for a picture of a Porsche cockpit so that I was effectively seeing my view whilst sat at the steering wheel. I found a picture of a Porsche cockpit that was taken from the driver's position that showed the steering wheel and all the instruments, the gear stick and the view out of the window, and I thought that's it. Rather than just have it in my goal document, I also put it on my phone as the screensaver. How interesting then, that when I ended up buying my own Porsche 911 I realised it had exactly the same cockpit, with same finish, the same instrument cluster, everything. Now there are lots of models of 911 and they change the cockpit regularly, so isn't it strange that a thing that I had been focused on, every time I looked at my phone, finally came into being? How often do we look at our phones? Subconsciously, every time I looked at my phone for three or four years I saw the same cockpit, and it is the one I ended up buying'!

You can use the law of attraction with money and deals, but it must be accompanied by action too. So, be very clear on the types of deal you want, and what kind of investor you would like and then let your mind direct your actions.

Locating the deal is where you earn your cut; the skill in this is not just finding a deal, but identifying how to sweat it, to get more money out of it, because that means you can offer higher than other people. Because you have learnt how to sweat the deal, you are able to increase your offer and know you will still make good money. That means you get the deal because you have put the highest offer in, not by overbidding out of desperation but by compounding your learning all the time.

After finding a possible deal, you will be assessing the property using desktop searches, viewing the property if worthwhile, analysing the deal and then making an offer. If your offer is accepted, then you enter the funding phase – that is the process, that is the flow.

This 'Go Large' system encourages you to develop buildings where you can use prior approval. There are two initial stages in finding the property: firstly establishing the prior approvals you are interested in, if that is the way you are going, or alternatively what your planning niche is going to be, and then secondly establishing the geographical area you are focusing on.

However, the initial search can be a bit chicken-and-egg, because you are looking for that combination of geographical area where prior approvals give you a decent deal flow, and also in the area you to want to operate in. It might be you have to test that a few times. Some areas might be great for some conversion niches but perhaps not the one you were considering as your focus. Try a few areas with a few different proposed niches at first and select the best combination after the testing phase. By all means test, look again, test again, but once you have a niche in a local area providing good deal flow, then you must make a decision and go for it. Don't get stuck in the testing loop and don't keep convincing yourself that whatever way you look it doesn't work. It is too easy to come to the conclusion that it doesn't work at all in your area, but it might just be that you are going to have to establish those networks to get the right deals.

For example, you might find that in your selected area there are quite a few shops around. They are not in key shopping areas, and you think the numbers work for your strategy, whether it is cash flow or building a cash pot. So, then you commit. You can't just keep waiting and waiting and testing every different area. At some point you have got to say, "yes there is a reasonable chance of success here, so I am going to commit". Your decision about where commit to should be based on a number of factors, the time you have available being one. If you have a full-time job, or maybe you are a parent with younger children, maybe you have older parents who need looking after, you are a carer to someone or maybe you can't drive and rely on public transport, these are all different factors to consider. But that's real life isn't it? These things exist in our lives and can limit what time you have available, but that doesn't have to limit your success. If you are lucky enough not to have many limitations, then you might have the luxury of going a bit further afield, but just look at the time you have available.

In your chosen area that fits with your travel time, what will you find a plentiful supply of that fits with your chosen prior approval/planning niche? For example, we are not going to find agricultural buildings in the centre of London, we are not going to find many big office blocks in the middle of rural England, so don't overcomplicate this, simply select something you are likely to find a good supply of. We don't live in an ideal world and you may have to travel to find an area which is rich in the prior approval type you want to settle on; be open minded about it, but be realistic about the limitations that your life imposes.

The benefit of setting an area, and the reason we focus on it is even if it is not in your immediate vicinity, is that if you pick one area and stick to it, you can get to know that area really well. Focus on that one area because we cover later in this book the usefulness of something we call the Ready Reckoner. The power of the Ready Reckoner is that by specialising in one conversion type, in one geographical area, all the numbers in your Ready Reckoner will become more or less fixed numbers in your mind and you will be able to mentally carry out a Ready Reckoner check in about 20 seconds. Looking at any deal in your chosen area, you will know within 15 to 20 seconds whether it is worth bothering with any further. You can save vast amounts of wasted time and effort by simply knowing the Ready Reckoner numbers for your niche in your area. But you will only reap that benefit if you focus on that one prior approval type in that one area. You will also build your reputation as a serious developer in that area much more quickly.

It is much easier to become a big fish in a small pond. If you spread yourself far and wide, the agents will have probably never heard of you before. But if you do three, four or five developments in the same area, everyone is going to hear about you and your credibility grows faster. You will build a reputation in the area as a serious developer and you will grow recognition, creating a deep understanding of the key factors, knowing the local planner's interpretation of prior approval or planning in that area, the development costs in that area and the contractors to use.

North/South Differences

In lots of areas in the north, your build costs aren't going to change that much from those in the south. The residential values are so much lower in some areas of the north than in the south that you would think the land value should be commensurately lower, but it is not as low as those numbers might suggest it should be. The differential between your development costs and your end values can start to disappear in large segments of the north. We all hear the stories about how people in the south travel north for rental yields, to places like Hull or Manchester, and all these people in the south were or are driving four hours up the motorway because the rental yields in the north are so fantastic. The downside of that is that the rental yields are in part high because the capital value of the houses up north are so much lower. So, if you are developing to sell, thereby generating a cash pot, there are lots of areas in the north where you are going to find that strategy difficult because land values are relatively high against development costs that aren't that different. The margins for you to play with are going to be reduced.

That doesn't mean the strategy doesn't work. We are merely proposing you do bigger deals because you are going to earn more money more quickly by adding more value and solving more problems. Other than the suggestion of using prior approval as a planning shortcut that removes risk, this is just developing as normal, which clearly happens all over the country. The normal rules of developing in the north and the south apply. If you are in the north and want to generate serious pots of cash (i.e. you want to sell everything), then you are going to have to find the pockets in the north where this works, which do exist. There are always areas anywhere where the richer parts of society live and where consequently capital values are higher. We know there must be, otherwise no one would ever develop anything to sell in the north. However, deals to sell for cash profit will be generally less prevalent than down south, and it is therefore much easier to sell for big pots of cash down south than it is in the north. Conversely, if you want cash flow and live in the south, you might be casting an envious eye to the north! So southerners looking for hold strategies may end up finding deals easier further north than the Watford Gap!

Accordingly, you might need to travel or consider joint venturing with people in that area who can be the 'boots on the ground'. The bottom line is, don't use geography as an excuse! With any strategy, you have to find a way of making it work for you. If you want big pots of cash and you live in the north, you have got a few choices. You can limit your opportunities and stay local, you can travel, or you can joint venture with people in the south. There will always be people that look for a reason why it's not going to work for them, because it makes them feel better about the fact that they can't make it work. And there are other people who will do whatever they have to do to make it work. If you are in that second category, this is a great strategy, but if you are in the first category, no strategy in the world is going to help you.

As an aside, always be aware that you may need to consider a different exit strategy, and by the way, you should always have at least three exit strategies. This, again, is just like any other developing. You should never rely on one exit strategy, because you always need a fall back, and you need a fall back to the fall back. So, even if you are targeting a sales strategy to build a cash pot, wherever you are in the country, look at your fall back options should that exit not be available. If you intend to hold, what options do you have if you are down valued and can't get all your money out, what agreement do you have with your investor? Always consider alternative exits from whatever deal you do, wherever you are in the country and whatever exit you have planned on.

A quick word on the opportunity afforded by turning commercial conversions into serviced accommodation (SA). There is much talk about passive income, about whether it is real, whether it truly exists or not.

Our view is that most systems aren't entirely passive, but they can be as passive in direct proportion to our own ability to outsource work to other people. Looking quickly though at the opportunity for relatively passive income from commercial conversions, let's assess a conversion of a block into apartments for use as SA. You will need to consider the planning implications with your planning consultant as serviced accommodation is generally considered C1 use and prior approval is for change of use to C3, but putting that aside, the income can be life-changing.

Take a relatively simple commercial conversion of a building into 10 units, which is a decent size to start with, and probably as big as you want to go when starting out. If it is in the right area for SA, each of those 10 units could quite easily make a net profit of £1000 pcm. How many strategies do you know where you can do one deal and have £10k a month after all costs, forever? We'll assume you found a person to run the SA business for you, so it is more or less a passive annual income of £120,000, plus the growth of the asset, plus the fact that no one can complain about it because you own the whole block! As mentioned, though, when locating a deal for SA, be very sure before you buy the conversion that the area is in need of further SA supply, and still have those other exits available should you find that the demand is not as expected.

There is a temptation to think that everyone knows about commercial conversions now, and you are a bit late to the party. A classic fear that strikes many of us when we hear about an opportunity is that somehow we have already missed out. That there was an opportunity but it is now gone, or the best has passed. How often do we wish we had started something 10 years ago, particularly in property! But what percentage of the population do you think really knows the stuff you are reading about? How many old commercial buildings are there that need converting? There are a lot more buildings than there are people who know what to do with them! This is a live opportunity for you right now, so don't let yourself become convinced you have missed the boat and that this book has come along too late for you. It may take a while to find your first deal. There is a lot to learn about how to assess each opportunity but if you stick with it, compound your learning within your selected niche, then eventually that first deal will come into being and you will be on your way.

Ready Reckoner

One of the propagated views, even within more enlightened training companies such as Progressive Property, is that this strategy is really complicated. It is suggested that maybe you should start with deal packaging, then you need to get some buy-to-lets under your belt, then maybe some buy, rent and refurbishments (flips), then get some HMOs and then perhaps you are ready to move on up to commercial conversions. In Glenn's view, when we distil property down, any property strategy is remarkably simple. The issue with any property strategy is that it generally is not that easy because issues come up, and we have to be committed and determined to press through. Why is that, because we are problem solvers? We are problem solving and that is what we get paid for? So, the strategy and the principle is simple, but not necessarily easy, because problems come up.

But in simplicity, it is remarkably freeing to know that you can use something like a Ready Reckoner and be able to assess deals at a meaningful level in just a few seconds.

The Ready Reckoner uses just three pieces of simple information: the size of the building you are looking to convert, the development price per sq. ft. (we will come on to what we mean by the development price), and lastly, the sales price per sq. ft. Those three pieces of information are magic, and if I had to sum up commercial conversions this would be it. With these three pieces of information, you will know within 20 seconds whether you are likely to have a deal or not. As the meerkat says, simples!

The more systems-orientated among you may want to turn the Ready Reckoner into a spreadsheet. Actually we made the mistake of allowing someone to turn it into a spreadsheet on one of our mentorship programmes, and we have since recognised that it is completely wrong. The whole point of the Ready Reckoner is that it is a mental model that you should be able to use in 15 to 20 seconds, and the moment you need to put it onto a spreadsheet you have made it too complicated. The Ready Reckoner is rough and ready, that is why it is called a Ready Reckoner. Its sole purpose is to simply to allow you to make a quick assessment to find out if the property is worth spending time on and possibly viewing. You are not going to offer based on the Ready Reckoner. It really is just a 15/20-second model to help you decide "am I going to go and view this property?" Does that make sense? The moment it gets any more complicated than that you have lost its original intent.

With the three pieces of information (development price, selling price and the size of the building) we work out the gross development value (GDV) of the building by calculating the selling price per sq. ft. by the size of the building. So when you have got this and you have done this a few times for your chosen niche buildings in your selected niche area, what you will notice is that the selling price and development costs per sq. ft. will not change much. For instance, the selling price in the Southampton area where Glenn operates is around £320 per sq. ft. The development cost (for office conversions) in Southampton is £150 per sq. ft. If you take £150 (development costs) off £320 (selling price) you get £170 left. This amount is the sum of the purchase price and the profit and in Southampton for office conversions, that leaves a £70 profit and about £100 per sq. ft. to buy the property because in Southampton that is about what offices cost – around £100 per sq. ft (at the time of going to print). That purchase figure doesn't change much, the development figure doesn't change much, and the selling values don't change much, so we are able to instantly look at the size of a building, and know whether it is priced in such a way that a conversion is likely to stack up or not. Let's say a 4,000 sq. ft. building comes up for sale. For Glenn's model in Southampton to work that building needs to be about £400k (4000 x £100). So, if it is on at £600k is Glenn going to go and view it? Why would he, it is overpriced, the conversion model on this occasion won't work. That is the Ready Reckoner in its simplicity

When you have got these numbers (development costs, selling price and therefore purchase price) for your area, you will be able to look at the size of the building and know almost instantly, "that will work", 'that won't", 'that will work", 'that won't".

A word of caution, let's say the building is up for £500k but your number is £400k – do you view? Yes, absolutely! We recommend that if you are within 25 to 30% of the asking price, you go and view because you can always offer low. Glenn's first deal was on the market for £500k. He did the numbers and thought it should be just £400k. However, he went to view and found out that he was only the third person to view and no one had yet offered, although that wasn't surprising because it was overpriced. He ended up going to see the agent who admitted that it was a vendor-led price. The agent had recommended £400k, which is the number Glenn had come up with. In fact, what the agent had said is £400k to £435k, so Glenn admits he made the rookie error of offering them £435k (doh)!, leaving £35k on the table. What he knows now is he should have said, "I am really sorry, I know you're probably thinking of getting another £35k but my number is £400k". He would probably have got it for £400k, but he acknowledges that he was desperate for his first deal and knew it worked at £435k so he did it anyway. It got him going, it got him into the industry and he also learnt a lot from that first deal as well as making a tidy profit. So let's get into the numbers of the Ready Reckoner a bit more...

Size of the Building

For our Ready Reckoner, we want the Gross Internal Area (GIA), i.e. the whole of the building including all communal areas, ideally including plant areas and the like as well. However, the agents are not always right about the size of the building, and they can be wrong by quite a sizeable margin. We need the GIA expressed per sq. ft., (it can be m², but what you will find is a lot of the agents use sq. ft. – just don't mix them up in the same deal). We need a reasonably accurate square footage of the building, but we do not always trust the agent's sizing, although it will generally have to be your starting point. When you are a bit more experienced, you might look at the size given by the agent and then look at the building and ask, "really?" Trust that instinct, as they might be wrong; we have had one or two examples where the agent is wrong and the building is much bigger than they said.

Agents' details will often provide a net internal area (NIA) rather than a gross internal area (GIA). The NIA is the area in the building that will be used for whatever its main purpose is. So if it is an office, this is the area of the building where you will get tables and chairs and desks and everything else. Simply put, the NIA does not include the lift, the toilets, the hallways or the fire escape – they are all excluded, as they cannot be used for the building's primary function. However, because you are going to rip everything out and, accordingly, you might be able to use the area of toilets, the kitchen, and some of the communal areas for your apartments, you should use the GIA. We need the area for everything, so if the agent's details provide NIA and there is no other way of getting the building size for doing a quick Ready Reckoner, simply add 20% to the NIA for a rough and ready GIA.

The other way of finding a GIA if you need to is to go to the non-domestic Energy Performance Certificate (EPC) register, because the EPC is calculated on the GIA. If you look up the government website for EPC, the wording used to describe the basis for the EPC is usable area, which is very misleading and would suggest they use NIA. Trust us though, because we have done the due diligence for you, the government actually instruct the EPC surveyors to base it on the GIA. So EPCs will give you the GIA but one thing to mention is that commercial buildings are generally assessed for the area of each separate lease. If you have a big building that is split by leases, each of those leases will have their own EPC and you will need to find each of them and add them together to get the GIA of the whole building.

Development Costs

The development costs – notice the words we're using, we are not using 'construction costs', we are using 'development costs', because they include the construction costs, what you pay the builder, but development costs also include your building warranties, utilities, professional fees and development costs of funds.

Construction Costs

Builders can give you the construction cost, which is, of course, only one element of the development cost. Builders are a good place to start, because with that price you can add on all the other elements that give you the full cost.

Project management firms are also really good for estimations. You can find them for the entire spectrum of deal size, and it is their job to know how much it will costs to develop buildings. You may need to pay a small fee for the information, but if you mention that you are moving into this field and are looking to build a pipeline, for which you will need their ongoing professional help, they may be forthcoming with free advice.

The other way to try and find local building costs is through your community and networking. There are people out there already using this strategy, and they tend to have a pretty good handle on the costs in a given area. If you were to meet us at a networking event, we would gladly tell you our development costs and how they are broken down. So use the community, go to networking meetings and find people who are doing what you want to do and ask them what the numbers are.

Building Warranties

If you are going to sell, you will definitely need a warranty of some sort. Whilst some might argue that you can 'make do' with a less expensive 'architect's certificate', this could seriously restrict the number of lenders that provide mortgages to your buyers, and we're not sure why we would make a minor saving that could severely impact our buying market. We would also strongly suggest that even if you are developing to hold, that you still get warranties on your development, because if you ever change your mind and want to sell, you may find it hard without warranties in place. Warranties are also very difficult and costly to achieve retrospectively. Before becoming developers, we might have only heard of the NHBC warranties that you typically get on new houses. But there are actually many warranty providers out there. If you search for 'building warranty provider' on any decent online search engine, a whole raft will come up. The ones we have tended to use are Premier, Checkmate and CRL, and we assume a cost of about £1200 per unit for the cost of our warranties.

Utilities

As a rule of thumb, we use £1500 per unit, per utility. Therefore, if you have water and electricity, it is £3k times the number of apartments you are creating. If you have water, gas and electricity in a scheme, it is £4.5k. There's a clue for you right there: why put all three services in when you can get away with two? Electricity does most things these days, and if you put gas in you are just adding to your costs. The flats we create are feeding the bottom end of the market. We are creating generally small one-bed flats for first-time buyers and investors, and they are not going to be that precious about whether there is a gas hob or not. You are not going to lose sales because there is no gas in the building, so why would you volunteer to pay an extra x amount?

Professional Fees

We simply add 10% of the construction costs for a professional fee allowance. In reality, the costs of professionals vary from scheme to scheme and can run anywhere from 7% to nearer 13%, but 10% is a good approximation at this stage and certainly good enough for our Ready Reckoner.

Cost of Funds

When we talk about the cost of funds, we are talking about the cost of development funds, not the equity investment. We will come onto the equity later. With regard to the development funds, there is much more of this in the funding section later in the book. For now, simply assume 15% of your *construction* costs. This should allow for circa 8% on your overall *development* costs for up to 18 months plus fees, and again, it is just an approximation for our Ready Reckoner, nothing more.

Now all of that together makes up the development costs which will become a set number for you in your niche. You need to understand that is roughly how the development cost is made up, so it is not just what you pay the builder, it's everything. It is the cost per sq. ft. of taking your dilapidated, empty commercial property and turning it into brand spanking new homes, roughly speaking. Remember we are still at the Ready Reckoner stage – you are not going to be offering on the basis of this rough and ready calculation, it is not your full due diligence, don't panic, this is just your "do I spend time and do I go and look at it?" test.

Where can we get the development and/or construction costs? Where can we find that number as we start our journey? We can get it from agents, because agents do the rough calculation that you are going to do with your Ready Reckoner. When they do it, they are doing it to value the building for their client. They know roughly what it costs to convert these buildings, as the agents are now very clued up about Prior Approval. They know a lot of these buildings are going to be converted and they know roughly how much it costs; they use that number when they calculate the value of the building. So they are a good place to start, particularly if you are new.

Selling Price

When considering our exit, whether selling or renting, we need to begin with the end in mind. If you haven't read it, Stephen Covey's The 7 Habits of Highly Effective People is a great book. It has been a business bestseller for many years, and one of the habits is "begin with the end in mind". You need a rough idea of what you are creating and whether you are selling or holding to do a basic valuation. Generally speaking, you will be creating the smallest one-bed units you can for investors and first-time buyers. So go to the estate agent and ask what that client base expects in the area, and what they will pay. What do they expect regarding specification, quality and price?

Now a word of warning. Estate agency is one of those things you can fall into with no education, training or background, other than the fact that maybe you can sell. So if you get an estate agent at the beginning of their journey, they genuinely don't know jack about jack and they are not going to be a lot of help to you. If on the other hand you are dealing with the Land and New Homes department, they tend to have been around the block and they have probably got a bit more of an idea. But if you are dealing with your local agency, you need to try and get the person at the back of the room. Don't take the Facebook person who sits at the front door, or the gatekeeper one desk back – the young keen one who is brilliant at selling but doesn't yet have the years to truly understand development. Don't even try with any of the Saturday staff! You need to try and get to the person at the back, who is often the expert. Usually positioned near the rear of the office, maybe even in a side room, try and find someone who knows what they are talking about and has some experience of selling developments.

If you get somebody without the requisite experience, you may be told that you will never sell units that are less than 45 m² because no one will pay for them. Or you might be told, yes, you can sell a unit for 30 m², but basically you just take the sq. ft. and you scale it right down, which means if you can sell a normal one-bed for £150k and that is 45 m², a 30 m² unit will be £100k because it is two-thirds of the size. This simply isn't true. In any area there is a minimum price that you would be able to purchase a one-bed flat for, and it doesn't matter how small it is, that will be the base price. So it is very important when you are getting the selling price that you are working with someone who you think has this perspective. But again, don't get too involved in any more detail just yet.

Don't forget, you can Use Rightmove sold house prices to find comparables. Get the square footage from the floor plans, as most agents now produce floor plans, although not all of them give you overall square footage. Sometimes you have to work it out, or you can go to the domestic EPC register, which works on the same principle as the commercial one. There may be a couple of premiums to add to your comparable prices for things like a new build premium (we usually allow 5-10% for the new build premium), or a parking premium. Flats with parking are going to sell for more than flats without parking, particularly in town centres.

As with any comparable, you need to try and compare like for like as much as you can. Try and find one-bed apartments that are as close as possible to the location you are considering. If you are intending to sell to the first-time buyer, or rent them on the open market, then don't use retirement properties as comparables because it is a different market. Always try to use comparables that could actually be the product you will be developing, in the area you are developing, to be used by the group you intend to target when you exit the deal.

The reason we need the selling price per sq. ft. is what we are going to do with it. Let's go back to our example and keep it nice and simple. In Southampton, the selling price per sq. ft. for a one-bed apartment is roughly £300. Don't get over complicated about this. If we can sell an apartment in the building for £300 per sq. ft. and the building is 4000 sq. ft. in size, what is the gross development price (GDV) of the building? Clearly, it is just 4000 x £300, so £1.2m. Yes, there is some stuff layered behind it, but ultimately that is all we're after. We need the rough selling price per sq. ft. in that area and we multiply it by the size of the building to give us our GDV.

Bear in mind that this is a Ready Reckoner, you don't need pound shillings and pence. You round it up to a rough number of, say, the nearest £2 per sq. ft., multiply it by the size of the building and you get your GDV. Now the smart amongst you will realise that we have used the GIA, but that we can't sell all of the GIA. Even in flats, you are going to have a communal area, such as corridors, fire exits, plant rooms, etc., but don't worry about that yet. The difference at this stage is not material and is actually countered by other things, such as the value of the freehold, which we haven't covered yet. Work on the GDV being the selling price per sq. ft. multiplied by the GIA, not the NIA. Don't make any corrections for communal areas at this point; trust us, it works. Don't forget: all we need to know is, "am I going to do any more work on this and maybe view the building?" Don't panic, you are not deciding anything other than is this particular deal worth any more of your time, or not. The most precious resource you will have is your time. You don't want to be going chasing dead ducks, and that is why we have this Ready Reckoner.

Another rule of thumb that is really helpful is to take your GIA and divide by 500; the resulting number is the minimum number of units you are trying to get into the building. If you really want to know how the 500 is made up, it is this: you are going to average no more than 415 sq. ft. allocated to each unit and the extra 85 sq. ft. is communal space (roughly 20% of any space is communal). So by taking the GIA and dividing by 500, we get the minimum number of units we are going to try and get into that building. You can then use that number of units and multiply it by the average selling value of a one-bed apartment in your area, and it gives you a quick check against the GDV in your Ready Reckoner. So we had a 4000 sq. ft. building, divide by 500 and you get eight, and if values in the area were circa £150k for a one-bed apartment, 8 x £150k is £1.2m. It is just another way to get a rough idea of whether our GDV number is about right.

What happens now is you have got the GDV, you have got your development costs and you put everything together to work out how much you can pay for that building. However, you need to work backwards. See the following example:

GDV – development costs = surplus (purchase price + profit)

Then choose your profit level. At this stage, let's presume 20% of GDV. Subtract the profit from your surplus, and you will then have what you can afford to pay for the building.

Let's again take our example from the Southampton area for a 4000 sq. ft. building. Selling price is £320 per sq. ft., development costs are £150 per sq. ft. and we want 20% of GDV as a profit.

GDV = 4000 x £320 = £1,280,000

Development costs = 4000 x £150 = £600,000

Surplus = £1,280,000 - £600,000 = £680,000

Profit target = 20% of GDV = £1,280,000 x 0.2 = £256,000

Purchase Price = Surplus – Profit Target = £680,000 - £256,000 = £424,000

To repeat, once you have done this a few times for your niche in your area, the development costs, the selling price AND the purchase prices (all per sq. ft.) will not change that much from opportunity to opportunity, leaving you with a very quick mental calculation to assess whether a deal is sensibly priced for your conversion model.

Don't panic if it doesn't feel second nature yet, it does become second nature, because what you are looking at eventually is £set per sq. ft. for the development, the selling price is £set per sq. ft. and the amount you can afford to pay for a building will become a set amount, per sq. ft.

The Ready Reckoner saves time: once you have got your numbers in your area, the Ready Reckoner will be incredibly quick to use. It means you are not looking at deals that are dead in the water because you will know that they are too overpriced. As mentioned, we suggest if it is within 25% of your calculated purchase price to go and look at it because you can always offer low. Assess the deal as you view, check for risks and adjust the purchase price, which we will cover in more detail in the next section.

Assessing a Building When Viewing

We have already mentioned Steven Covey's 7 Habits, and in particular, one that is pertinent to us is "begin with the end in mind". That is your job: when you look at a building, what do you see? What can that building become? Begin with the end in mind. Then if you think the building may be suitable for a deal, use the Ready Reckoner. If it passes the Ready Reckoner, then move onto desktop searches. At this stage, use the KISS principle – keep it simple, stupid – and don't get over complicated yet. You are just making a quick assessment; you are beginning with the end in mind. What do you think you can build? Remember the rule of thumb, how many lots of 500 sq. ft. can you get into the building? Use your Ready Reckoner to ensure is there a deal. Use your desktop searches to back it up, and then maybe bounce it off your planning consultant and if you are using permitted development, check whether there is any reason you can't use permitted development or prior approval in the area. Is there anything you need to be careful of? We will go into some details of that later. And are you likely to get planning, if you need it? It makes sense to keep it simple.

When viewing a property, here are some things you need to consider with examples: environment, shape of the building, land, roof, windows, floor plate and services.

Environment

What do we mean by environment? If you have been assessing a deal and you have done your Ready Reckoner, and you think the building may be worthwhile, and you have moved onto your desktop searches, you will need to start using online facilities such as Google Maps from your desk. So even before you go and see the deal, you can find out what the environment is like by looking at it online. What is in the area? Use the satellite view and the street map view to assess what it would be like to live there, where are the local amenities, where could people pop out to, to get bread and milk? What kind of area is the building in?

This was a deal Glenn was offered in Basingstoke and the building offered for sale is somewhere in the middle of the industrial estate pictured. Now look at the industrial area around it, who thinks that is a nice place to live? The bottom line is that although the unit itself may be perfect for conversion and the numbers in this instance stacked up, who would we sell it to? Who would want to live there? There is nothing residential around it, the views are horrible, surrounded by your typical industrial unit service road, there are no local amenities, not enough land around it to screen, etc. We didn't even go and look at it; that is the benefit of a desktop search – we didn't even waste time going to look at it.

However, would I have looked at the other building highlighted in yellow? Yes. I would have done. It is close to residential, you would never know because you can't tell on Google Maps, but there could be an underpass here with a Tesco Express just on the other side. Further, this has got quite a lot of land in front of it and it looks like there is a grass verge, which means we might be able to screen it off from the rest of the industrial site. So if I can get in from the main residential road and the site is overlooking residential with greenery around it, and there happen to be some local amenities, that could have become a good development. The great thing is that if you find anything like that you have got a really good deal because the price per sq. ft. will be low. But you have got to think carefully about environment.

Contrast that with this building in the perfect residential environment, surrounded by 'chimney pots' and with all the residential feel and amenities you could wish for.

One is definitely a residential opportunity and one is clearly less so. On occasion, it may be worthwhile to drive by and have a look, but very often we can tell what kind of environment the development is in, simply by checking online.

Shape of the Building

When developing a building, we are always learning lessons. Along with his JV partners, Glenn bought both of the buildings shown above. One epitomises a good building to buy, and the other, one not to buy! However, we used this strategy with both buildings and, necessity being the mother of invention, we found solutions to each of the issues thrown at us.

The building shown in the top left picture on St Mary Street is too deep. Notice how square it is, and therefore how deep the building is. Imagine trying to get daylight into the middle of the building. That is the issue with deep buildings... Light. If you can't easily get light into a building, the layouts will be compromised. We knew the layouts wouldn't be perfect in the St Mary Street building, but it isn't the most salubrious area of Southampton and we bought it at way less than £100 per sq. ft. We knew that there was a base value in Southampton and that we could still make money on the deal, but we also knew that this building was going to give us layout difficulties. If you were looking in a prime area, you might really suffer with a slightly less appealing layout.

The building highlighted as 11 Queensway, however, has a better layout. Pretty narrow back to front, perfect for a corridor down the middle with units to one side and units to the other side – absolutely ideal. Moreover, the units to each side won't be very deep, so without making the flats too large, we would be able to give good sized windows to both the bedroom and the lounge/diner.

The perfect width or depth of a building is about 13 metres, because you can have a corridor in the middle that takes out one metre, which leaves 12 metres – six metres deep on one side and six metres deep on the other side. Now what you can do is go down to about 11 metres, because then you have got about five metres for each flat and you can just make them broader. That is a rough rule of thumb. The moment you get to a building and it's 20 or 30 metres across, you need to be thinking a lot about natural light and how you are going to get light 15 metres into a building. We need to buy and develop buildings where we can sell all of the square footage. Good luck with getting light 15 metres into the centre of a building in a unit that is only going to be 30 m² (our optimum size to maximise sales value) as you will have just created a flat that is 15 metres long and two metres wide! Think about the shape of the building and about natural light getting into the building.

Land

One point to note with regard to commercial properties is that they often sit on reasonable chunks of land in the middle of town centres.

The site above (the building with the large car park behind it) is in a town on the south coast, very close to the new civic offices, which was a conversion from an old office block that was completely revamped and given new life by the progressive local authority. Close to Sainsbury's and the beginning of the town high street, and with green space opposite, this was a perfectly located conversion opportunity. Additionally, given its proximity to the town centre, any land in this area is likely to have significant value of some sort. In this town, the area in which this building was located was known as the Renaissance Zone, which encouraged high density housing, which to you and me is flats! Accordingly, this land at the back of the site had far more development value than its value in its current use as a car park.

Remembering that part of the original assessment is a quick check with the planning consultant, enquiries were made about the prospects of getting planning to develop the site further. The planning consultant in this case is quite reserved and doesn't over promise, so when she replied that we were unlikely to have any problem at all, we knew we were onto a winner!

We didn't know then how much of a winner it would be, though. We ended up getting planning to develop that and an adjacent site, and given the locality of the land and the importance to the council of getting exactly what they wanted on the land, they made an offer to buy the site from us. We banked 80% of the profit we thought we could make by developing the whole site, but without doing any of the work! These are the things that happen when you have control of land; land is valuable. If you start buying land, you never know what can happen, so be very aware of the land around any site you assess.

Roof

Contrary to popular belief, with regard to commercial conversions, flat roofs can be very good news. If a building has a pitched roof, be aware of its condition. If it has a pitched roof, your warranty company is likely to want to make sure it is water tight and they need to know with confidence that it is going to last another 15 years so that they can give you a 10-year guarantee on it. So you may need a timber treatment on the joists, you may need the tiles redone, you may need to renew linings, you could even end up having to rebuild the whole roof. Be aware of the condition of the pitched roof and see if you can find any existing warranties on the building which you can pass on. Look at the condition of the structure and think about the guarantee. On the other hand, if it has got a flat roof, unless it is new and you can give a guarantee from the people who put it on, you are going to have to work on the basis you will need to replace that flat roof. The good news, though, is that flat roof technology has moved on – it is now much more reliable and doesn't cost very much to replace.

Windows

You remember the two buildings we showed earlier in St Mary Street, which was too deep, and Queensway, which was perfect?

This is the St Mary Street building from the side.

This is 11 Queensway from the side. What do you notice about the Queensway windows? They are old casement windows, so they are going to need replacing.

The St Mary Street building, in fact number 63, was actually only built in 2002, so the windows were all UPVC and are all still covered by a guarantee, so no replacement was required. But also notice the volume of glass in each window pattern. On 11 Queensway, see how many windows there are, what a nice staggered pattern there is and how big they are – plenty of natural light. Now look at 63 St Mary Street; they look plentiful on first glance, but look closely and you'll see there aren't that many of them and they are not large. It is not the worst, but we would ordinarily recommend looking for more windows. One trick for really 'seeing' the volume of glass is to instead look at the brickwork. If you compare the two pictures above, there is much more brickwork/blanking panels on 63 St Mary Street than there is on 11 Queensway. Always bear in mind where the windows are and how much natural light you are going to get into a building.

Floor Plate and Pillars

Simply put, when assessing the floor plate and pillar positions, we are making a cursory check to see whether we consider the floor plate easily divisible into suitable apartment sizes, and that the pillar positions are evenly spaced and not too numerous. Once we are a little bit more experienced, we may consider how they work with our prospective corridor layouts, etc. Don't worry too much about either of these factors though, as long as they seem relatively sensible, your architects should be able to make most things work.

Value Add Planning Applications

We have already covered the added value afforded by land. The other value adding opportunity to consider is that of the airspace above the building you are looking at. Airspace is wonderful because it is effectively free, as you have already paid for the land the airspace 'sits' on. If you already own the airspace, consider the extra profit in those upper floors. Of course, the units in the new floors that you get permission to build will cost more to build than the existing building is going to cost to convert, but that is more than compensated for by the 'free airspace' afforded to you.

Commercial buildings are built to more stringent stress testing and strength requirements than residential ones, so if you buy a commercial building, you can often get more floors on top without adding significant additional structural elements, by using lightweight construction on the new upper floors, such as timber, MetSec, SIPS or other lightweight construction methods. As a rule of thumb, one would normally be quite safe adding a fifth and possibly sixth floor to a traditionally constructed four-storey commercial building. Accordingly, always look at whether there may be an opportunity to go up. Look at the buildings around the site to see whether they go higher than the building you are considering.

However, it is important to state that one should never buy an opportunity based on an added value opportunity. Your deals should stack up on your prior approval conversion, with nothing further added. If you are using planning, then you should be offering subject to planning.

The reason for not including any added value uplift in calculating your offer for a prior approval conversion opportunity is demonstrated very well by our 'perfect' conversion at Queensway. When we started looking at the structure of Queensway to put extra floors on top, we had a bit of shock. Whilst it was a traditionally constructed building in most senses, we found out that it was an unusual structure, being of 'sway frame' design. The implications of this transpired to be that although the building could indeed take the vertical loading of an extra floor or two, it would not be able to withstand the extra lateral loading caused by extra wind to the increased façade. That extra loading would cause the building to 'sway' beyond its designed limits! As a result, we have had to spend a significant amount of design time and cost coming up with a structural solution that is relatively expensive to put additional floors on top.

Something might look good on paper, and you might even have planning for it, but you should never go through planning or include any additional element in your thinking until you have had a structural engineer look at the design and the building itself. This may also require 'opening up works' so that the engineer can be sure of the building's structure. You could spend a lot of time and money getting some very beautiful architect plans drawn, getting it through planning and you all celebrate and go and drink the champagne and then the structural engineer comes along and says you can't build it. So never include 'hope' value in your offers.

Reviewing Your Visit

Having completed your viewing, and having assessed the variables we have just covered, the key question, if you are using prior approval or permitted development, is there any reason prior approval won't work here? Have you discovered anything that undermines your major assumptions? If the Ready Reckoner told you that you had a deal here, your planning consultant has confirmed the planning/prior approval opportunity, you have assessed the building during viewing and found no major issues, and possibly, too, your imagination has found an added value opportunity such as land, extensions or additional floors, then you might just have found yourself a deal.

Before we move on, just a quick word on ugly buildings: they can work! What's more, they can work wonderfully well because other people may have been put off. Architects can do amazing things with buildings to 'disguise' ugliness and it doesn't have to be too costly. Your architect's job is to not let it stay ugly. You have the vision to know ugliness can be resolved, let your team solve the problem and by doing so, you get paid big profits. Glenn had to persuade his JV partner on 11 Queensway for quite some time to buy the building. The environment was poor, surrounded by social housing and a decrepit old fruit market. He knew, though, that the environment was going to improve, as there was a massive regeneration of the fruit market planned, so what was an almost derelict and nasty looking old fruit market was to be completely redeveloped into residential housing. Furthermore, the housing was only to rent rather than for sale, so even though the value of the area would increase by becoming less of an eyesore, it wouldn't affect the sales rate. Indeed, we expect the sales rate to increase because the area is becoming more desirable but there will be few properties in the area for sale.

Once again, the local knowledge that comes through niching pays high dividends. Although Glenn had to persuade his partner in the first instance, when Ocea's architect presented to their Mastermind Group he actually used it as an example of the perfect commercial conversion. The architect confirmed it was the right shape, enough windows, an ugly looking building that can be easily skimmed to refresh its look and with another couple of floors on top it also comes with an added value opportunity. So don't be afraid of ugly, your job is to improve it.

To summarise, when you review your visit, there is a key question: is there any reason why I cannot use this commercial conversion using prior approval? If you are going to use prior approval, that is your key question. The secondary question is can I create more value? So number one: is there any reason why I can't use prior approval? Number two: how can I add value if possible?

Deal Analysis and Your Deal Analyser

Having reviewed your visit, if you come to the conclusion that there might well be a deal available to you, it is time to assess the deal in detail, in readiness for your offer. It cannot be stressed too highly that your analysis tool must be as robust as possible with lines for almost every eventuality, reminding you to consider all the various costs that are applicable in property development.

There are costs associated with buying, designing, planning, constructing, financing, selling and investment. There are all kinds of costs at every stage, and whilst in every deal you will find costs that you may not have considered, or perhaps factored in accurately, you need to give yourself the best chance to ensure that you are no more than a few percent out.

Let's list some of the lines you should consider in your appraisal tool:

- Purchase price

- Finder's fees

- Working capital

- Stamp Duty

- Conveyancy fees

- Insurance

- GIA ft2

- Number of units

- Build cost per ft2 (ex. VAT)

- Subtotal build cost (ex. VAT)

- VAT

- Contingency

- Contamination provision

- Utilities

- Lifts

- Total build estimate

- PD preliminary planning fees

- PD architects first stage (incl. VAT)

- Surveys (asbestos, flood, environment, contamination, drainage)

- Mechanical and electrical engineer

- Party wall surveyor

- Building control (£240+VAT per unit)

- SAP & EPC

- PD architect and planning fees – second stage (incl. VAT)

- Prepare specification for works

- Tender preparation and contract docs

- QS

- Architect project management

- Project management

- CDM consultant

- Section 106 payments

- Council fees (e.g. transport contribution, deed and monitoring fees)

- Interior design

- Guarantees

- Landscaping

- Other professional fees necessary for your opportunity

- Sales agents fees

- Legal fees on sale of units

- Marketing costs

- Brochure costs

- Dressing of units

- Cost of funds for bridge, development finance, and investor funds

This is by no means an exhaustive list, but it does cover most of the usual considerations for a commercial conversion. Work these into your spreadsheet model and continue to iterate it until you have a robust and comprehensive model you can use to assess your deals.

The following flow chart provides a clear system for finding your deals up to the point of making an offer:

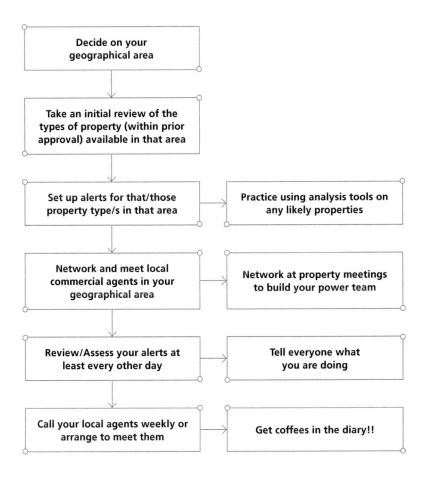

Making an Offer and Other Considerations

You see an opportunity, do the Ready Reckoner, you assess the deal, is it worth viewing? You view the property and think it is probably worth putting an offer in, so then you fill out your deal analyser and come up with an offer price; at this point you might even be talking to your joint venture partner about it. The offer gets accepted, you get into the deal and at that point you might hire somebody to fill in your deal analyser and use it for sensitivity analysis and variance tracking. Does that progression make sense?

This is what we use our deal analyser for. It is not just for calculating our offer, it is for ongoing monitoring of the project and it is at a high level of granularity – in fact, as high a level as you desire or require. And the bonus is that you can use it for sensitivity analysis of your future offers, as you become ever clearer about how much each thing costs within your model over a succession of deals – another benefit, by the way, of niching and building up your expertise in one area. The analyser we use also allows us to test 'what if' scenarios, such as *what happens if it takes six months to sell, not three months? How much extra will the cost of funds be? What happens if all the units sell for £5k less than we have assumed? What happens if the cost of money goes up?*

When investors ask a lot of *'what happens if'* questions, the best way to answer them is to have a powerful deal analysis model that allows you to respond by saying "let me just change that for you... there is the end result". Do you think your investor has some comfort then? Think that might win you more investors? Absolutely, it will.

When we are looking for deals we are looking for profitable, not perfect: there is no such thing as the perfect deal. If you ever find one it will go wrong – they don't exist, so don't look for it, don't waste your time. There will be something niggling you about every deal, that's just the way it is.

You have to use all the learnings in this book to mitigate most of the risk. If you have a 20 to 30% margin on cost, you can accept things going wrong, you have enough fat to play with. So don't waste time looking for the perfect deal, because you will never get one over the line.

Conversely, remember there is always another deal, so this is the opposite: don't get too precious about any one deal. If you can't get the deal at the right price, let it go, even if it is your first one – there will be another one along. Isn't it amazing that when we find the car we love that has been on the forecourt for months the salesperson has just happened to have had five phone calls that day from people who are going to come and view it because it has suddenly become the most popular model in the whole of Southampton? The salesperson is playing on our fear of missing out. Properties are just the same, and agents will try it on. Part of you being taken seriously is that you need to show you will walk away if it ceases to become a viable deal. Remain detached – don't get too attached to a particular building. At the end of the day, this is a business.

Speak to your agent. We cannot stress enough, for most of you we believe your first deal is likely to come from an agent, even if you find it on Property Gazette or Rightmove. You are going to have to build a rapport with that agent to get that deal over the line. Speak to your agent – don't try to befriend them, just try and be honest and explain, "this is the kind of thing I want to move into, I would really like to work with you closely, I am backed by pretty much unlimited funds". We will cover funding later in the book, but for now, accept that you are backed by almost unlimited funds – the world has got enough money for all of your deals put together. Once you have spoken to your agent and he has asked you to submit an offer, it is important that you send in an offer that further strengthens your standing as a serious developer.

Sample Offer Email

Here is a sample offer email. Read through it, then we will look at some of the elements.

Dear Sir/Madam,

Following our viewing with Mr John Smith and associated conversation, please find herein our offer for Building A, Newtown.

Having completed our due diligence, our unconditional offer is subject only to the issuing of a VAT 1614d and our offer is £x,xxx,xxx (£xmillion, xxxx-xxx thousand) and we are content with the normal deposit level of 10%.

The buying entity will be a new SPV to be set upon confirmation of an accepted offer, to be called Building A Developments Limited. Our solicitor is Jade Smith of Newco Solicitors LLP, Newtown. We work with HNWIs and will not be reliant on a mortgage, although we may choose to access some bridging for less than 50% of the purchase price, thereby requiring a valuation, but this is easily achievable within the prescribed timetable. We work closely with AlwaysInTheMoney Corporate Finance (main contact Mr Loadsa Dosh) and they will confirm our track record for fundraising and will also confirm that we will have no issue with raising funds in the given time. Furthermore, our solicitor, who has acted for us on many occasions, will also confirm that we have never withdrawn from a transaction due to a lack of funds.

Business Partner and I represent 100% of BigCo Group Limited (Group Parent Company) and accordingly have all the authority required to make this offer. In various SPVs, BigCo has undertaken a number of similar, larger and smaller projects and we attach a copy of our property CV. We also invite you to review our website at www.bigco.com.

We will exchange within 4 weeks of receipt of CPSEs, draft contract and receipt of all searches, and complete 4 weeks thereafter. We require access for surveys and opening up works before exchange, but of course will make good where/when needed. We will also need early sight of the Asbestos Report.

We are dedicated prior approval developers with an established track record, with references available from Number One of Commercial Agent 1 (Newtown), Number Two of Commercial Agent 2 (Bigville) and Number Three of Commercial Agent 3 who represents us in this transaction. Current developments have a GDV in excess of £YYM.

We look forward to hearing from you regarding this offer.

Picking out some of the main elements of this offer email:

Unconditional Offers

If you are using prior approval and your planning consultant has confirmed that there is no reason not to be granted the consent you seek, then you are well positioned to make an unconditional offer. This places you at a distinct advantage against less well educated bidders that only submit conditional offers. Otherwise, unless you are buying something that already has a planning consent that you intend to implement, you would be wise to offer conditional on planning.

Use of SPVs

It us usually wise to incorporate a new SPV whenever you take on a new development project. You will need to consult your legal advisors and tax accountant for professional advice in this regard.

HNWI – High Net Worth Individuals

By stating that you work with HNWIs, you are making at least two very good points to the agent. You will not only be making it clear that you are well networked with ready cash available to you, you will also be removing a large amount of risk to the vendor/agent by removing the need for a mortgage. With rundown, partly or fully vacant premises this is important as most commercial buildings are valued primarily on their revenue producing capability. Whilst there will always be an underlying 'bricks and mortar' value, it will usually be significantly less than the value of a well repaired, fully tenanted and income producing asset. Accordingly, it can be very difficult to raise a good level of mortgage funding against commercial sites that are up for sale for anything other than investment.

Bridging

It is our experience that agents are quite relaxed about the use of bridging funds at a relatively low LTV in the deal. It is generally readily available and doesn't therefore represent huge risk, but explains why we will need valuers visiting site, which for cash purposes may otherwise not be required.

If the building is opted to tax, your offer should always be subject to issuing a VAT 1614D to disapply tax. If you are converting a commercial building into residential, you do not have to pay the VAT on the purchase. This relaxation of VAT is applicable if you are immediately going to convert the building to residential use. So if you are going to use the building in its continued commercial use for any period, you will not be able to apply the VAT 1614D. Another couple of quick things: 1) you don't want to pay the VAT if you don't have to, 2) the tax man charges you SDLT (Stamp Duty Land Tax) on the purchase price including VAT, so you end up paying tax on tax! So unless you are feeling particularly generous towards our lovely government and you want to give them a tip for introducing permitted development, you don't want to pay SDLT on VAT, because unlike the VAT, which you can get back even if you pay it, you can't get the SDLT back. One other benefit of stating that you need to issue a VAT 1614D is that you are communicating to the agent that you know what you are doing.

Exchange Dates and CPSE

The important thing here is not the period, whether it is four weeks or six weeks or whatever, but that you should say in your offer that you will exchange xx number of weeks after the receipt of the CPSE and draft contract. CPSE stands for Commercial Property Standard Enquiries. Nobody calls it Commercial Property Standard Enquiries, so if you put that in your email they will know you are a newbie. CPSEs are issued with every sale of a commercial building. They can be fairly useless, as it is a very long questionnaire that asks the vendor all kinds of questions about the property, such as "have you had a boundary dispute?", "do you have a right of way across your property?", "are you aware of any of this, this and this" etc. There are many pages of this stuff, and for that reason most vendors can't be bothered to answer it properly, so they just write unhelpful things such as "the buyer should rely on their own enquiries" on most questions. So there may not a huge amount of useful information in there. What we are communicating again to the agent is: 1) we know what it is and that it must be issued, and 2) we know this is often the last piece of information that comes because the vendors can't be bothered to fill it in.

By linking our timetable to this often delayed enquiry form, we also tend to buy ourselves a little more time to get ready for the exchange.

Surveys

There are more surveys to do with commercial conversions, so to save time we suggest you ask for access for surveys between exchange and completion. If you can get it in before exchange, great, but many vendors will be very nervous about granting you access before exchange, especially if they still have tenants in as they may not want to tell the tenants they are selling the building. Definitely, though, between exchange and completion.

Conveyancing and Completing

Your power team are doing most of the work now as you have done your work. You have located the deal, assessed it, negotiated it – now it's time to hand over. If you are currently in a job, then just one of these deals could change your life and give you enough money to leave your job and go and do property full time. Until then, though, once you found a deal and put it together with the money, you must hand over the detail and get your power team working.

Asbestos Reports

You should always receive an asbestos report when buying a commercial building, that should be supplied by the vendor. Don't be too worried by the asbestos word, there are some very low level asbestos risks in buildings, but you can also find some very high-risk asbestos that is very costly to remove, so would you rather know before you set out what risk you have got.

Other points on the purchase if your bid is successful:

Insurance

Insurance requirements are forever changing for a developer. The insurance required on a vacant building is different from that required on a building that has a contractor on-site, which is different once again from a finished building that is not yet occupied, which is different again from a building that new owners are moving into! If you do not have the right cover, then if there is an issue the insurer may not pay out in full, if at all so get a good insurance broker that specialises in this field and keep them informed.

Transfer of a Going Concern

Some of the best opportunities on the market at the moment are part vacant buildings. Why? If you are looking at something that is beginning to come to the end of its useful life in its current use, then there is a high chance that the landlords are attracting getting good quality, high-paying tenants. Whether it is a shop on the high street, an office that is not very attractive any more, or a care home that hasn't got all the people they need to make it work because it isn't very appealing any more, you will often find something that is being sold with some tenants *in situ*. These can be fantastic opportunities, for a couple of reasons: 1) there is an income, 2) you can get them cheaper, and 3) there is less competition. The other thing is that you may find that you are buying a company with tax losses, so you can offset any profit you make against tax losses made by somebody else! The downside of buying such an opportunity is that you have got to do a lot of due diligence, but you should be doing that anyway. The upside is that you can find a lot of deals that other people would pass by because they think buying something as a going concern is too much hassle.

If you are going to buy with tenants in situ, you need to be clear how you are going to get your tenants to leave. This is part of your due diligence, to establish how you can exit the tenants when you need to. Essentially, if they are inside the 1954 Landlord and Tenant Act they have certain rights that if they are outside the Act they don't have. Inside the Act they are entitled to an automatic renewal of their tenancy when the current lease term ends. However, if you are re-developing the building, it is considered to be one of the circumstances under which a landlord can give notice to tenants inside the Act, paying a pre-determined compensation based on rateable value. If the tenant is outside the Act, then the day their lease ends, you can effectively change the locks the day after their lease ends without paying any compensation. Furthermore, many tenants are open to negotiation to move if you are able to incentivise them in some way.

VAT

If a building has tenants in situ, you are effectively buying a small business. So if the building is elected for VAT (i.e. they are paying VAT on the rent) and you are buying it as a going concern, there is no VAT payable on the purchase. The great news is that usually we can reclaim the VAT on our professional fees too in this circumstance, because it is part of the transaction, so there can be lots of upsides of buying with tenants in situ.

Locating the deal is about momentum, and it may not happen overnight. We need to build up our knowledge, our relationships and practise our deal assessment. That is when the rubber hits the road, because some of you will give up on this strategy before you find the first deal. You will convince yourself that you are different, that your area is different and that somehow the universe works differently for you in your patch. And yet next door someone could be doing exactly the same thing; they stick at it a bit longer, and the day after you have given up they walk straight onto their first deal, giving them momentum and the resultant success.

Case Study – Never Give Up (by Glenn)

I mentioned earlier in the book that when I heard the webinar by Rob Moore about doing bigger deals, I immediately went off to try and find a bigger deal. I found a deal in a place called Romsey, fairly near to where I lived, that had been used as offices. I tried so hard to buy this building. I tried every which way, I had an investor who was an experienced developer to mentor me through the process, and he was telling me how to put my basic analyser together, most of which came from him. He told me all the things I needed to think about and consider, and we put multiple offers in. I worked really hard for that deal and I broke all the rules because I fell in love with the deal. This was THE deal, this was the one that was going to change my life, this was the one that was going to help me step onto bigger deals.

But I didn't get it. In the end, it was sold to an owner occupier. The thing is, that could have been a great deal, and the number we were offering would have made it a good deal (for us), but owner occupiers work on a very different valuation. There aren't many of them around in the market at the moment, and it just so happened in this case that the building was perfect for their needs.

I felt like I had been kicked in the teeth. We had been through months of negotiating, several rounds of offers, I had visited them several times, I had built rapport with the vendor, I'd had coffee with him on numerous occasions. I had built bridges and done just about everything I could, and then still lost the deal. The sad thing is that losing deals is very common, and we have to decide how determined we are, because I could easily have given up at that point.

Thereafter, because I hadn't yet picked a niche, I then looked at something entirely different! Here is a little tip for you: talk about what you do, wherever you are, whatever environment you are in. At the time, I was operating as a consultant for an IT company and I had just talked about the fact that I was a property investor. A lady came up to me with an opportunity. She told me her stepmother had a property but was a really private person who didn't like dealing with agents. She wanted to sell her property and thought that there was some development potential. "This is what you do, isn't it?" my colleague asked. Truthfully, I considered the chances of this opportunity being something suitable were pretty slim, but I said I would take a look, to see if I could help this colleague as much as anything.

I went along to see if I could help, intrigued but not expectant. What I was shown was a bungalow in one-third of an acre. I thought it might be a bit more interesting than I expected. I had a chat with the stepmother and it was clear she wasn't going to sell it below value, but her value was the value of the bungalow and not the development value of the site. She knew the site had development value, but she wasn't interested in getting into all that, being a very private person. She didn't just not want agents involved; the worst thing on her mind was the prospect of developers flooding her with offers and coming in trying to outbid each other – the thought just filled her with horror. All she wanted was to be paid what the house was worth without any agents or any hassle. If I could pay that, then I could have it. Hey! The price was agreed and a deal struck, and now I needed to find the money.

Sound familiar? My network of investors wasn't as developed as it is now, and I was desperate to get this deal over the line. So when I met someone who knew someone who might have a bit of money, I went and had coffee with them. I was so desperate! I was where many of you reading this book are, and investors can smell desperation. This guy put me over a barrel, saying he would put the money into the deal but it was going to cost me a fortune. He would also only fund the process of applying for planning and then he wanted to exit. He also wanted to take most of the cream for getting planning, but I justified this 'expensive' money with the consoling thought of getting on the property development ladder. After all, we were moving towards exchange and I needed the funds and with an undeveloped network I had few other options.

About a week before exchange he pulled out. He gave no real apology as he felt he had been doing me a favour, but he had found something else to do with his money and wasn't interested in the deal anymore. I now had a deal due to exchange imminently and no funds, the stuff of nightmares?

There is a reason for telling you this story. Two days later I was with my new network at the Progressive Property Training Academy, sat at a table on a PPN Post Training Day. In an effort to boost my visibility and credibility (more of that in the networking section), I had taken on a Progressive Property Network (PPN) meeting as a franchise. I found myself sharing a table with a chap we will call Bill, who I had seen on some of the Facebook forums, and he seemed to be well known at Progressive. Bill was the host for a London PPN and we got chatting in the lunch break. He asked what property strategy I was using and I told him I was looking to go big. He said, "I really like the idea of going big too. I am fed up with messing about with these small deals". We got chatting about 'going big' and as we talked he asked about my past and how I had ended up in property. We discovered that we had both worked in Albania, of all places. It transpired he had worked there as a missionary, and my father was a vicar who had also ministered in Albania!

As we chatted away, building ever more connections, he got round to asking me tell him more about 'going big'. "Have you got any deals of the kind you are looking at?" he asked. Of course, I showed him the bungalow site and he became very animated, exclaiming "this is exactly the kind of thing I want to be doing". I explained the plans to knock the bungalow down and build seven downsizer units for retirees. The more we chatted, the more animated he became. "This is exactly the kind of deal I want. Tell you what, if you get any more deals like this can you give me a call?" And then he looked up at me to ask" I presume this deal is already funded", to which I was able to respond, "well, funnily enough I lost my investor two days ago". We shook hands on the deal 20 minutes later: a 50/50 profit split, with him putting the funds in and me doing the work. He had solved my lack of funds and I had satiated his desire to get into bigger deals.

Having agreed our first deal together, he went on to offer to fund any more big deals I found. Bill and his business partner then funded my first office development too. Reflecting on what happened, I could have given up when I lost the first office in Romsey. I could have given up when I lost the investor just a week before we were due to exchange on the bungalow. At any point, many of you, some of you, a few of you, I hope, might have given up, but if you are in the right community and the right networks, I sincerely believe money will come to the right deal.

I am often asked what comes first, the deal or the investor? In my view you should always be looking for both, but you will need a deal for investors to get involved with. I find it easier to have the deal first. Bill and his business partner went on to fund (so far) over half a dozen deals with me. The moral of the story is, don't give up. Don't give up if the first deal falls over, don't get too wedded to any particular deal, and get involved in networks and communities, because you are going to need good connections to provide the money and the deals.

Graphical Representation of the Deal Finding Process

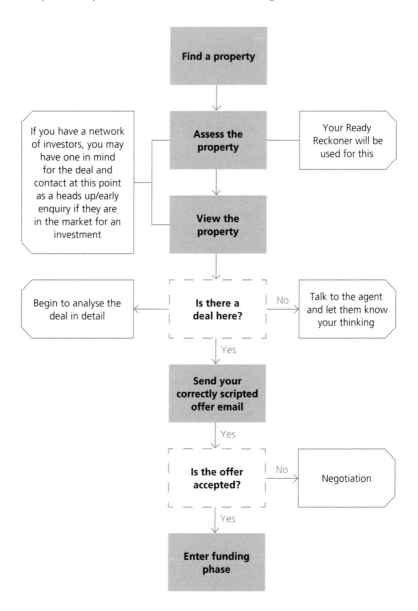

Chapter 9: Arranging Funds

Types of Funding and Where to Find Them

Funding is required for two elements: in basic terms, you have got to purchase a property and you are going to convert the property by developing it. So you need to fund the purchase and the development. Together, the purchase and the development are collectively 'the costs'. What we refer to from now on as the costs is the purchase of the property and the development combined, and the costs are financed by a combination of equity investment and development finance. It is no more complicated than that until we make it more so, but that is the essence of funding.

Development Finance

You might consider that we are going to start backwards, but actually development finance drives your equity requirement, so we are going to start with development finance. The first good news is development finance is plentiful in the market at the moment; in fact, they are tripping over themselves to lend to people. They are competing with one another for the business and therefore lack of experience is not necessarily a barrier to entry. There is a caveat: don't try and make your first loan £5m on the back of simply reading a book, because that might be a barrier! But if you go and find a deal to convert a shop to maybe for our five units and you need £200,000, you might find that someone might lend you the requisite development finance.

'Bank' is a broad term these days. It is much broader than the main high street banks such as Barclays, Lloyds, HSBC and NatWest. There are masses of challenger banks out there, some of which you might never have heard of. You might have heard of Metro Bank, or Shawbrook or Aldermore because they do HMO funding and have become slightly better known in property investing circles. But there lots of others that you may never have heard of, such as Zorin, Paragon, BLG, Close Brothers, LendInvest, United Trust Bank, and many, many more. There are masses and masses of these lenders – they are competing for business and will lend anywhere between 65 and 80%, sometimes even 90% of loan to cost. But if you have a relative lack of experience at this stage, you are likely to be nearer the 65% mark, which means your equity requirement as a percentage of the whole is going to be higher. This is another reason why you might want to start with smaller deals; we will come back to that later.

Loan to Cost (LTC)

As stated above, together the costs are the purchase of the building and the development cost, and the banks will gear their lending against the overall cost of the deal. The 80-90% loan to cost (LTC) finance offers will open up once you have done a few deals, obviously based on track record. Clearly, if you have done a few deals and haven't performed well, that might not open up the 80% loan to cost offer, but hopefully if you are employing this system you won't have lost money, and you have gained a good track record and then the funding ratios will open up for you. It is not just about the loan to cost that will change for you, it will also affect the interest rates they will charge you. In the early days, the interest rates might be higher because you are more of a risk; that also goes for equity investment, by the way, when we get to that. You might find you have to give more to equity providers at the outset, even acknowledging that although you may have learnt a lot by reading this book and you might be very excited, you are still more of a risk to people than you will be in a few years' time when you have been doing this for a while.

Let's work an example through. Let's say we are going to purchase a building for £500k and are going to develop it at a cost of £750k. Overall, therefore, the costs involved in this project are £1.25m. One way or another, we have got to find £1.25m. How many of you have a spare £1.25m lying around? Not many of us. The good news is you don't need it – it's all going to come from other sources, every penny. If you do this right you don't need a penny of your own money. £1.25M looks like a fairly scary number at the moment to many of you, but it doesn't need to be, and by the end of this chapter you will understand why.

Let's say you are offered 75% loan to cost on £1.25m – that's £937,500 in development finance. A quick word on how development finance works. You don't go along, sign the paperwork and end up with £937.5k in your bank account the next day. Once you have an agreement with the lender to lend you up to £937,500, you will usually start drawing it down against development costs on a monthly basis. The costs get validated either by a QS, an architect or a project manager, who in so doing, confirms to the lender that that portion of the costs has been expended appropriately, and that funds can be released accordingly, safe in the knowledge that that portion of the works has been completed. For instance, the builder will say "I have spent £100k", the QS will say "I can see £100k of work", that gets sent off to the development finance bank and the development finance bank releases £100k of the £937,500. This process will be repeated until the development is finished. They simply release the money as the work is done and as you need to pay the builder.

Given that the development finance covers £937,500k against £1.25m costs, that leaves you with an equity investment required for £312,500. You may have thought it was going to cost YOU £1.25m, even at a relatively low loan to cost, but this means that your equity requirement is not very high. With project costs of £1.25m, which probably means that that project has a £1.6m GDV, you might have thought, "wow, that is way out of my reach", but actually the only equity you have got to find is £312,500. You may know people with that amount of money, and we guarantee that when you go to networking meetings, there will that kind of money 'in the room'. You will have met a lot of people with a lot more money than that, and you would never have guessed it in a million years. You passed them by none the wiser to their wealth. It is this balance of plentiful development funds and equity that makes this strategy more accessible than you may have previously considered.

You may have noticed that the equity didn't quite cover the cost of the building at £500k. The equity investment of £312,500 is £177,500 short of the purchase price, and you will also have purchase costs such as stamp duty, local fees, valuations, finders'/agents' fees, etc. So the development finance is going to need to cover some of the purchase and associated costs, as well as the development costs. That is entirely normal, but it does lead to some interesting things, which we are going to come to. The advantage is that the equity required is lower than you might think. You might look at a building and see it is £500k, then you add on the stamp duty, and then you add on all the other buying costs and then think, "flipping heck I have got to find equity of £600k" and suddenly it seems twice as far out of reach as it does when it is only £300k. The development finance will cover this uplift, but first we need to understand how the financing market works.

Metrics for Funding

The development finance companies have some metrics, which we need to cover. We have talked about loan to costs (LTC) and that they will have a maximum amount of percentage of LTC that they will lend to you based on your experience. They will therefore lend less to you at the beginning of your journey, given your lack of experience. But that's okay because you are going to be doing smaller deals, which means you are going to need smaller equity anyway.

There is a rule of thumb regarding LTC that is quite helpful, although it is only a rule of thumb. Generally, finance companies will lend up to 100% of the development costs and up to 50% of the purchase costs, and that usually comes out at around 75 to 80% LTC overall. We have established that when we see a building and it is £500k, we don't need £500k to £600k of equity investment, but instead just £300k to £350k. If 80% is their maximum LTC, this is the over-riding measure of what they will lend. So if, for example, you could buy a building and 50% of the purchase price plus the development costs was to exceed 80% LTC, then they would lend less against the purchase. Accordingly, whilst 50% of the purchase price and 100% of the development costs is a helpful rule of thumb, it is just that and the banks lending will be determined by their LTC metric rather than anything else.

Development finance lending rates are typically between 6% and 9% per annum (at time of writing) and again, when you are starting out, it will be at the more expensive end because you are a bigger risk. As long as you put the cost in your deal analyser, and your deal analyser calculates it for you, then you know where you are and whether the scheme can afford the cost of funds. They do sometimes measure their loans against other things, such as loan to value (LTV), more accurately described as loan to GDV (LTGDV), so you might see that as well, but whether they measure it using LTGDV, LTV or LTC, their overall loan to any development is likely to be the same.

Importantly, you will only get access to development finance when you have a consent that you are *going to implement*. Therefore, if you buy a building before you have got prior approval, are you going to get development finance on that building? No, because you haven't got a prior approval you are going to implement. What might happen is that you find a building that has got planning on it, but it is not a particularly good scheme that doesn't maximise the opportunity. Or it may even have an existing prior approval, but you consider there to be an option to add more value, maybe by intensifying the scheme. What currently seems to happen in the market is that vendors have heard now about prior approval, so they think they will increase the value of their building by getting prior approval on it. The problem is they don't know how to sweat the asset or how to maximise the value of the development. They don't know what they don't know, and nor do their architects! They will phone up their mate or an architect they might have used in the past who also knows nothing about prior approval, and they create nice big units that meet all the national minimum space requirements and they go to planning and get the scheme approved. The issue is that because they have rarely maximised the value, the consent acquired is about as much use as a chocolate fireguard.

The only benefit of that current prior approval is it shows and demonstrates to you and your investors or lenders that you can definitely get prior approval on the building. But if it has got national minimum space requirements or hasn't fully taken advantage of the space available, you are going to be throwing money away if you implement that strategy. Unfortunately, therefore, you will still be in a position where you can't get development finance, because although it has got a prior approval on the building, it is not the one you are going to implement. The key words are having a consent that you are going to implement. Only when you have approval for the scheme you intend to build out, will you be able to access development finance.

Bridging

So what do we do in the meantime? We do what we usually do when there is a finance gap in property: we bridge it. At the mere mention of that word, many of you have just gone shivery cold. Oh no, we are going to use bridging? Bridging is brilliant. If you are scared of it, it's only because you don't have a context in which to put it safely. Too often, bridging has been used when there is no realistic prospect of getting out of it. That's when we end up coming up to the end of the bridge, we can't get out of it and we know the costs are going to double, and the bridging company can take the building off you, and there is a horror story just waiting to unfold. It is a horror story regularly told at networking meetings and on social media, but is largely propagated by people who rushed in without a real plan, or maybe took a risk with planning, were uneducated or are stories merely being retold to make it sound like they are experienced – a bit like the man down the pub!

Don't get me wrong, there are bad bridging companies out there, but good bridging with reputable bridging companies is brilliant. Just because you have been on a bad date, doesn't mean you stop going out on dates, so just because there are bad bridgers out there doesn't mean you can't go out and use bridging. You need to know how to make it work and how to use it in the right way. In the situation where you have found a building that already has prior approval or planning, but you are unlikely to use it because they haven't maximised the deal, bridging can provide a wonderful stepping stone to cover the time gap until you have secured the consent you intend to build. Accordingly, in this scenario you can purchase the building by using your equity investor for the equity to purchase, and using bridging finance for the balance, including all those associated purchase costs and working capital.

Remember, our equity portion in our example was £312,500 but the building is £500k, and the rest will come from bridging. Bridging is more expensive than development finance – it is between 10% and 12% per annum, and there are fees associated with it as well, which we will come onto shortly. As long as you put the price of the bridging into the deal analyser and the deal still makes a profit, is it a problem? There is an expression taught by a property training company which is brilliant and has always been a useful memoir: "when you are digging for gold, don't worry about the cost of a shovel". You don't care how much money costs as long as it is in the deal analyser and the deal can afford it, and still pay you a healthy profit.

In the early days, the cost of your borrowed funds is going to be more expensive than you would like, but you need to get over it because it is just the cost of a shovel for you to dig the gold out of the ground, and the more experienced you get, the cheaper that shovel will become. You have to accept that you are a higher risk when starting out and you also have to accept that bridging is going to cost you more, because not only are you a higher risk at the moment given that you are new, but using bridging at any stage means you don't have an implementable scheme, and therefore whatever your view, however well you know prior approval, the banks still consider it a higher risk than if you have a scheme you could immediately implement. What do they do when they are going to take on more risk? They increase the price.

Generally speaking, in our scenarios where we are just bridging until we have a prior approval, we won't need it for more than six months. Of course, if you are going for planning you might need it for up to two years, and that is when bridging can get a lot riskier! That's not a joke either.

If you are going for planning we would not recommend you take on a bridge that went into default after a year, because how can you be super confident that that planning would be granted within a year? We would want a bridge that we could have for up to two years without going into default. It would be expensive, but that is the true cost of planning and the risk associated with it. However, if you are going for prior approval, you are likely to only need bridging for about six -12 months depending on the scheme, and once you are experienced and have a good team around you, it shouldn't take anywhere near that long to get your prior approval in place.

You need to look for the best deal in terms of bridging, and sometimes the best deal is secured by finding a development finance company that won't lend you development finance at the beginning (because you haven't yet got a scheme that you are going to implement), but they will bridge initially, and when you have got the planning consent or approval, they roll the bridge into development finance. Once the bridge is rolled into a development finance loan, the borrowing rate will decrease and you may have also saved on quite a number of fees by staying with the same lender. That process can work really well and there are a lot of lenders offering that type of product in the market at the moment.

Family Offices

A family office is simply ultra-high net worth individuals (UHNWI) who create an office to look after their money! Obvious, really! It is their family money and they create an office of staff to look after their money, investing it in various entities and markets. They will often take a debt role and an equity role and can be very good investors to work with, because they are very sophisticated and tend to understand the markets they enter. The reason we mention family offices at this point is that a lot of these family offices are currently entering this banking space and offering bridging into development finance, as well as equity, all in the same scheme. It may not be cheap money, but they also come with very good networks, and just by getting into a JV with one family office, many other doors can open subsequently. Furthermore, given their experience in different sectors, and often many years of making money work for them, JVs with family offices are frequently worth many millions of pounds in future profits just through lessons learnt during the process.

But the current 'banking' space is so competitive that sometimes that you may end up taking up bridging with one company, you then get the scheme that you are going to implement approved and then a whole raft of other lenders will come in and offer you much better finance rates and products. We do need to be cognisant of the fees associated with moving from one lender to another, and you will need to factor that into your calculations, but it can work out better to leave one lender and go with another one for the second 'development finance' phase.

Working Capital

It is important to factor in working capital when calculating your bridging finance. Once you have bought your building, you are going to carry out all the activities required to secure the prior approval you want, which means you are going to need a measured survey, you might need a structural engineer, you will need architects to draw up your plans and you are going to need a planning consultant to submit your plans. You are also going to have to pay the local authority, although it is only £80 for the prior approval submission but there may also be business rates to pay. So as well as borrowing the extra funds to pay the associated buying costs, you also need to borrow enough to fund the appointment of the professionals to get your prior approval through. And you might also want to do some detailed design to get ready for a tender. All this can be a significant amount of money, even on a small development. It might be £40k, £50k or £100k depending on the size of the development, so you won't want to fund it out of your pocket! You need to borrow enough to ensure that the combination of the equity investor and the bridge must be enough to cover all those expenses. Additionally, if you choose to soft strip the building (more on that in Get It Built) you will need even more funds so be sure to calculate your working capital figure as accurately as possible and allow for it when applying for your bridge and equity.

Development Finance Fees

There are lots of fees associated with development finance and bridging that we need to factor into our cost of borrowing. There is often an 'in' fee, which you pay to get into the loan, and it is usually between 1% and 2% of the loan value. This should all be in your deal analyser, so that all you need to remember is to fill it in, using your deal analyser as an 'aide memoire'. There can also be an 'out' fee. Although it can sometimes be zero, more often it is 1 to 2% again. Sometimes it is charged on the loan, but make sure you don't sign up for a loan where you pay an out fee linked to the GDV, which can work out very expensively. It's difficult to understand a bank that asks for an out fee linked to GDV. It is you who has added value to a building, and instead of paying an out fee based on the loan given to you by the lender, you are paying an out fee based on all the value you have added through your own efforts and expertise. Don't ever sign up to that.

Valuation fees tend to be one-off fees. If a lender is going to lend against a building clearly, they want an independent valuation to make sure the building is worth the money they are paying. These fees vary significantly by lender, valuer and area and need careful policing.

Assuming you use a broker to scour the market for the best deal, you will also be paying a broker fee of typically 1 to 2% on debt. It will be nearer to 2% if you are at the beginning of your development journey, because they will have to work harder to find you a good deal, and then you will negotiate it down as your track record improves making their task easier. You will also pay brokers 3 to 5% on any equity they raise. Similar to debt, it may be 5% at the beginning, and then you negotiate it down as you go. Again, if it's in your deal analyser and the deal can afford it, the broker fee is just part of the cost of the shovel, and a good broker will save you more than their fee by finding you the best deal.

As previously stated, a lender will want to make sure that the amount that is released every month to pay the builder is a sensible amount, and they ensure this by hiring a monitoring surveyor. Most of them appoint a monitoring surveyor who comes along to the site meeting every month and signs off on the amount the lender is going to release. You have to pay for the cost of that monitoring surveyor, and that is usually about £500 to £1000 per visit (i.e. per month). The monitoring surveyor fee is only payable whilst the contractor is on-site, as this is principally when you will be drawing down development funds.

All those fees must be in your deal analyser to ensure that they are always accounted for. I also want to bring some terms to your attention that you might hear. You don't need to understand these at the moment; if you do then great, if you don't, don't panic because your corporate finance broker will walk you through them.

The principal development finance loans are usually described as senior debt, and this term is used for lenders that have the first charge on the building/SPV/asset. Their loan is backed by collateral, putting them in the 'senior' position. A senior debt lender will always take first charge. Stretched senior debt is simply when they stretch their level of comfort, so let's say they have a senior debt of 65% loan to cost, but they will go up to 80%. That is 'stretching' their enthusiasm and their appetite, so consequently they will charge higher rates. They consider the larger LTC loan to carry more risk, so it is more expensive to borrow.

When you hear about mezzanine debt, it means the lenders are now so beyond their normal senior debt that they introduce a hybrid of **debt** and equity **financing** that gives the lender the rights to convert to an ownership or equity interest in the company in case of default. It is riskier, sits behind all senior debt in ranking and consequently is the most expensive debt of all. It can sometimes be used by some equity investors as 'quasi equity', allowing them to charge a fixed interest rate at quite a high level, whilst securing them a greater equity position if things start to go wrong. There can also be some tax advantages to investors to invest in this manner, but that is way beyond our remit in this book.

At this stage you just need to understand senior debt is the basic loan, it will carry a first charge and it will have a cost associated. Stretch senior debt is stretching their appetite, so it is going to cost you more money because they are taking a risk, and mezzanine is even more risky and has accordingly higher costs.

Now all of this should be enough to convince you of the merits of finding a good corporate finance broker who comes recommended. You need to go into the communities and do exactly the same thing as we have talked about before: ask people which corporate finance broker they are using. Find the people who come recommended and are spoken well of, introduce yourself to those people, and it is likely they will do exactly the same thing for you. As soon as you have got a deal, in part because they want their fee, they will come and sit down with you and walk you through how they are going to help you, how they are going to put the debt package together and then they will go out and get the best deal for you. It really is that easy if you get someone who is recommended.

A good corporate finance broker is essential. Whomever they are, they are one of your five key power team people because they are going to help you put the money together. That sounds like a pretty good plan, does it not? The other thing about corporate finance brokers is that they can find you equity as well as development finance, as a lot of them are in contact with family offices, and as we have seen, family offices often take an equity position as well as a debt position. They will also know high net worth individuals who have been in touch with them saying "if anything comes up, I am looking for a way of getting my money into the market". Some angel organisations also lend equity into property, so if you hear of one, always note down their details for future reference.

Brokers are likely to charge you 1 or 2%, maybe even up to 3% when you are new, on debt and 3 to 5% on any equity. When you start, start with the smaller deals – you might be able to fund the equity part of those deals from your network. Friends, family, community, local network meetings, property networking meetings, business networking meetings, flying clubs, health clubs – all the stuff you have heard about. They are generally pretty good for getting you equity funds when you are starting out.

Money is everywhere though. Always talk about what you do because money springs out of the most surprising places. Glenn found his first JV funder sitting in a training room at a Progressive Property Network (PPN) Host Training Day, and one of his fellow PPN Hosts asked what he was doing in property. Glenn replied that he had just moved into doing bigger deals and when he asked about what that involved, Glenn showed him a deal. Glenn and his fellow PPN Host shook hands on the deal funding 20 minutes later. He then became the funder for Glenn's second deal, which was his first office conversion. The funding Host then introduced Glenn to someone he knew who became a funder of three more office conversions and before he knew it, Glenn was involved in a network of equity funders. One of his next funders was a taxi driver taking him to the airport! They got chatting about what Glenn did and some months later entered into a JV together!

However, when you scale your projects both in number and size, you might get to the point where your deals exceed your current network's ability to fund them. That is where corporate finance brokers are very good. At the time of writing, Ocea has just done a deal with a family office and that family office manages billions of pounds. Having just agreed to fund their deal, Glenn found himself sitting next to someone worth £billions in Prezzo, having lunch. Three years ago, he had debts of £140k, had no money and no clue; do you think the billionaire would have sat down with Glenn then? Of course not, they didn't exactly mix in the same circles! But as you scale, you might need people like this, and that is where your corporate finance broker comes in.

See how important these people in your power team are to you? And the great news is they grow with you. If you find someone that is good at what they do, you go on the journey with them and they can become friends, confidants and supporters. When dealing with all your professionals, remember they are massively important to you and they may grow with you. Treat your brokers well, don't resent their fees, and the great news is that they can help you access almost unlimited funds.

Other Bank Gates/Metrics

There are further metrics that the banks may or may not use, and they are great for you because it helps to double check whether your development proposal is as strong as you consider it to be. If a bank won't lend to you when money is so plentiful and they are so keen to get it into the market, could that be an indication that you are extending yourself either beyond your expertise, or that maybe the deal isn't as good as you think it is? The answer is yes and no to be truthful – some banks are just very conservative. Other banks, though, are not, and if they decline to lend they may be giving you a very important message.

So here are some further metrics you need to watch. Most of them will want the profit in the deal to be 25% of the costs before you take off the interest, i.e. before the cost of funds is considered. Or they will have a metric that says they want 20% of costs after the interest has been taken into account. These very common metrics effectively mean the bank won't lend you development finance unless you are making a 20% margin on cost. Now that's a good indication to you that 20% is where is most developers should play, because it is a sensible number is it not? But it is a good check and balance, because you should never do a deal for less than 20% profit on costs, it is too tight. So if the bank won't lend to you, it will probably be helping you out.

In our example, our profit pre-cost of funds was 25% of £1.25m, which is £312,500 (this is only to give you a rough idea, so don't do the maths exactly). Let's say you had 8% per annum development finance on that remaining £937,000, and in 19 months (roughly the time it takes to do a development), the interest on that loan would be about £125k. That is a lot of money, isn't it? Don't worry, it is the cost of the shovel. As long as you have allowed for it and you are still making money, it is just the cost of the shovel. Now you will probably have about £25k of fees on top of that, so that is now up to £150k. Adding the £150k onto the original costs, your overall costs now include buying the building, developing the building and all the costs of funds; your overall cost is now £1.4million. £312k profit target over £1.4million is 22% after your cost of funds, so it is more than your 20% gauge. You are good to go, and the good news for you is that this is also the bank's way of checking you are not about to do something silly.

The profit doesn't mean anything to the bank other than margin of safety for them if things go wrong. Quite frankly, they don't care if you make 20% profit or not – what they are using this metric for is as a margin to ensure they are never going to be in a position where you can't afford to pay them back. We are just using this as an example so don't get overworked on the detail.

In summary, you probably need less equity than you thought, have a rough idea of the metrics the lender is using to assess your deal, and your deals may cost more when you are digging for gold, but don't worry about the cost of the shovel.

As a rule of thumb, try to have only one investor per deal, where you can. Investors are lovely people, but they are all created different, all wanting different amounts of information, different levels of stroking, preferring different methods of communication, and if you have got more than one investor in a deal you are going to have to work harder. The more investors you have in one deal, the harder it is going to be. Having suggested that you should only use one investor in each deal as it will be a lot less hassle, we should also emphasise that where you need to, you should use as many investors as required to get underway. The biggest killer in this strategy is when people don't get underway before giving up, either because they can't find that first deal, or they can't find the investors to get on with.

Once you have got momentum with this strategy, it builds and builds and builds, partly because your belief does, but also because your network starts to see credibility in you as you are doing deals. The most amazing things happen when you have got one deal, because agents seem to take you that much more seriously, they start phoning you with other deals. Investors see more happening and become interested in investing, opening up more deals, which gets the agents excited and so it goes on. That's how it goes. It might not seem fair, but that's the way it works.

Working With Your Equity Investors

Investors provide the equity portion of the funding if you can't. If you are in a position to fund your own deals, we actually don't know whether to congratulate you or not; if you are sitting on £200k, you are now naturally going to limit yourself to one deal where the equity amount is £200k, which in turn is going to limit your journey. Having a bit of money is great in that it makes it easier for you to get into that first deal, but it is not great if you allow it to limit your mentality to using only your money. Conversely, the good news for those of you who don't have £200k or more lying around is you don't need it. You are released into the freedom of knowing and finding the equity investors out there. You are going to be able to find them, you are going to present them a deal that solves their problem and they are going to want to fund you.

Investors are looking for returns as a profit share – that is a true equity position, so they are going to share the upside and maybe even the downside with you. It might be a 50/50 split on profit, or they may say in the early days they actually want 70% of the profit because they are taking a risk on you. So what? Be generous and allow them to help you get underway. Remember, once you get momentum, deals and money flow, your credibility increases and the deals structure will change in your favour. Alternatively, they may say they want a fixed return, commonly called a coupon. It could be 1% a month, could be 15% per annum, might be 8% per annum. The amount is not really relevant, but what is relevant is they might ask for an element of fixed return. Furthermore, sometimes they may request a mix. So they might say, "I want a coupon of 8% and then I will take 50% of the profit". The good news for you is that if you put all that in your deal analyser and the deal still makes money, it is still all in the price of the shovel. So investors provide the equity proportion of the funding if you can't, that is what they are looking for.

The final note is just thinking about this and understanding this. Let's say an equity investor says, and this could be very fair in the early days, "I would like 1% a month as a fixed return, so that is 12% per annum, and then I also want 50% of the profit". Is that expensive money? Yes and no. No, in that it can help you access this amazing wealth creation strategy. But yes, in that equity is nearly always the most expensive money in the deal. Think about it. Let's say you have got development finance at 8% per annum (in this particular example, the equity investor's coupon alone is worth more than that), and then they are going to take 50% of the profit. Now let's say the equity investor didn't take a fixed coupon but just said "I will take 50% of the profit", is that equity investor likely to still be taking more than the 8% on the loan? Yes, the equity investor is always the most expensive part of the deal, which is why you borrow as much development finance as you can, and use as little equity as you can.

Development funding is cheap at the moment, but equity is expensive. Equity is going to cost you a much bigger part of the deal, but you need it. One of Ocea's strategies for exiting developments as a business is to become their own investor. They will multiple their returns from each deal as soon as they can invest their own equity into a deal, even if they are developing it themselves. They get two bites of the cherry if you like – their equity return and their developers' return. Then eventually, they are going to go that one step further and say they aren't even going to find or develop the deal, they are just going to be the investor, because the investor always earns a great return. But of course, that is why the investors are there to work with you, because you are going to give them a great return with them doing little of the work. The bad news is it's expensive, but the good news is that's why they are in – because you are going to earn them a high return on their money.

We see a lot of frustration on Facebook in property communities from people saying "I don't get it, I can't get any money". "Everyone tells me there are investors out there, but I can't find them". There was a time when a certain rumour became fact just because people kept repeating it – you know how that happens, you know it's complete nonsense, but someone says it often enough and they say it on the stage and someone else repeats it and it becomes a self-fulfilling prophecy. One fact that was going around was that a decent return for an investor might be 1% a month. So, people were going out there looking for investors, offering them 12%, and wondering why investors weren't tripping over themselves to lend them money. The would-be developers were focused solely on fixing their own problem, their own need for money. They were not focused on adding as much value as possible to their investors and so the investors were investing elsewhere, with people that were adding more value.

Be generous. When you are starting out on your development journey, you are a risk. So offer great value to your investors by being generous, and watch the funds flow in. Ocea raised £10m in joint venture finance in their first year, for probably two simple reasons: 1) they had discovered a system and were in the early stages of creating the system you are now reading about, and 2) they were generous. You are a risky proposition at the beginning. Yes, the investors might want a fixed return but so what if you get underway, and if there is a fixed return element in their equity return, make sure you are realistic about timescales, because that is money you are paying out for as long as their investment is in there – make sure you are being very realistic.

On that note, in general, we don't believe that a commercial conversion can realistically be turned around in less than 18 months from start to finish (deal sourced to deal re-financed or money in the bank from all sales). It can be done, but it usually isn't that fast. Even a smaller deal can take this amount of time because a smaller deal is normally being done by someone inexperienced, so they will burn time learning skills, short cuts, etc. And then once they become more experienced, they scale the deal, making it harder to do it in less than 18 months. 18 months to two years is the figure we use, and we are usually kind of in the middle at about 21 months. What we would encourage you to do is if you think there is a fixed return element in the equity investment, base it on 21 months, just to be sure you can afford it.

Mixed returns are where they lock in a certain amount from the fixed return, and then blend it with a profit share too. Now clearly if they have an element of fixed return, they should reduce the amount of their share of the profit at the end. It might be unreasonable to ask for a 15% coupon, and then also ask for 75% of the profits. However, there are people that do it, and actually, if they are putting in a lot of money and it might be your only choice of getting the deal done, it just becomes the cost of the shovel. One of the deals Ocea has done is based on a 12% coupon and somewhere between 65% and 70% of the profit. Why did they do it? Easy, they had to put a lot of money in, it still met the Ocea profit criteria of earning at least £500k, if not £750k from each deal, and there was no-one else in play for the equity when the deal was available. So they either did the deal, offering them 12% and whatever the other percentages were of the profit share, or let the deal go and be £750k poorer. It was an easy decision! It keeps coming back to the price of the shovel.

Sophisticated, Non-Sophisticated and HNWI Investors

It is really important to know who is investing with you, and whether the proposal you wish to offer them is considered appropriate for them according to the rules. Accordingly, you need to know how FCA13/3 applies to you. If you haven't heard about FCA13/3, it aims to clarify the kind of people you can and cannot do joint ventures with, and what kind of joint ventures you can do with them. It is designed to protect the less experienced would-be investor from being ripped off by unscrupulous scoundrels who want to con them into investing in some dodgy scheme.

The bottom line is there are two main forms of investors you can do anything with: sophisticated and HNWIs. Currently, roughly speaking HNWIs have to own over £250k of assets, not including their principal house (and other vehicles) or have earned over a £100k a year. Sophisticated investors need to have invested in different unlisted vehicles, run a company turning over more than a £1m or been involved in the private equity sector. The qualifications are different, but the effect is the same: if they are either an HNWI or a sophisticated investor, you can enter into various forms of JV with them. So for sophisticated or HNWIs, you can form any kind of JV with them that you like. It can be a coupon, it can be equity, it can be a 50/50, it can be a 70/30 or you can come up with any weird and wonderful structure you like, because the government has decided that they should be savvy enough to understand what they are getting themselves into. That is the nature of the legislation.

With anyone else, however, you can only enter into a loan, so you couldn't do an equity share with them, you can't offer them a fixed coupon mixed with a profit share, but you can offer a fixed coupon. This legislation does have teeth – and rightly so, given its purpose – so do please familiarise yourself with both the regulation and the impact it has on what you want to do.

Where to Meet Investors

When Glenn was in the Royal Air Force, he remembers they talked about 'target-rich environments'. He remarks that it was as often about the weekend nightclubs as it was theatres of combat operations, but that is an entirely different subject! However, it is a great expression to sum up some of the best advice we have heard about meeting investors: "hang out where the money is". Put yourself in a money-rich environment. That could be networking at business angel events, clubs, charity balls, hospitality at major events... we could go on, but it is really just about anywhere that you find money. Let your imagination take you to places that attract wealthy people. Just a very quick word on clubs though: when joining clubs with the intention of finding investors, why not do what you love? This is a business reason to spend the most money you can afford doing something you really like doing. If you want to meet high net worth individuals and you like playing golf, is there any point in joining a local municipal course? You will find a load of beaten up white vans with paint falling out the back, and sorry, whilst that is such a gross generalisation, it conveys a certain truth.

Case Study – Mixing Business With Pleasure (by Glenn)

In the past I have really loved my golf, and I joined a wonderful golf club that is truly a hidden gem. It is number 43 in the top 100 golf courses in the country, and if you go into the car park you won't find any white vans there – unless the club is having some work done on the club house! You will find Ferraris, Maseratis, Porsches, Aston Martins, classic vintage cars, you get the idea. I went for a roll up one day, where we all just turn up and the balls are thrown in the air to decide who you are playing with. I ended up playing with a chap who I had never met before, and ended up getting introduced to a former British Formula One world champion. Would I have met him down the local muni? I joined the best golf club I could afford – the kind of club where there is money – and met an ex-Formula One world champion. This chap is still connected to Formula One, he knows all the drivers and everybody on the circuit. Do you think he might know other people with money? Do you think other Formula One drivers might be a bit too busy to do their own commercial conversions? It is not why I joined that particular club, but it makes the point about the calibre of people you meet in higher quality environments. If you love something, whatever it is, join the best club you can. Go where the money is. Oh, and by the way, check out with your accountant how much of the expense is allowable.

Any investor relationship is a partnership, you have to think about what you are offering. To offer the right thing, you need to know your investor. The only way you can know your investor is to give them a damn good listening to. Go in naked without an agenda. Listen to them and then let them make you an offer; it is incredible how often people will offer you what you need when you just listen to them for a while and let them tell you what their priorities are, what their fears are. Even if they don't eventually offer something to you, then you can at least be in the best position to pitch them a tailored offer.

When listening to them, be ready with some great questions to keep them engaged. Questions such as *what are you trying to achieve? What would you look for in a JV partner? (That might be a bit forward, unless you are referencing it to a third-party JV possibility.) How would you measure success? What does success look like to you? How would you evaluate a deal, and what does good look like? And of course the killer question is, what is most important to you in a joint venture?* Don't miss out the word MOST, otherwise you will end up with a shopping list with no real idea of their priorities. Remember: help others, solve their problem and you will be amazed how quickly the world pays you back.

If you do everything we have said, you will know what the investor needs to hit their criteria, so all you do when presenting any deal is make sure that your offer hits their criteria, which will make investing with you a relatively easy decision for them. But they will still want to know what happens if...? Investors will often want to know what happens in certain scenarios, and you can give them a lot of comfort by being prepared for the kind of questions that frequently come up. You might get asked *what if the market fluctuates? What if the GDV goes down? What about the market softening?* (Remember, you are feeding the bottom of the market by creating one-bed units to sell to investors and first-time buyers; I am not saying you won't be affected, but the model you are using will be one of the last to be affected.) *What if there are project delays, with the cost of the money accruing all the time? How is that going to affect us if it takes six months longer? What if your investor wants a bigger profit share? Is there a certain return on investment they are looking for? What if we can get more or less equity?* You should also remember to structure your deal analyser so that you can model the different answers to the questions – it will blow your investor away and give them huge confidence in you.

JV Agreements

There is no such thing as a standard JV agreement because there is no such thing as standard investors who always want the same thing – every investor is different. You have to listen to them, you have to make sure you can give them what they want, which means you have to draft the agreement from scratch to meet their needs. OK, it may be possible to have a template that you work from, but it will always need a lawyer to amend it to fit the criteria and arrangements you have mutually agreed. Secondly, it costs maybe £2000 to get a legal agreement drawn up and even less if working from your own template from previous deals, and the only reason you would want a standard one that you would never change is that you are a cheapskate who doesn't want to spend £2000 on a deal that is going to make you £200k. There is no such thing as a standard JV agreement, but that doesn't mean you don't have any agreement. There is only one thing worse than having a standard agreement, and that is having no agreement at all.

Sadly, we are aware of people in our community, the commercial property conversion community, who have borrowed money without legal agreements. We are embarrassed about it, but there is nothing we can do. It is not under out control, but it is wrong and it is scary, and you know what? That kind of slapdash approach is almost always taken by the kind of person who is going to lose investors' money. And then there is no legal paperwork and it all goes horribly wrong – usually very publicly – and if you are involved in it, it is going to tarnish you as a developer, as you won't be taken seriously by anyone else. As stated, the one thing that's worse than a sloppy or standard agreement is no agreement at all.

Personal Guarantees

Generally, when borrowing money as development finance, lenders will often ask for collateral, such as a charge on an unencumbered building. Should that not be available, they will invariably ask for personal guarantees. The amount varies across the lenders, but it can be anywhere from 10% of the loan up to 100% of a bridge, in exceptional circumstances. Investors will not usually give personal guarantees because they have got equity in the deal. Many investors will flatly refuse to risk their hard-earned wealth by providing a personal guarantee on a development they don't have full control of, so be aware that this is likely to be requested of you as the developer.

Chapter 10: Redesign

The principle requirement of the redesign process is to add as much value to the building we are converting as possible. Why are we adding value? Well, the simple answer is we are adding value because that is what we get paid for. Remember, wealth mindset expert T. Harv Eker says that you will be paid in direct proportion to the value you bring to the world. If you bring more value, you get paid more.

So how do we start adding value? The odd thing is, and it might sound strange, but one of the first things you should start doing when you start thinking about adding value is strip out everything that is there. This isn't like smaller developments or house refurbishments, where you walk around the building to see what you could save – can we save that boiler? Can we use that wall? Do we really need to take the plaster off that wall? – because you are cutting costs. That isn't likely to be the case with your commercial conversion, because in fact what you need to do is strip the building back completely to find what is wrong with the building. We recommend you instruct a soft strip as soon as possible, and often under a separate contract from the main development contract. When we get into contracts later, we are going to talk about the tendering process, and that tendering process is going to be reliant on you having a design that takes into account the faults and problems with the building –when contractors tender, they want to have clarity on what their risks are. If they don't have clarity, they will price for the unseen risks, probably costing you more than if you told them everything that was wrong in the first place.

There was a conversion undertaken that highlighted a number of issues that don't reflect well on the original builder and for that reason we won't identify the site. The conversion of that building proved to be a huge learning curve, and some might call the development a bit of a lemon! However, the profit on the project was circa £700k, and that isn't a bad return from a lemon-type development. That, again, demonstrates the power of this strategy and the safeguarding aspects of using a proven system. The building being converted was actually a modern building built in 2002, so it should have met all modern building regulations and should have had no real issues at all. Nevertheless, we stripped the building out, and when we ripped the interior fittings out, we found a couple of things that really shouldn't have been there. We found a problem with the roof, as it appeared that they had not used galvanised nails to fix the roof tiles on the mansard. After 12 years, all the nails had pretty much rusted through, and the slates were starting to fall off. So firstly, the roof got condemned, which was a shock.

This was a typical modern construction office building comprising a steel frame with concrete slab. You often see them being built by the side of the motorway as you are driving along; the first thing you see is like a Meccano set – lots of steel. Then what you will see is lots of concrete, whether pre-formed or poured on site, but you will see lots of slabs going across the metal frame. That is your typical construction: very simple, very strong, very robust, which is why it is used extensively. There are few issues with steel frames, but one issue is that steel is a pretty good conductor of heat, among other things, which makes it very good at transferring fires around buildings. Accordingly, building regulations offer several options to mitigate this risk, including cladding around the steel, and using intumescent paint within that cladding. When we stripped the building back, it appeared that they had coated the steel in intumescent paint, but only where the inspection holes were! Having removed all the cladding, most of the steel wasn't covered in intumescent paint. Now that was interesting – scary interesting – but actually it didn't have a massive direct impact on our costs.

However, the other fault we found was a problem that could have had very significant cost implications if we had not discovered it early, before the contractors got going on-site. When you typically lay a concrete floor, you see a concrete slab and what usually happens next is they block work all the communal areas like kitchens, lift shafts and communal toilets, placing all the permanent walling. They will then finish the final floor level, and when they screed the floor to that final level they should screed to a datum, so it doesn't matter what side of the block wall you are on, it will be the same level. That appeared to have been too much trouble for the original contractors on this particular building. What they decided to do was just screed to whatever level they felt like. So, when the block walls were taken out, as the communal toilets and so on weren't required anymore, we had gaps in the screed of about 40mm, which we were expecting because that is where the blocks went. However, what we weren't expecting was that on one side of the wall the screed would be at one level, and on the other side of the screed it was at a completely different level. In some places, across the 40mm gap, the level of the screed varied by as much as 80mm!

Now imagine you haven't stripped the building out, you have already got your contractor on site and your contractor is now laying floors for you. I'll tell you what happens: the contractor calls you and tells you there is a major problem. He probably tells you it's going to cost huge amounts of money to fix, and by the way, they now want an agreed delay to the programme, so they will ask for your agreement to increased costs and a delay to the project. Whatever way it happens is not going to be good news for you, and if you don't agree, they may even stop works – indeed, they might have to stop anyway, because it might require such remedial work that they can't do anything else until the floors are sorted out.

Even in the cold light of our detailed design period when we stripped the building out, we were actually in a tender process, so we went to all the four tendering companies with the problem and asked them how they would each suggest we fix it. What a great way of finding out how great your companies are! One company came back and said "well, you are going to have to completely re-screed the whole lot at a huge uplift in cost". Another company came back and said "we will chip it all out in one area and re-lay that area", which was also a very large amount, but the company we ended up going with said "it isn't that serious and we can level it out locally". Exactly how they did it is not relevant, but what is relevant is that given time and space to come up with a resolution, they sorted the issue out for around £60k less than any of the other bidders.

So the point of stripping out is to reveal the buildings secrets, because then you can allow for them and get them designed out in the calm, controlled design period. The solution gets planned into the design, goes into the tender and all the contractors price for it. From the contractor's perspective, if you have stripped the building out to reveal all its secrets, the contractor will be comfortable that you have eliminated most of their risk and their pricing will be tighter. If you don't eliminate their risk, they won't have a line in their contract that says risk, they will just hide it and your contract prices will be higher. It may be counterintuitive, but the first thing you do is strip the building out as soon as you can, which may seem an odd way to start adding value!

Next, you need to get a measured survey done as quickly as you can. You may remember earlier in the book we mentioned how inaccurate the agent's details can be. So, especially if we have managed to get the building stripped, a measured survey will confirm exactly what we are dealing with. Our project managers are authorised on our behalf to go and get three quotes for a measured survey as soon as we have agreed to purchase a building. Often, we will end up paying more money for a company that can get there just after exchange, rather than wait for somebody cheaper that can't get the report to us for four weeks or more afterwards. You have to make that judgement call.

The results of this survey will be passed directly to our architects, who will normally have to hand our ideas for how to layout the building. At this point, we need to understand how some aspects of prior approval may help us if we are using that strategy.

Minimum Size Requirements

The minimum size requirements of the new national space standard do not apply to prior approval applications. The implications of this are that you can put in much smaller units than would normally be allowed. That is something you really need to grab hold of and understand, because it helps you add a lot more units into a building and in so doing, add a lot more value.

As mentioned before in the book, apartment prices don't just continue down on a scale. There will be a minimum price in an area and you will know if you are scouring the markets and looking in your area what the minimum price for a one-bed is in your area. There will be a price below which you simply can't pick up a one-bed flat. That is the price you are interested in because then you can create a 30 m² flat and it will be that bottom price. Consider this: if you are getting that bottom price for a 30 m² flat that some people can only get for a 38 m² flat, you are getting more per m², i.e. you are making more money out of the building you are developing. This is gold dust to us as developers. As a reminder, we use no less than 30 m² because this tends to be the size below which it is difficult to get a mortgage.

Planning Your Design

We need our experts to inform our design based on whether we intend to sell or hold the final apartments. You need to know your end users, what problems are you solving for them? If you are starting with the right mindset, you would never just build something out and then wonder who it is right for?

Multiple Agents

Right at the beginning, you are asking your agents for information, advice, valuations and estimates. Note the plural: don't ever take the word of one agent, use three. A quick note on that: you are not going to get away with using three agents for all that input for very long unless you feed them all with a bit of work. You have to let them all win sometimes, and since you are going to become a developer and you are going to have multiple schemes – that is what you tell them. You can be really honest and upfront with them, you can say "look, I can't give you all my work, I can't instruct you on every scheme I do because I need three sets of information. I promise you will win some, but I have to be fair to the other agents as well". In your area, the agents will talk, they meet down the pub, they will know you are getting advice from other agents so just be upfront and be fair. Make sure that you give them all some work – otherwise why would they take the time to help you and give you really good specialist advice about who you should sell to, what the product should look like and how much you can get for it? Use your agents and your experts to tell you who you should be preparing these units for; speak to your agents.

Student HMOs

Generally, in our companies we are aiming at a market of young professionals, investors and first-time buyers. These are by far our biggest markets, and between us we don't have a single scheme for students. The reason is simple: Southampton, like many university cities and towns, has become a hotbed of major companies and pension-backed firms building huge bespoke housing schemes for students. Many landlords in our city with HMOs that are let out to students are seeing reduced demand and rents, because the quality and volume of new student accommodation going up in the city is sucking away their traditional market. For those who are develop HMOs, it is of course an opportunity. Where other people see problems, entrepreneurs see opportunities! How can you solve a problem of dropping demand for student HMOs? Well, you might buy a tired old student HMO that is already a multi-let in a city that maybe has an Article 4 Direction preventing more houses being turned into HMOs without explicit consent, and you upgrade that old HMO into one that is suitable for young professionals. But that is not our model and it doesn't seem like a market to target with commercial conversions in our area. Mark does use commercial conversions to create multi-let units (covered later in the book), but only when he intends to hold with his primary market being professional tenants.

First-Time Buyers and Investors

Having established that our market is essentially first-time buyers and investors, our end occupier is quite well-defined. We need to provide affordable, good-quality, hardwearing apartments that are well positioned for young professionals, blue collar workers and young couples (usually without children). They may or may not have a car, will almost always be employed and will often work locally. Being relatively younger, their tastes will be influenced by current market trends and the latest finishes in the bathroom and kitchen shops, as well as taste represented in fashion magazines, all of which is going to inform their view of the finish to our apartments. Investors may be less fussy about the finish, but they will want functional, well-presented and hardwearing apartments that give them few maintenance problems and where their tenants will be happy to stay for many months. We probably don't want to go into a full-on redesign process of our final finishes every time we do a development, so the finishes need to be broadly appealing and be non-gender specific.

All of this informs both the layouts of our design and also the finish. Furthermore, as developers, we want to provide the finishes that our end occupiers seek, but at the lowest cost to us, thereby maximising our margin. By keeping the design ostensibly the same each time, we are able to leverage our supply chain, source materials more competitively and enhance our margins whilst also making life simple for ourselves. To this end, we have two main considerations as we set about the redesign process: 1) layouts, and 2) finishes.

Layouts

Put simply, to maximise our profits we need to squeeze as many units (whether apartments or rooms in multi-let apartments) into our building as we possibly can. If using full planning, then your architect will be using their skill to fit as many apartments as possible into your building, whilst always remaining compliant with the National Minimum Space Standard (NMSS). This will reduce the number of apartments you can fit into the building when compared to a prior approval development. This equation is much more flexible if using prior approval given that the NMSS does not apply to prior approval developments. To maximise the benefit of this, we need to reduce the size of the units to an optimal point between achieving attractive desirable and functional apartments, always ensuring that they are large enough to attract mortgage lending, and yet not so large that our profit margins are compromised.

Mortgage lenders tend not to lend on any unit of less than 30 m². Accordingly, we use 30 m² as our minimum size and never develop anything smaller. Even when we change to a hold strategy, I would maintain that approach of a minimum size for two reasons. Firstly, even when holding, we want to leverage our portfolios with a sensible level of debt, and any lender may take a view on their security being adversely affected if the flats in the portfolio don't attract mortgage lending if sold off. Secondly, we might decide ultimately to sell off apartments if they don't function well in the letting market, and again, we wouldn't want to limit our buying market to just cash buyers by ruling out mortgage lending.

Having established the smallest size of apartment for us is 30 m², we then need to decide how large we want to go. In this regard, I learnt a valuable lesson when selling my first development.

Case Study – Small IS Beautiful (by Glenn)

Experience tells us that for some of you, the idea of creating 30 m² flats is a bit of an anathema. You might consider it almost unethical! Is producing such 'tiny' apartments the very epitome of being an money-grabbing developer who really cares nothing at all for the person that is going to live in the rabbit hutches they produce? Or is it a genuine service to the community and adding real value?

In your developments you will often find you have a mix of sizes, because in conversions, the existing shape of the building often means you can't create perfectly symmetrically shaped boxes. It doesn't work like that, because you have to work around the structure, and as a result, even if you have identified a perfect unit size for your model, it generally won't fit quite like that!

We were converting an office into nine units and within the development we had a real mixture of flats. The largest was 44 m² and the smallest few were 30 m². I was really excited about this – it was our first development, I didn't know what I didn't know, and I hadn't sold any units prior to the completion. More of that later in the section on exiting. So we hadn't sold any units in advance but I was excited; the development was finished, we had dressed a couple of show flats and we were about to have our launch open day with a number of viewings booked in.

In the development, we had a 30 m² unit next to a 44 m² unit, so we fully dressed the 44 m² unit and we half-dressed the 30 m² unit – by that I mean that we dressed the kitchen and the lounge and the bathroom, but in the bedroom, instead of having the bed we had a sales desk so that the estate agent could take reservation fees in that room. I was so excited about this day, this was the fulfilment of everything I had been working on until then. I was 18 months into my journey and we had five or six developments on the go at this point, but this was the first one to come to sale and the fulfilment of my hopes thus far. It was our first 'child' in development terms! Given my excitement I wanted to be at the open day. To this day, it is the only open day I have ever attended but at that point I went out and bought bottles of champagne, and cards, and chocolates and flowers to give to anyone who paid a reservation fee. I put all the champagne and chocolates in the fridge, hid the flowers and cards away and then pretended to be one of the estate agents, kind of just hanging around to watch and listen to what people thought of the development.

About two hours into the open day, a young lady with someone who it very quickly became apparent was her mum, arrived and went into the show flat. I was really nervous, trying to earwig without it looking like I was earwigging, and they were enthusing profusely. "I can't believe it, this is just what I have been looking for. Oh Mum, this is so much better than all those crummy flats we have been looking at. Ah, this is what I really want". Then suddenly, I think it was Mum who reminded the young lady that she couldn't afford the large show flat because all the prices had been issued and of course it was a bigger flat, so it was more expensive. She suggested that they went next door to look at the one they thought might be for her.

At that point she entered the 30 m² 'sales' suite, obviously only two-thirds the size of the big show flat, but here is where finish and style of finish become relevant: the small flat had all the same finishes, and though smaller, it still appeared beautiful to the young lady. She commented out loud that it had the same style doors, the same kitchen, the same lovely feel. "I can just imagine myself in here" she said. Her Mum pointed out that it was small, not a lot of storage, and... at which point her daughter cut in and said, "Mum, don't take this the wrong way, but I would rather live here and struggle with storage than stay at home with you". If her Mum was hurt she didn't show it. They continued to walk around the flat until the daughter declared that she wanted this flat.

It transpired that she had been very sensible and had been out before the viewing and secured an agreement in principle from the bank. Accordingly, she knew exactly what she could afford and it was exactly what this flat was up for, so they decided then and there they were going to buy it. They went and sat with the agent and signed the reservation form! Yes! It was a lovely moment for me to hear someone gushing about our hard work, and to then come out and surprise them with champagne, chocolates and flowers, at which point she promptly burst into tears!

I think we made five sales from nine flats on the opening day, and of all the sales that is the one I remember. To hear someone so full of excitement at what we had created was lovely. Imagine my surprise and shock, then, when about four weeks later the estate agents contacted me and told me that she had pulled out of the sale! I couldn't believe it, it didn't make any sense. Why had she done that? Apparently what had happened is that when she had arranged the agreement in principle, she hadn't taken into account the service charge payable on a flat. So when the lender had reassessed affordability, having now taken account of the service charge, she could borrow £5k less than she had originally been told. She had no choice but to pull out, because she had no more money available. Everything she had was already being piled up and put into the deposit, and she simply couldn't get the £5k from anywhere. Despite being terribly upset, she had no choice but to withdraw from the purchase.

This shows how price-sensitive the market can be. People are stuck either in rental accommodation or living with Mum and Dad because property prices have separated from salaries. Many buyers can't afford bigger units and their affordability is so stretched that even £5k on a 30 m² unit can make a difference. This young lady had no prospect of getting £40k more to go into the bigger unit.

Sadly, in its desire to help people, the government has determined and dictated that under normal circumstances you should not get less than 50 m² for a one-bed two-person flat. The problem is that a 50 m² apartment has 50 m² of costs associated with it. Space costs money and developers have to make margins. What the government have inadvertently achieved in trying to be helpful and protect people and give them 50 m² is to price people out of the market. Standard developments of 50 m² are more expensive, leaving price-sensitive potential customers frustrated, living in rented accommodation or with Mum and Dad.

So now, I would ask you, are we money-grabbing heartless developers, or are we providing a service to a sector of our community and our society that otherwise would not be able to afford to buy their own place? That lady was distraught. She had lost her dream home because she couldn't afford the extra £5k, let alone another £40k for a bigger unit. Effectively, a 30 m² unit can be the answer to someone's problem, and what do we get paid for? Solving problems and adding value. Do you think we were adding value to that woman's life by providing a unit she could see herself in, that she delighted in, that got her out from her Mum and Dad's place and put her on the property ladder?

I expect you want to know what happened, don't you? Well yes, this money-grabbing heartless developer discounted the property by £5k and she did buy the apartment. We all like a happy ending!

Now the point of that story is this: 30 m² units can be beautiful and a genuine solution to somebody's problem if you get the detail and focus right. Let's focus on a few of those details:

Schedule of Finishes

It is really important to provide all the final finish details in a schedule that you give the builder. It doesn't matter what building contract you use, every building contract will rely heavily on your schedule of finishes. However much you like or dislike detail, this is an area where, at the beginning of your journey, you will benefit from putting some work into it, to get it right from the word go. You will end up with a version of this for every development you do, and it needs to cover everything in detail, so it is well worth spending some time on it first time round. We might tweak it sometimes – if the price point is a bit higher we might put a higher-level specification in – but generally the specification changes very little from development to development if you have picked a niche and are sticking to it.

Among other things, your schedule of finishes needs to cover: the paint you will use on the walls, ceilings and woodwork by room, the floor coverings throughout, tiles on the bathroom floor and walls, kitchen units, worktop, appliances, white goods including waste fittings, taps, numbers and types sockets throughout, lighting throughout, doors throughout, door furniture, including hinges and handles, blinds/window treatments, locks, bathroom fittings such a toilet roll holders, etc., specification of shelving in cupboards, cupboard door types, skirting and architraves specification, threshold finishes, light switches, letterboxes, light fittings throughout, etc... The list goes on and on, but once you have done it, you avoid the countless calls from the builder, usually when you least need them, asking you to make one of a hundred decisions on matters such as paint colour or where sockets should be positioned.

By sourcing your own preferred product and being exact in your schedule, you will also have tracked down the price that you expect to pay. Using buying groups such as Landlord National Property Group can grant you access to heavily discounted pricing, some being as low as government contract rates and even less expensive than your builder can source at. You can give flexibility to the builder by offering them the opportunity to either supply the exact product you have specified, or similar with your approval.

The issue with the contractor can be that they may have a vested interest to get their supply from somewhere else, and therefore they use that opportunity to add a little bit extra to their profit margin rather than add extra to your profit margin. As an example, they might try and convince you that a boiler that they have access to is as good as the Worcester Bosch boiler in your specification. So proceed with caution when approving 'similar' and make sure it's clear that any changes have to be approved by you.

You need to know what you actually want and it really focuses your mind when you fill in a specification sheet. How many double sockets do you want? Are they going to be white, or they going to be satin chrome finish? If they are satin chrome finish we would suggest you put them in the kitchen at high level where they are seen and make everything else in the flats white as this will save you money, but it is up to you. But what you can see is that when you start specifying detail such as "am I putting a pendant light in, or am I just going to put a central point where I put a four spot fixture or am I going to put spots all over the ceiling", it will really call you to focus on the detail, including the cost of each choice. For instance, if you investigated putting individual spotlights all over the ceiling, you will find that it is expensive as you are puncturing insulation for each one, every one of them needs its own wiring and every one of them needs finishing by the decorator. It is much more sensible generally to go with a single spot and have a fixing with four or five spots on it. When you have to go through that schedule of finishes it focuses you, you then become very clear about what you want and that means that you have put it in the contract and the contractor has to deliver what you specify. The alternative of answering queries as you go along will cost you money, cause you grief and ultimately there will be all kinds of arguments when trying to agree costs at the end of the project. Time you spend now is very much saved later.

Things to Consider in Your Specification

Commercial buildings often benefit from high ceilings, helping make the apartments feel bigger, but you should also paint all the walls white and use light coloured flooring to enhance the feeling of space. Having painted everything white and kept everything basic, you should still spend money where it counts. Think about what people will notice and physically feel and consider how you can ensure these 'touch' points can convey a message of quality. For example, why not spend money on doors such as the Mexicana door that Magnet produces. It is a hardwood door finished in oak that looks fabulous and always elicits comments on how lovely it looks and the quality it conveys. We put lovely door furniture on the doors – we use solid hinges and a really lovely handle that feels solid when you put your hand on it. Some people are tactile and their first impression will be the first thing they see (the door) and the first thing they feel (the door handle). Your front door and its handle can either communicate flimsy and lacking quality, or subliminally and subconsciously you can communicate high quality and a beautiful finish.

Once they have opened the door, generally speaking your buyer is going to move into the hallway or the lounge and open plan kitchen, so flooring is the next thing they will 'touch'. Do not skimp on flooring by installing the cheapest horrible laminate which sounds like "clack clack clack" and which will chip horribly. We used to put relatively expensive engineered wood flooring in, but some laminates now are so good that we don't have to. We currently specify Quickstep laminate, which is available in many beautiful finishes, is affordable, durable and is a fairly sensible choice. The great thing about good laminates is with so many choices of finish, you can match it to whatever you are doing with the kitchen. It is likely that you are going to use the same flooring throughout the apartment, other than in the bedroom. As you enter a flat and walk into a hallway, your eyes are immediately drawn by how spacious and welcoming it feels, and that is going to be down to your paint finishes, your door finishes and your flooring.

Everybody knows that kitchens and bathrooms sell houses. You find that out if you have been around property for five minutes, so don't skimp – but don't spend money you don't have to. We specify Magnet kitchens for one simple reason: they offer a contract price to key accounts. With the country's biggest supplier of trade kitchens, Howden's, every time you want a kitchen you currently have to go and negotiate a price for that kitchen with the local depot. They don't have contract pricing, and even their trade discounts are negotiable because the stated trade price is actually the starting point for negotiation! You can't run a development business like that. With Magnet, and particularly if you use a buying group such as LNPG, you can specify a kitchen and know what price you are going to pay all over the country, whatever depot is local to your site. With regard to quality, we do not specify the cheapest kitchens that are made of chipboard and will warp as soon as they become wet. Of the five levels of trade finish, we are somewhere between level 2 and level 3 in our choice of finishes, depending on the demographic of the area we are developing in. We are now specifying AEG appliances where they are visible (i.e. the worktop and oven) and for the integrated fridge/freezer we specify a lesser brand that will cost less money. Put brand where it is needed to convey quality.

With bathrooms, we order half-height tiling to everywhere other than the wet area. If you have got a shower over the bath, which is our normal specification, it will be full-height tiling around the bath with half height tiling everywhere else. It offers a significant saving compared to doing full-height tiling, given that you're painting where otherwise you might be fitting porcelain tiles. Half-height tiling where you can is a good compromise, but we don't suggest you go to the other end of the spectrum and do almost no tiling with only tiny little splashbacks behind the sink, because that just looks naff! You have got to find that middle ground where it conveys quality but at a price we can afford as a developer.

Use proper porcelain tiles and, again, don't skimp. We specify porcelain tiles but we find other ways to save money. In this respect, we recommend you make your bathrooms as small as you possibly can. People don't live in a bathroom; it is functional space, but they do need to feel warm and cosseted in it. Your strategy is to create small units, so you cannot afford to waste two or three metres of floor space in an oversized bathroom. There are much better areas to put those square metres. For some reason, architects seem to love big bathrooms, but we would advise you to squeeze them into the smallest size you can. However, for balance, don't use anything smaller than a 1700mm bath, because that begins to feel really cheap and nasty. Over the bath, we specify a proper waterfall type shower over it with a thermostatic control and with a hand-held unit on it as well.

If you get to the point where you can't get a 1700mm bath into your allocated bathroom space, then you are better off putting a walk-in shower in there. There was a time when you would never sell a flat without a bath, but that time seems to be behind us. Most people would seem to rather buy a place these days that had a luxury walk-in shower with a really beautiful shower head on it than something that had a nice big roll-top bath and a tiny shower cubicle. By the way, don't put a cubicle in of less than 1 m² – nothing will turn buyers and tenants off faster than a tiny shower cubicle with a measly looking shower head in it!

For the bedroom, a simple wool carpet will do, and given that the bedroom will not be oversized, the price will be acceptable.

In summary, spend money only where it counts, but where it does count, spend money!

Windows

Try and specify UPVC windows in a standard size. Try not to use aluminium windows where you don't have to, because they are expensive by comparison. If you have fairly standard sizes without any one window being particularly large, you can get good UVPC windows that can now be coloured too. We currently specify anthracite grey on the outside of properties and white on the inside, so when you go in they feel big and are obviously new, but on the outside you have that contemporary finish.

Other Redesign Considerations

Parking

Although with prior approval developments there is a highways test to be satisfied, this is a lot less onerous than might have been the case. There was a major landmark battle won by a developer in London on one of their first developments. The prior approval application was refused by the local authority because they said there wasn't enough parking under their normal parking standards. The developer appealed and won, with the appeal court stating that the regulations are quite clear that there just needs to be some form of sustainable transport plan. So if you are in a town centre, which many commercial buildings are, and you have got bus routes, or you can cycle to work, or there are trains, or local amenities and work opportunities within walking distance, then why would you need parking? Indeed, many local authorities are reducing access to parking for new home buyers by limiting the parking provided by developers as a means of encouraging more sustainable transport use.

Whatever the situation for you locally, generally speaking the highways requirements for all prior approvals is now interpreted in the light of this court ruling and parking is only one aspect of a sustainable transport plan. This can make sites available that otherwise couldn't be brought forward for development.

On the flip side, if parking is available, it is a valuable resource. Given that we are taking existing sites and converting them to an alternative use, parking ratios of availability to each apartment rarely works out perfectly. One strategy for dealing with less than one parking space for each apartment, is to sell all the apartments without parking, and to sell the parking spaces separately on a first-come-first-served basis. The price of the parking space is simply added to the purchase price of the flat for mortgage purposes and proceeds as a normal part of the transaction. We would normally allocate one space to any two-bed apartments in a development, and then sell the balance to the one-bed buyers on the first come first served basis mentioned above. If we have more parking than one to one, we simply allocate one space to each apartment and then put the balance up for sale in a similar manner, again on a first-come-first-served basis.

Stacking Your Design

Stacking is important; more accurately, the stacking of the services through the building. You are unlikely to be able to do this in Victorian buildings, but what you need to try and do is replicate the floor layout on every floor of your development, and that means all your services will run straight through the building. Just one floor that is different can cost you tens of thousands of pounds. We had the lemon scheme, where we had a different layout on the ground floor, then we had three floors with the same layout, and then a different layout on the top floor because it had quite steep eaves/skillings, so there were issues with going into the eaves space. So we had three floors stacked in the middle, the top floor and ground floor were not stacked, and therefore instead of having three service risers through the building, we have seven; each of those risers are somewhere in the order of £10k to £15k. Make sure your architect stacks wherever they can, and if you can, try and do it all the way through the building.

Another aspect of the benefits of stacking is the increasing need in any multi-floor building for smoke stacks. This vertical shaft is where, in the event of a fire, the smoke shaft is either mechanically or naturally ventilated, drawing smoke away from the escape stair. To meet current building regulations with regard to smoke management, shafts are increasingly required, and it is very difficult to put a smoke shaft vertically up through a building if your design changes on every floor. The moment the smoke shaft isn't vertical, you are likely to have to put in mechanical ventilation, which generally speaking for four or five floors of mechanical ventilation, will cost you £40 or £50k. With a vertical shaft of sufficient size, it is possible that the mechanical ventilation will not be required, that saving representing another positive aspect of being able to stack your design vertically throughout the building.

Building Regulations

Do not, do not, do not get involved in building regulations. They seem to change every five minutes; they have just reissued them again and even the building regulations experts are struggling to keep up, and building regulations apply differently for each kind of conversion you are trying to do. Some of them will have to be part 'M' compliant, thank you, some of them won't, and if you don't know what part 'M' is, congratulations, because it is not your job. Get a building regulations expert in; at most, you should be paying £240 per unit to get experts to advise you to ensure that your development is compliant with the current building regulations. Do you really want all the hassle of finding out what a building regulation is and whether you are compliant when you can outsource that hassle for £240 a unit? It shouldn't even be a discussion, so get your building regulations expert in. You do have to comply, it is about safety, but outsource it to a genuine expert who will do a great job and charge you a very affordable amount for their expertise.

Thermal and Acoustic Separation

You will sometimes hear that you can covert flats for £25k, £30k or whatever number you may have heard. Treat such claims with extreme scepticism. Even if true, they may be creating entirely different products in different areas and they may be excluding all sorts of costs that you would normally include. Conversions such as those we covering in this book are considered new builds and as such they must meet the thermal and acoustic separation requirements of modern buildings. If you have a Victorian building that used to be accommodation of some sort and then became an office or a shop or whatever else, and now you are converting it back to accommodation, intuitively you would think that should be easy? It used to be accommodation and you are just converting it back. But this is where modern building regulation requirements can bite you, because taking an old Victorian building and getting it up to modern building regulations for thermal and acoustic separation can cost you somewhere around £7,500 to £8,500 per flat. That's a very large chunk of just £25k or £30k!

To enhance safety (thermal) and comfort (acoustic), the current regulations require that each apartment meets stringent standards for acoustic and thermal separation, essentially making each apartment into a 'box' that is thermally and acoustically separated from its neighbours. Bringing old buildings in line with these requirements, such as they apply, can be costly, so please let the experts advise you, and ensure that you make adequate allowance for the sometimes costly nature of the conversion, such as thermal and acoustic separation.

When you have finished your development, they will come and test your building for your thermal and acoustic separation. If it fails the tests, you may be required to take everything back out, upgrade all the insulation and the put everything back. That might hit your profit margin a bit! You do not want to risk failing the thermal and acoustic tests, and if you do fail, make sure it is someone else's problem by relying on your professional team. Use specialist sound and fire engineers to design the thermal and acoustic separation, because whilst this might mean that you over specify it (they will err on the side of caution and slightly over-engineer the solution), that is better than under specifying it. Let them decide what is going to be done to achieve thermal and acoustic separation and then make it a condition in the contract that the contractor is responsible for it, and that if it fails the tests, the contractor has to go back and make it right at their own cost.

Loft Spaces

People think they buy floor space, but they don't, they buy volume! You can walk into a 10 m² room, if the ceiling height is less than two metres it will feel small. You could walk into the same sized (floor space) room with a vaulted ceiling and think oh my goodness, this is very pleasant. Good architects know that, so even if you have a loft space that you can't use as an extra room, using it as a vaulted ceiling can make a small room feel bigger, and can improve the quality of life for the people that live there at very little extra cost to you.

If you are thinking of converting loft space, make sure it is in your numbers and it is worth doing. Many old commercial buildings have such high slab-to-slab heights, particularly on upper floors, that there can be opportunities for installing mezzanine decks to add an extra floor. Sometimes entire floors can be added into voids available too. Voids in buildings are simply another aspect of 'airspace' that we may want to convert and in the case of prior approval developments, any internal change of use of space is allowed.

Windows to Doors

Under prior approval, you are not allowed to make external changes; however, a lot of local authorities will allow you to change a window into a door on the ground floor, particularly if it is a less obvious elevation of the building. It is worth asking your planning consultant to have a word with the local authority and check their attitude with regards to adding minor elevational changes to the prior approval application. We have certainly had a number of schemes where we have just thrown it into the prior approval with the agreement of the local authority.

If you can't do that under the prior approval, don't panic. All you do is you leave the windows in for the prior approval application, and then you go back with a planning application to make the external changes.

Elevational Changes Under Prior Approval

Prior approval is predominantly for internal change of use and usually precludes external changes to the building. However, many of the buildings we are converting can be relatively unsightly or possibly downright ugly and in desperate need of a facelift! Permission to make whatever changes the architects recommend is simple to achieve by putting in a separate planning application, either along with the prior approval application or after you have received your prior approval, depending on your planning consultant's advice. The separate application should be warmly received by the local authority, because if the building is deemed to be changing to residential use, then both you as the developer and the local authority now have mutually aligned aims – you both want to improve the street scene and amenity for the future residents. There is also no Section 106, affordable housing, CIL or viability to be negotiated, so in most cases the application should be approved with little delay and without too much negotiation. We show an example of the changes that can be made to a building by implementing some simple external changes.

Communal Areas

Good architects will keep your communal areas to a minimum, but at the same time enhance the feel of the quality of the building with good design. If the architect can get the communal area down to 20% of your building, they have done well – in conversions 25% is not unusual. Do you remember the rule of thumb we gave you? We recommended allowing 500 sq. ft. GIA for a 415 sq. ft. apartment. We advised you to divide the space by 500 to give you the minimum number of units, and that is because it gives you 415 sq. feet for your one-bed apartment and 85 sq. feet for your communal area, being roughly 20% of the 415 sq ft.

In your communal areas, you have a number of other considerations. You need to think about security, letter boxes, bin stores, bike stores, apartment numbering, lighting, robust flooring, access systems, trades access, external landscaping, gardens and parking, among many other items that may come up from time to time. With prior approval, you are not required to provide any information on many of these considerations, or indeed to even provide bin stores, cycle stores or amenity space! In many prior approvals, some of these considerations are completely excluded, but who wants to live in a block of flats that doesn't have anywhere for the bins? This is one of those areas where even though you are not required to provide these facilities, or information pertaining to them, you are going to have to consider them all in reality.

Bike Stores

The provision of bike stores can help to support a sustainable transport plan in developments with limited or no parking. By using cycles as an alternative means of transport to cars, along with adjacent bus services, train routes, and local amenities within walking distance, it can be argued not only that parking is below the normal standards acceptable, but that it can be a positive aspect of the development by reducing cars and associated pollution and promoting sustainable and healthy living.

Lighting

Communal lighting needs to considered carefully. It can enhance the visual appeal of the building at night, but importantly, it can help make it feel safe and welcoming. However, the designers need to make sure that the lighting helps the residents enter and leave the building, but doesn't annoy the residents inside the building.

Lifts

If you have got an existing lift, work on about £10k basic cost plus £10k per floor to refurbish it. If you are considering putting in a new lift, don't bother with any building with three floors or less. If though you are going to buy a building with four floors and it hasn't got a lift, you are probably going to have to put a lift in; work on £20k per floor and you won't be a million miles away.

Prior Approval With Planning Uplift – Design

When you use prior approval, there may be an opportunity, as we have mentioned before, to add some further value with planning. As a reminder, the process is to get the basic prior approval first. When considering going for a planning uplift, we would strongly suggest that unless you are adding at least 30% to the original space, i.e. sq. footage, don't do it. If you are not adding at least 30%, the uplift is not likely to be worth your time. Get in, get out. Sometimes you will make more money just undertaking the easy, smaller option, because of all the risks and additional costs of developing with planning.

As well as the cost of the funds while you sit there in the actual development you are seeking planning for, there is also the cost of lost opportunity because you haven't come out of the development and consequently you can't roll your funds into the next one. If you spend six or nine months getting planning for an extra three units on a 12-unit scheme, you would have been much better off just doing the 12 units really quickly and rolling the money into another development, which you might have scaled by then and could be 20 or 30 units! You get the point. So our advice is this: if you are not adding at least 30% to the volume of the building, don't even bother thinking about it.

Additionally, even if you can add 30% or more, be careful and change course if it starts to look too difficult.

The picture above is the architects impression of the additional floors we are seeking to add to 11 Queensway, Southampton. If we had known the ramifications of it being a sway frame building, we would have simply got in and got out by developing the existing structure. Given the complexity of this structure and the lengths we have had to go to to design around the limitations, we have now been holding this building for far too long. It took months and months to work out how we could develop the extra floors on the top, and even though we are about to get the planning for the extra floors, it took so much longer than we thought and it is far more costly than we calculated. We now know that we would have made more money if we had just developed the building as it was, and just got out. So while the rule of thumb is don't even bother with planning unless you are going to add more than 30%, we would add another part to that: unless there are real technical difficulties, in which case fall back to get in and get out! The moment a structural engineer comes and says "oh my goodness, this could be a complete nightmare", walk away! The moment you think that planning could be a nightmare and take you a whole lot of time for maybe not a whole lot of upside, that is the time you should bin the idea. Only if you get all green lights, i.e. it is easy structurally, it is going to be an easy planning decision and it should all be done in about six months, maybe then you pursue it if it is going to add more than 30%.

Layouts of Cluster Flats

A key component of a cluster flat is getting the layout correct. Mark usually specifies that all bedrooms need to be 11 m^2 plus a 2 m^2 minimum en-suite. This ensures that the rooms let easily and that they meet HMO regulations. Mark also provides a kitchen/lounge/diner of at least 20 m^2 to enable six tenants to have enough space to eat and socialise, and the worktop, cupboard, oven and fridge space also needs to be carefully considered. As a rule of thumb, each cluster flat of six rooms seems to average around 140 m^2, which is useful when calculating the size of a commercial building you are viewing to convert, allowing a quick decision with an agent. Fast rules of thumb like this are important as they save you a lot of time and help you make quick decisions, which is what vendors and agents usually want to see.

Unlike some operators, Mark also puts lobby areas off the front door in each cluster flat to reduce noise and have a separate utility room to house the washer and dryer, which you need to provide in these units. At the time of writing, there is a consultation out on effectively making almost all HMOs licensable, which means it's especially important to make sure you meet current and proposed future regulations on these units. Windows that are sized to be at least 10% of the floor area of the room and that have an area that opens to at least 5% of the floor area of the room are also mandatory, along with fire doors to every room and flat, fire blankets and interlinked smoked detectors.

Full HMO standards can be found within the document at the link below; read them and set them as the minimum specification your builder needs to follow, as they will save a lot of extra expense later:

https://www.nihe.gov.uk/hmo_standards.pdf

There are lots of areas where rules are frequently bent in property, but fire shouldn't be one of them. When it occasionally goes wrong, people can end up dead – and this also usually ends up with a developer or investor going to jail. Ensuring fire risk assessments are done in each of these buildings and implementing the recommendations in the report should protect the people in the building – and you from losing your liberty. Mark has included an illustration below with a couple of example cluster flat layouts to help illustrate a layout that works for these types of units.

Chapter 11: Get it Built

Having set up your team, found your niche, located a deal, arranged the funds, gone through the design phase and got the planning consent you intend to implement, you are finally ready to get building. We are really making progress now, but although we can conceive of the most beautiful plans in our minds, if we are not able to communicate them in a contractual fashion to our builder, we could still be heading for disaster. Almost anyone who has tried to achieve anything in property will have horror stories to share about their experience of issues with builders. And do they have to be large schemes to have issues with builders? Absolutely not!

Having experienced horrendous problems with builders on relatively small jobs – from refurbishments to loft or garage conversions, small or large extensions, or possibly even building or refurbishing a whole property – most people merely assume they could extrapolate those issues if they were crazy enough to consider taking on bigger schemes. Certainly, if you don't get the principles right in a bigger scheme you definitely could have even bigger issues with your builders. But here is the really interesting thing: as you move up the value chain, the quality of the people you work with gets progressively better, and dealing with them can become at worst no more problematic than much smaller projects – and in many cases, relatively trouble-free.

At the bottom of the value chain, when undertaking small schemes, you might be dealing with one man and a van. When does the one man and a van turn up for your job? When he likes! Is it when you agreed? No, generally not. When you get to the end of the job with the one man and a van, is the cost less or more than you expected? Generally much more. Do you remember the beginning of the job where he went "ffffwwww" (large intake of breath)? That "ffffwwww" becomes a "no guv, nah, that was never included, no mate sorry". Or what happens if there is an issue with the job, how easy is it to get him to come back? It can be almost impossible.

However, as you move up the value chain, your one man and a van has become a contracting firm. It is not one man and a van anymore, it's probably a number of people, in multiple disciplines backed by a head office and run as a business by someone experienced in the industry.

For Glenn's first development, he hired a main contractor. They weren't particularly large, taking on jobs of up to £500k – possibly a little more, but that was their sweet spot. The company was essentially one man as the main contractor, with a loyal set of sub-contractors that had been with him for many years. He relied heavily on reputation to secure his pipeline of work. So how did Glenn find him? By reputation, word of mouth. Glenn's architect had worked with the contractor on several large house extensions and new builds, and when Glenn approached his architect for suggestions of names to go into the tender process, this chap was one of them. By moving up the value chain, using networks of trust to find a credible and reliable small contractor, we ended up with someone we could trust.

That job went really well, and that was only a small step up from one man and a van. He was a man with a van, a loyal set of sub-contractors and a reputation to defend. Furthermore, he had been around for years and had built a significant cash pot. There were no requests for money upfront to 'buy materials'. He was content to work within a good contractual framework and to be paid for work he had carried out, but in arrears and it was a good indication that we had a strong and reliable contractor.

Never, ever pay money upfront for works or materials. This approach screams of a lack of funds on the contractor's part, which indicates either lack of track record, financial mismanagement or worse, impending collapse. In our efforts to find the right contractor, we should always be minded to ensure we are working with well-funded and well-run companies that are highly unlikely to go bust while they are working on our schemes. Not only would this cost us money, but it could have a catastrophic effect on the programme – and it can be hugely difficult to find a new contractor willing to step in to a project half completed by somebody else.

As you then scale your projects in size, your contracting firms will also scale. The larger firms have an office with possibly tens of people in it who are running the administration for a fleet of contractors; they will have an estimating section, a finance and accounts section, a fleet of vehicles and a track record of delighted customers that you can take references from. OK, maybe I'm getting a bit carried away with 'delighted customers', but at least generally happy! The benefit of scaling your projects and dealing with the larger firms is that they get ever more professional. The larger developments also come with larger professional fee budgets, and your dealings with these companies are likely to be through project managers and QSs that you have hired to represent you, such that even the reduced hassle of dealing with these more professional contractors is mitigated further by the fact that a lot of that legwork is being done on your behalf by somebody else! Your involvement may be limited to one or two meetings a month and the occasional email from your project manager. In this way, it can be simple to run a number of projects concurrently, building your pipeline of larger developments and opening the door to life changing profits.

So this section is about how to get it built, ensuring that this beautiful development we have conceived in our minds is not left to the mercy of a man with a van, who turns up when he feels like it and then says, "no guv, it wasn't included"! Instead, we get to a point where that beautiful thing you have conceived in your mind and agreed with the estate agent gets delivered with a set of keys that you can hand over to the estate agent, and it is eminently achievable.

One of Glenn's favourite movies is Apollo 13. There is a scene in the film where the NASA Flight Director, Gene Kranz, has gathered his team of experts around him to brainstorm the nightmare scenario created by a serious systems failure on the Apollo 13 spacecraft. After being briefed by his various experts, determining the main issues, he is just about to dismiss his team to their various urgent and important tasks. But as they begin to disperse, he utters the words, "We've never lost an American in space and we sure as hell ain't gonna lose one on my watch. Failure is not an option!"

Failure is not an option! It's a great movie if you haven't watched it, but why do I mention it now? For a number of reasons: 1) do you think that Apollo missions are well planned, well-funded, well thought through and rehearsed with extensive training? By the time of Apollo 13, NASA's missions were so well planned, so well delivered and had actually become so routine that the world wasn't so interested any more. When the crew were doing a TV broadcast from Apollo 13, the networks didn't carry it because it had become samey and predictable. The world was bored with Apollo missions! This was Apollo 13, and they had seen the previous 12 Apollo missions, which had all gone well. Nothing had happened and the public were no longer impressed or interested. The process had been funded, researched and carried out 12 times, and it had becomes so predictable and so boring that the world just didn't care any more.

If something unexpected can go wrong with a well-funded NASA programme that has been tested, simulated and carried out for real 12 times, do you think it could happen to you on one of your developments? Yes, of course it can. Not only can it, you can be rest assured that at some point, it will. Yes, absolutely it will. And if that scares you, this strategy, or indeed anything in property, might not be for you. However, it shouldn't scare you, it should actually excite you, because we get paid for what? Solving problems! If you undertake numerous developments, be assured that problems will occur. But also know this: you are not on your own. Gene Kranz was an ex-fighter pilot. He wasn't an expert in all the systems on a spaceship, he didn't know all the spaceship systems off by heart and he probably had no idea himself how to solve the critical issue that was crippling Apollo 13 and endangering the crew. But he did know how to lead a team to a mutually agreed end – and he had an awesome team around him.

What did Gene Kranz do when there was a problem and his experts – or rather at times, herd of cats – were crying meow all at the same time? What did he do first? He listened. Sometimes you are going to have to filter out the noise from the really important stuff. When the scene described starts, what they're actually talking about is the fact that the crew has an oxygen problem, with only enough oxygen left for 45 hours of travel. That wouldn't be enough to get them back to earth, but at that point, that is the main problem they're going to work on – the critical path, if you like. Gene Kranz is still listening to find out what the real problem is though, and ultimately a power systems expert points out that they have a more critical problem: that they're going to run out of power in 16 hours and if that happens, everything else will fail and the crew will die, long before the oxygen runs out! At that point Gene takes control, he is calm, he listens, identifies the real issue, makes a decision and takes action. At the end of the scene, Kranz despatches his team with urgent instructions to each go back their specialist teams and to work the issues.

Did Gene Kranz go and do it? NO. Did Gene Kranz try and learn about electrics to check the guy who said it was 16 hours? NO. And nor should you. If you have got the right team around you, you don't need to go and double check them because they will have forgotten more than you could ever learn. They are operating in their profession, their expertise. And really, that scene of Gene Kranz 'working the problem' is a little picture of your role as a developer, because things will go wrong, problems do happen, and you are either the kind of person who will look at a problem and go shrink and hide, or you are going to be the developer who says "great, more value to add". That is why we get paid the big bucks.

We make that point particularly at the beginning of this section because contract law, contracting and contractors are where you will really need to rely on your experts, as it is a very technical area. When you are appointing a contractor, our number one rule, as with most of our experts in our team, is to work only on recommendation. You never use sites such as checkatrade.com, you never Google and you never meet the guy down the pub who knows a man that can do it for you and just happens to have a gap in their schedule right now! You get the point. Use your network, ask your experts, ask your mentor or mastermind group, work in the community that you are in – go anywhere other than checkatrade.com or Google. Always select a contractor by reference, even when you are starting out and are doing a smaller job. Try and have a minimum of three contractors tender for work.

When you have got one or two trusted contractors, you may be able to skip that step (we will come to that later) but at the beginning, if you are doing a £500k build for the first time, don't use the contractor you have used for your £50k HMO because they may be out of their depth. By all means include them in the tender, but get other people who are used to doing £500k contracts involved in the tender – you may suddenly see why your guy has previously been doing £50k HMOs and nothing more when you compare them with someone who is used to doing bigger contracts. That principle holds true as you scale up through the contracting firms too. We have a chap that we use for our £500k to £1m contracts, and there is no way that we would put him into a contract of £2.5m. Quite apart from anything else, he hasn't got a big enough team, so the job would probably take two and a half years!

It's horses for courses, and the people you currently have in your team may not be the people you need in your team in the future. "What got you here may not get you there" holds true in this scenario. Find a good recommendation, get at least three people to tender for the work and take the advice of the team around you when making your final selection – after all, that is the same team that will be with you and the contractor when the big problems need solving down the line.

What do contractors want?

Clarity

Good contractors like clarity, whereas bad contractors don't mind confusion because that provides them with an opportunity to drive a train through your budget, and to charge you far more than the initial estimate. Bad contractors love the lack of clarity, because they are going to charge you extra for it, or they deliver a load of rubbish knowing you can't hold them to account because you weren't clear enough. You can't tell them they didn't deliver what they should have delivered, because you can't prove it if you didn't give them the clarity.

However, good contractors like good clients and good clients know what they want and have a detailed tender pack. Who pulls that pack together? No, you don't, the experts do. What you will pull together is your schedule of finishes and that only makes up part of the tender pack. The rest of the tender pack is a contractual document and that will be pulled together by your team. If you are developing smaller projects, the tender pack might be pulled together by your architect (covered later in this chapter), but when you are getting onto the bigger contracts, you might be using a project manager and it will be your project manager or QS who pulls together your tender pack. You won't have time, and it is not your area of expertise, and unless you have been a building contract lawyer you are going to miss some stuff out. Like Gene Kranz, use your team, because the tender pack and contract are really detailed and are a lot of work to put together.

Reliable Payment

Good contractors will want to know that they are going to get paid. They want clarity on what you want, and they want clarity on the fact they are going to get paid; good contractors are not going to work for someone who they think is not going to be there when they want their bill paid. Good contractors are not going to work for someone who says "yes, I know I owe you £300k but do you mind waiting six weeks because I have got a bit of a cash flow problem".

Contractors ordinarily work on a project with very small margins of circa 7 or 8%. Consider, then, that you sign a contract with a contractor for works of say £1m, the contract profit to them is just £80k after their costs. That is not a huge amount of money and can easily be eroded by unexpected risk. Furthermore, in 'down market' conditions, contractors may even take on a contract for 0% profit just to keep their labour employed. In doing so, they will accept they may not make a profit just to earn enough to keep their team employed and keep everything ticking over. In that context, it becomes clear how important it is for them to have confidence that they are going to get paid, because they don't have a lot of room for manoeuvre. How you are going to pay will depend on the contract type, but more of that later in the chapter.

Wiggle Room

The other thing any contractor will want is wiggle room! You don't want to give them wiggle room, but they will love it. When you are only making 7 or 8% on a contract, an extra 2 or 3% that you make by taking advantage of a little wiggle room might be quite handy because it could increase your contract profit by as much as 30-50%. Good contractors really like good clients with a good tender pack and clear requirements, and who are well-funded, but who are not perfect and have left a little uncertainty or perhaps small omissions in the paperwork. That seems to be the reality. And that is why they are going to play the 'variation game' – we'll come to that later.

Tendering Process

The size of your project will determine your approach, but generally speaking you will either be using a cost consultant/architect to put together your tender paperwork for smaller deals, or you will be getting into the realms of using a project manager on a scheme, who will put together the tender for larger developments. If you get a project manager to put this together for you then they will probably have a QS working for them within their team. Principally, there a couple of ways you can tender, one being a single-stage tender and the other a two-stage tender. But first, a quick word on how many contractors you need to invite to tender for your project.

Ideal Number of Tenderers

One of the issues with tendering is that it is a lot of work for the contractors. The bigger the job, the more work it becomes, and contractors don't want to waste their time. Accordingly, if they discover they are only 1 of 10 contractors being asked to tender, they aren't likely to bother. Indeed, the higher the quality of the contractor, the more likely it is that their order book looks healthily full, and therefore the less likely they are to compete in such a big number of tenders where their chance of success is low.

The converse problem, though, is that usually during the tender process, a number of contractors will drop out. It is likely that at least one of them withdraw from the process, maybe because they win another job, taking up their pipeline capacity and they don't need or want your contract any more. You have got to understand that contractors are very limited by capacity, as it is not easy for them to expand quickly. Being a good contractor, they will only want good tradespeople working for them, and good tradespeople are unlikely to be sitting around just waiting for the phone to ring. So when they start the tender for your job, they may well want the job, but if they win another tender in the meantime they may suddenly decide they don't need your job and they can't fulfil it, so they withdraw from the tender.

Ideally, you want at least three good tender returns to compare, so if you are going to work on the fact that one is going to drop out, then it follows that you need at least four contractors in the tender at the beginning. Three is not enough because one then falls out you have then only got two costs. Another possibility is that a tenderer decides that they don't really need the project, but submits a super high price such that should they win the tender, they would make so much money that they could afford to 'sub in' the extra labour required, paying higher rates if necessary. Consider, therefore, if you have only got two tenderers, you might get someone whose tender return is poorly considered and lacking in quality, and someone who is giving you a really high price because they don't need or want the work. You may have wasted four to six weeks getting a tender price that isn't workable/acceptable.

Accordingly, four is generally the right number, but sometimes it could be as many as five. We have never put a tender out to more than five, because if they find out there are more than five in the tender they won't bother and they may not consider us in the future either.

SINGLE-STAGE TENDER

With a single-stage tender, you send out all the detailed information of a full tender pack and give it to the four or five tenderers. The tenderers consider the information, come back with a detailed cost and then you make a selection based on your criteria. There are advantages and disadvantages to this single-stage approach, as follows:

Advantages

This approach will provide you with a clear cost at the outset. In just one round of works, typically taking between four and six weeks once the tender pack is submitted, you have got four or five firms bidding for the work on the same basis. If the tender pack is well put together, the tenderers should each have returned their response in the same format, ensuring that is easy to crosscheck each tender return against the other. It should be clear where some firms have priced lower than others, and, conversely, where they are more expensive. This can help flag errors but also highlight an innovative approach to a problem that provides excellent value.

Even in the event that a firm returns a tender in a different format that makes it hard to make direct comparisons, you will have learnt something. If we consider the mantra of "how you do anything is how you do everything", if a contractor cannot follow instructions on how you want a tender returned, they are unlikely to follow your instructions during the project. Additionally, if the tender return is sloppy and vague, why should you expect their work to be anything other than the same?

So the advantage of a single-stage tender is that you have got a fixed cost at the outset, it is very easy to compare the contractors and easy to assess their ability and appetite for the work.

Disadvantages

However, a single-stage tender takes an awfully long time both to draw up, and then to proceed to completion. In all that time you are incurring costs, and if work is plentiful, then contractors may fall out of the process.

Depending on the complexity and size of the development, the detailed design required to provide the requisite information for a good-quality tender pack can take anything from four to 16 weeks. The tender pack itself may then require one to three weeks to be pulled together. The tenderers will then require four to six weeks to respond, ordinarily. Once the responses have been received, you may need a week or two to interview any contractor being considered for the contract based on their tender return. Invariably, there will then be a requirement for the firms to consider and price up amendments to their original submission, which may be another week or two. Only then are you in a position to select a contractor, who may then of course need a number of weeks to mobilise and arrive on your site! From start of this process to having a contractor on-site can easily be 16 weeks, and will often be nearer six months for larger projects. It is suddenly clear why we need enough tenderers in the process to ensure we have at least three good prices to compare, but that it can be hard to achieve. It is for this reason that some may consider two-stage tenders.

TWO-STAGE TENDER

With a two-stage tender, the process is simply split into two parts. In the first part, a lot less detail is designed before the first tender is sent out, and you will probably get away with sending it to a few more people, say maybe five or six contractors, because they are going to have to do a lot less work. The tender information is at a much higher level with much less detail. Given that there is less detail to consider, the returns from the prospective contractors should be received more quickly, and on the basis of the overall submitted tender prices, you select one contractor to work with further. The selected contractor will then work with your design team, and their own in-house experts to provide a firmer price based on a fully worked-up scheme. The contractor presents that price with a view to signing a contract with you, and your expectation is that their considered and detailed price submission is similar to their initial submission. So with a two-stage tender, you are using a higher level, quicker, shorter process with lots of contractors to come up with a basic price, that you then work on to refine that price with one contractor.

Advantages

It is much easier to get contractors to engage in a two-stage tender because they have a lot less work to do. Clearly, because the process is so much quicker, the developer also gets faster access to information about the likely tender pricing, and gets to build a relationship with the final contractor earlier, meeting them after two weeks instead of six weeks.

Disadvantages

However, the major disadvantage of this tender process is just how 'flexible' the tender price often becomes after the first stage. The weakness of the two-stage tender is that the contractor can provide a price to get through the door, and then suddenly everything seems a bit more complicated and costly and the costs can ramp up. Once the contractor is through to the second stage, they think they are 'in'. The following case study gives an example of just such a project.

Case Study – Flexible Pricing (by Glenn)

Do you remember our lemon? I told you it was a lemon, in that everything that could go wrong did go wrong. With the lemon, we entered into a two-stage tender, and on the back of the process we chose a contractor that submitted an acceptable price. They were well established in the area, of a good size, well financed and with a good reputation. Before we went too far into the second stage, we agreed their price looked good, but to be sure we were on the same page we asked them to show us one of their current developments, in which they were hitting the same price point of £115 per sq. ft. for the construction. So they took us to a site near

Woking, where we found the works to be pretty much spot on for the kind of standard we were looking for. On the back of that visit, we agreed to proceed to the second stage of the tender. I can't remember the exact numbers, but I think on the basis of the £115 per sq. ft. we were looking for a tender of circa £1.4m. Imagine our surprise when the final tender price came back at £1.85m.

With an additional £450k in the basic tender price, we then added on a contingency of 5% and found we were getting into the best part of £500k additional cost, which would all come off the bottom line – off our profit. When you are making a 20% profit on a £3.5m building, (i.e. circa £700k) that is most of the profit gone. We decided the problem was that they thought they were in, and that they had an opportunity to 'gild the lily' a little. There were some clues to the fact they were hiding extra profit too. All contracts have a section for preliminary costs, which can be a bit of a grey area, but generally includes things like site setup, fencing, welfare facilities, administration support and some contractors put an element of profit in there too. Ordinarily, prelims should be somewhere between 7 and 13% of the contract value, but in this contract, they came in at 18% – and more worryingly, with very little breakdown of the associated costs.

We very quickly assessed that in our view the contractor was trying it on and insisted on them breaking down the prelim costs into defined amounts. They completely, totally and consistently refused to comply with our request; one can only assume they thought they had us over a barrel. Now this was back when prior approval on offices was due to run out in May 2016 before it actually was made permanent. They thought they had got us, they thought we didn't have time to find another contractor before the deadline was up and that we would have little choice but to accept their price. We concluded that we had no choice but to go back to the market, despite the risk of running out of time. It cost us a lot of time and some money because we had to put a single stage tender pack together, but we went back to the market. When we got the prices back we didn't quite hit our £1.4m target, but it did come in at £1.5m, £350k (plus contingency) cheaper.

Given our experience, we suggest that you are careful about using two-stage tenders. The only time we would recommend you enter into a two-stage tender would be if you had a number of contracting firms tendering that you had dealt with previously. Proceed with firms you have worked with previously, and that you know and trust and that have delivered for you on multiple occasions before.

Negotiated Contracts

There is another approach that you take when you have a bit of experience. If you have a few contractors out there you have worked with, and you really like them and they have done a great job for you, you can enter into a negotiated contract. Ocea has just done this on a scheme in Basingstoke with a contractor who delivered their scheme in Hemel Hempstead. The contractors workmanship was excellent, the show flats were beautifully presented, they were quick, and they are great people to deal with. So Glenn approached them with a similar scheme in Basingstoke and asked them if they could deliver it for the same price per square foot they had delivered Hemel for. They appraised the site and agreed they could deliver it for the same price. Ocea saved the cost and expense of doing a detailed tender pack, saved money on having to do a detailed design because the contractor knew their specification and what Ocea want, and have committed to producing exactly the same specification at the same price. Once you have an established product that has already been delivered well by a contractor, the negotiated contract can be a good option based on mutual trust.

Joint Contracts Tribunal (JCT) Contracts

Contracts themselves are a very technical area, so as ever, use your experts. This overview is intended to give you a working knowledge of the main contract types and some of the terms you might come across. A JCT contract is generally the one that is most used, and whilst there are other ones, the JCT contracts are the ones you are most likely to come across. It is a standardised contract with standard terms that can be varied each time you enter into one. The JCT has become almost an industry standard, largely because it supports a number of functions that are synonymous with good contracts. The list is as follows:

- use of valuation certificates

- retention

- liquidated and ascertained damages

- determination

- employer's requirements document

- minor, intermediate, major project

Valuations Certificates

Every month, usually the QS and/or the monitoring surveyor for the lender will attend the site to assess the work done by the contractor. Their role is to agree the amount of work the contractor has done and to certify a fair amount to be paid for that work. The contractor applies for payment using the issued valuation certificate and the lender will send out the money for that valuation. This process protects the contractor by ensuring they get paid promptly for works carried out and materials used, and protects the client by ensuring they only pay for works completed. The lender also has comfort that funds lent to the scheme have been spent sensibly on the scheme, and not used elsewhere.

Retention

By retaining an agreed amount from the payments made to the contractor, it is ensured that the contractor is always incentivised to return to site to resolve any problems. Somewhere between 3 and 5% of the contract sum as it is drawn down is in the normal range for retention. If you are not holding some of their 'earned' funds, imagine how difficult it is going to be get them back to fix snagging or resolve the inevitable issues that arise.

After the agreed Defects Liability Period (DFLP), the contractor will revisit the site to resolve outstanding items such as plaster cracks, small leaks, etc. and once that process is complete and signed off, the retention is released to them.

As a tip, don't allow a gap between when your building warranty kicks in (usually 12 months, but it can be up to 24 months) and the DFLP ends. Most contractors want the retention to finish after six months, but the problem is the warranty that you have procured for your apartments is unlikely to kick in until 12 months. So if the DFLP finished after six months and the contractor's retention was released to them, but an issue occurred between month six and month 12, then you as the developer are solely responsible for sorting out the issue. The contractor has gone, has got their money and will only come back if they are paid, and the warranty provider's cover hasn't yet commenced. Accordingly, ensure that your DFLP runs sequentially, straight into the commencement of the warranty cover so that at any time, any problems that arise must be resolved by others.

Liquidated and Ascertained Damages (LADs)

LADs is the little stick at the end of the contract that makes it clear to the contractor that they need to finish on time, and in the event that they fail, they will be charged £x amount per week for every week they overrun. You calculate the amount as an assessment of your actual loss caused by their delayed completion. It could be £3k a week, £10k a week, whatever your loss is, but it is designed to incentivise the contractor to finish the contract on time so that they are not incurring those damages.

This is a good point to remind you of the fairly small margins contractors are working with – LADs can have real teeth. However, LADs cannot be penal; you cannot say it will be really quite inconvenient if you are going to be a week late, so I am going to charge you £1m as soon as you overrun. It doesn't work like that, and the courts would throw it out because such a large amount would be considered penal. It has to be a true assessment of your costs, but you can include costs for all sorts of expenses and losses, such as cost of funds, delays in sales process, management time, and many more. You will have to justify every cost line by line by line, so it has to be a real assessment of the cost to you of that delay.

Nevertheless, LADs can still be very significant. When Glenn was still employed and was overseeing the building of the spectator stands at The Rose Bowl, he had significant delays at the beginning of the project and the contractor had a lot to do in about four months after those delays. They went from almost no progress to hundreds of people crawling all over the building site like ants at all hours by getting permission from the local authority to work nights and weekends, all because the LADs were huge. It had been easy to justify substantive LADs, because a few weeks after the contract was due to be finished, the ground was due to host a one-day international featuring England versus Australia. The ground was sold out, the new spectator stands were due to be filled with 9,000 spectators, the hospitality boxes were full with people paying top money for hospitality and the ground needed the toilets and catering facilities in the stands as well. So the very real loss to The Rose Bowl had the stands not been finished on time was so enormous that the LADs were extremely heavy. It had to be a massive stick because the losses – both real and reputational – were enormous.

Following the early delays, the contractor looked at the LADs and realised there was no way they could afford to pay them, or shoulder the reputational damage, so they threw people at the project. But you can see that The Rose Bowl were able to demonstrate real loss. The end of that story is that they got so close to the wire, that on the day of the cricket match literally as the hospitality guests starting walking in the door at one end of the suite, Glenn reports that he was kicking the painters and carpet people out of a door at the other end of the suite.

Contract Determination

Contract determination is the right to stop the contract if you need to. Let's imagine you have a dispute with the contractor, and the contractor decides to walk off site. Under a contract without determination rights, you may not be allowed to put another contractor on the site. It is their contract, and the fact that they walked off site wouldn't give you the right to take the site back and give it to someone else. Therefore, under a JCT contract, if the contractor does effectively repudiate the contract and says they are not fulfilling the contract, you can determine the contract and get somebody else to build it out. This right of determination is also important when the contractor goes bust. Without this clause, you would have to wait for the whole of their liquidation process to be completed and for the receivers to work out any payments due before you could put anyone else onto the site.

Employer's Requirements Document

The employer's requirement document includes your specification, your schedule of finishes, your plans and lots more besides. It tells the contractor exactly what they have to deliver for you and as such it is very long, complicated, detailed and technical – which is why you get your experts to draft it.

Project Size

It doesn't matter how big your project is, there is a JCT contract to support it. The JCT contract comes in three main forms: minor, intermediate and major.

By the way if you are really excited about this opportunity and you go and do what you consider to be your first 'major' project of your first commercial conversion, and the build cost is £250,000, don't be upset when it comes back as a 'minor' contract! JCT contracts can be used for large construction projects of many millions of pounds, so the Minor Works Building Contract goes up to circa £250,000. The JCT Intermediate Building Contract is designed for construction projects involving all the recognised trades and skills of the industry, where fairly detailed contract provisions are needed, but without complex building service installations or other specialist work. Intermediate Building Contracts are suitable for projects procured via the traditional or conventional method, whereas The JCT Major Project Construction Contract is designed for large-scale construction projects where major works are involved. It is used by developers who regularly procure large-scale construction work, and the work is carried out by contractors with the experience and ability to take greater risk than would arise under other JCT contracts. Major Project Construction Contracts are suitable for projects procured via the design and build methods mentioned later in this chapter.

Fixed Price Contracts

Even with smaller projects, a JCT contract can be used, but should you be in a situation in which you have little more than floor plans to work with and you are content to let the builder sort out the design with the architect, you might just go to a fixed price contract with a builder selected through a small tender process. In this case, you might not come up with a full employer's requirement document with a full detailed design. Instead you just give them your specification, and the price quoted by the builder is the price you pay.

Variations

Once a contract has been signed, based on the delivery of an agreed product at an agreed price, any variation to that contract will be noted as a variation. If you have changed your mind or not been specific about what you want, or discovered something that wasn't known that requires the design to be changed, a variation order will be raised. Sadly experience shows that something that would have cost £100 before you signed the contract, seems to somehow cost £300 the moment it becomes a variation after you have signed the contract. Despite agreed scale rates in the contract for the various trades, costs for changes always seem higher, and savings for omissions never seem to quite yield the saving we might have expected!

It might be helpful to see variations as a tax on incompetence and indecision! So if you take up that challenge, accept the fact that if the contractor manages to charge you significantly more on top of the agreed contract price because of a long list of variations, you take it is as a tax on the fact that maybe you haven't done enough due diligence and work upfront. That is why your schedule of finishes and a good detailed design are critical. If you follow the advice of the old adage to "measure twice, cut once" you will seriously reduce the risk of excessive variations. Do the real work upfront before you sign the contract, and then resist the temptation to change your mind unless absolutely vital.

One of the things we do to reduce the risk of late changes and expensive variations is to take the floor plans and 'project' them into the building space by means of painting the designed layouts on the floor of the building as soon as it has been stripped out. By 'walking through' each apartment layout in the reality of the building context, we have often identified design that looks great on paper but doesn't work in reality.

Design and Build (D&B) Contracts

As suggested by the name, with a D&B contract the contractor is required to do a predetermined (but variable) portion of the design, and then build it out. It is not the design of the floor plans and all your final finishes though. The design they might undertake is the detail as to how they achieve your final finish and the employer's requirements. To give you a simple example, let's say that you want hot water to appear in the taps in the bathroom between a certain pressure range because if the pressure isn't high enough you will be waiting impatiently for the basin to fill, and if the pressure is too high you end up with water splashes all over your trousers, which for us men is particularly embarrassing. So you need the water to arrive at a particular pressure range and a particular temperature range. Now you don't care how they do it, you don't care how they get the water there, you are not worried if they use a pump here or a pump downstairs or where the piping goes, what kind of piping they use, whether the system is pressurised or gravity fed or any other such matter. Your requirement is for the end result, without any particular concern about how they achieve it. That is the essence of a design and build contract. You don't tell them how to do it, you just tell them what you want and it is up to them to design it and build it.

The amount of design you undertake before tendering on a D&B basis will affect the amount of risk that contractors price into the contract. Furthermore, the more design you complete yourself, the tighter your end product will be to what you envisage, and you will probably also see a tighter price range in your tender returns. However, over-designing your product incurs cost, time and may obviate an opportunity for a contractor to present a creative and better value solution. Accordingly, the design carried out by the developers team on each project is variable and negotiable.

Advantages

The D&B contract is what they call an all-risk contract, i.e. because they are responsible for the design, all the risk goes to the contractor. This is great news for you. You have had to do less work and they have had to make sure they have got it right or they have to carry the burden of the extra costs incurred, not you. The responsibility for the site goes to the contractor so you have very little to do – they are responsible for site safety, site access, people wearing PPE and all other aspects of on-site operations.

Disadvantages

Given the contractors don't yet fully know how they are going to design the end product, they are going to price in risk. They have little choice, bearing in mind the small percentages they are working with. They could be fulfilling a £1m contract and only making £70 or £80k, so they can't afford to take huge risks; they are simply going to price risk in. This goes back to when we mentioned that the first stage of redesign is to strip the building out, because if the contractors are confident they have identified as many of the risks as possible, then your design and build contract will be tighter since they are not worried about what they don't know.

Whilst giving control of the site to the builder has its upsides, there are downsides too. Arranging access for viewings by potential buyers must be pre-agreed and under conditions acceptable to the contractor. If you need show flats half way through the build, this must be pre-agreed in the contract, including access arrangements. The contractor will have to give you control of that part of the site back, so what will often happen is that you will have a completely separate entrance into your show flats. They will hand you the flats, passing responsibility for that portion of the site to you, insisting that any damage done to those flats by people wandering through is not their responsibility. You are now in control of that part of the site. This 'staged handover' needs to be in the contract, otherwise the contractor may refuse to provide both the show flats and the access.

All access and control of the site has been passed over, as has control of the specification. The moment you sign the contract, if you have not made it clear what you want delivered, they can actually deliver less and as long as it meets what is laid out in the employer's requirements, you will have little or no recourse.

Reducing Contract Risk

How do you reduce your risk? In summary, use your experts, produce a good quality tender pack, produce an excellent employer's requirement document, make sure you know what is included and excluded ensuring you get someone to explain all the inclusions and exclusions to you before you sign the contract. Look at the preliminaries and confirm they look sensible, make sure your liquidated damages are defensible and are appropriate and a true reflection of your costs. Consider your retention and make sure it crosses over with your warranty.

Novating Professionals

Although it is rarely required, novating professionals of your choice is an option to you. Novation is the assignment of one of your design professionals, such as your architect, to the contractor. Maybe you come up with a beautiful design and you particularly want your architect to work for the contractors, because they know what you want. By novating them you 'force' the contractor to use your chosen professional. It doesn't happen much because: 1) usually the contractors are used to people who work much more commercially and cost a lot less, and 2) even if you do novate them, the professional is actually then working for the contractor from the moment they are novated; they are not working for you any more. Probably the biggest advantage of novating professionals is the passing on of accumulated detailed technical knowledge that might otherwise be lost from the project, or take many hours to pass on.

Construction and Design Management (CDM) Role

Whilst it is a contractor who directly employs or engages construction workers or manages construction work, and therefore has an important role in planning, managing and monitoring their work to ensure any risks are controlled, it is the overall responsibility of the developer to ensure that CDM practices are being followed. This role can be delegated to a principal designer, but it is important to understand that this doesn't mean that the role can be abdicated.

Generally, a developer will delegate their responsibilities to a principal designer, thereby ensuring that a knowledgeable and appropriately qualified person is overseeing safety. According to HSE, "Principal designers have an important role in influencing how risks to health and safety are managed throughout a project. Design decisions made during the pre-construction phase have a significant influence in ensuring the project is delivered in a way that secures the health and safety of everyone affected by the work.

Principal designers must:

- plan, manage, monitor and coordinate health and safety in the pre-construction phase. In doing so they must take account of relevant information (such as an existing health and safety file) that might affect design work carried out both before and after the construction phase has started

- help and advise the client in bringing together pre-construction information, and provide the information designers and contractors need to carry out their duties

- work with any other designers on the project to eliminate foreseeable health and safety risks to anyone affected by the work and, where that is not possible, take steps to reduce or control those risks

- ensure that everyone involved in the pre-construction phase communicates and cooperates, coordinating their work wherever required

- liaise with the principal contractor, keeping them informed of any risks that need to be controlled during the construction phase."

People die on building sites every year. Developers must take the appointment of principal designers seriously and ensure that the role is monitored.

Case Study – Tragedy (by Glenn)

When I was running The Rose Bowl, I was overseeing the construction of the new spectator stands. We had experienced quite a lot of delays, it being one of the coldest winters in recent history. We were due to have the steel frame going up in January, and just as it was about to go up, all the concrete factories froze. Normally you can use admixtures with concrete so that by adding accelerants it doesn't matter how cold the concrete will go off. The problem on this occasion was that it was so cold that the concrete factories themselves froze that year. The process used to produce the concrete ground to a halt until the temperatures picked up again. Once we could get concrete delivered for the foundations to the steel frame, we were well behind schedule. Suddenly, though, over the next few weeks the metal frame went up very quickly, like a giant Meccano set.

When building modern stadiums, the first thing you do is get the steel frame up. Then you lay the concrete slabs on the frame, and then fix the seats to the concrete slabs. Then you put the walls up, put the roof on, and hey presto, you have a stadium... more or less! Stadiums require massive concrete slabs to support the dynamic loads of people on them. Stringent load testing assumes that all the spectators jump out of their seat at the same time and land at the same time, thereby causing massive flexion. So these are massive bits of concrete that are craned into position on the steel frame.

In our case, when they started adding the concrete slabs to the steel frame they started with two of the biggest pieces of concrete to provide the vertical walls for what they call the vomitory. The vomitory is the walkway that you proceed through when you enter a sports stadium. When you enter or exit a stadium through a long concrete corridor, you come out to see all the seats are raked in tiers below you or going up either side of you; that corridor is called the vomitory. You can imagine that the front of that vomitory wall isn't very big, but because of the rake of the stands, the back of the vomitory walls are massively tall. So because they are big and vertical, for our stands they were the first pieces to onto the steel frame.

On 8 February 2010, as the managing director I was chairing a management meeting of the senior staff. We were using one of the meeting rooms overlooking the cricket pitch. The Rose Bowl has an oval pitch, with seating in a bowl configuration curved round the pitch and the main pavilion above the seats at one end of the pitch. Our meeting room was in the main pavilion; from where I was sitting in the meeting, given the curve, I could see the new West Stand being built. It was a very exciting day after all the delays – this was the day that the first big concrete slabs were being delivered to the site. It was a beautiful, sunny day, one of those quite frosty but very clear, still days with almost no wind at all. No movement, bright sunshine and not a cloud in the sky. That was great news for us to crane big bits of concrete into place, so we knew that finally we were going to see some material progress, with concrete slabs appearing on the stands. Sure enough, we could see the lorries rolling in with the big slabs on the back and we could see the cranes waiting to crane them into place. Exciting times.

As we were sat in this meeting, the contractors were getting on with what they were doing, and then we heard this strange sound that's difficult to describe; it was almost like a low, loud but softened sucking sound. Then there was this kind of eerie silence. Then we heard what I recognised as the sound of running feet – one or two at first and then gradually many running feet. There are times in your life when you just know something is wrong, and this was one of those times. I instantly stopped the management meeting. As the managing director of The Rose Bowl I had overall responsibility for the building site on our venue, so I went straight out of the door that opened up onto the concourse, which then allowed me to run the 80 yards or so to the building site. What I saw that day will never leave me.

The vomitory walls that were meant to be standing upright were lying on top of each other, and underneath one of them was a dying man. Between the two walls there had been another man, but when the first wall had started moving he had seen it and got out. Unfortunately though, when one big concrete wall falls against another it's like dominoes – the first one is slow but because of the mass, the next ones fall more quickly. Phil was working behind the second slab. He couldn't see the first 'domino' moving, so when the first slab hit the second one, it was moving so fast that by the time he saw what was happening, he couldn't escape and was crushed underneath two huge falling slabs of concrete. I hope you never see what that amount of weight does to a body. I saw Phil take his last breath, but he was dead from the moment the concrete hit him.

Very soon afterwards, the ambulance arrived, then the police and then the health and safety executive. The site was shut down because it had now become a crime scene. Eventually, some months later I would meet Phil's family for a memorial service and discover much about his life. It was one of the most traumatising events I have ever experienced, but my trauma was nothing compared to that of Phil's family and friends.

Why am I sharing this? Later on that fateful day, we all had to give statements to the police and the health and safety executive. The site was shut down for about six weeks. Nothing moved. We weren't allowed to move the crane, or indeed anything on site. Nothing can move.

The incident resulted in a criminal case that went to court and I was called to appear at Winchester Crown Court as a witness. Sometimes terrible things happen. Sometimes it is avoidable, sometimes it is not. There are deaths on construction sites and sometimes they are accidents that couldn't have been foreseen. But sometimes deaths are avoidable, and you have a role as a developer that you are not allowed, and nor should you want to abdicate. According to CDM rules, you are the person required to oversee safety on your site, and I can tell you that if you are unlucky enough for anything to ever happen like that terrible incident that I experienced, when everything has calmed down there are going to be two questions in your mind. The first is a moral one: did I do everything I possibly could have done to keep everybody safe? Can I look that family in the face knowing we couldn't have done anything more? The second question is a legal question, because when people die or are seriously injured on site it gets serious – and rightly so. Your second query will be: have I done everything I should have done?

The first question is have I done everything I could have done? And the second one is have I done everything I should have done? There is a chance that you might end up in prison if you didn't.

Now I am not sharing this event with you to scare you. I am sharing this with you to impress upon you how you need to understand CDM.

As a developer, one of the things you do is make sure you are visiting the site. Make sure you make time for that in your calendar, and that you are there at the site meetings and the project review meetings.

Utilities

Utility companies tend to be incredibly disorganised and a hugely onerous administrative burden to work with. It is easy to parody the companies, because their internal processes are so poor and their internal departments don't communicate – there are so many different departments that a simple job often has to be attended by five or six different people because they all carry out separate tasks. One might dig holes, one might lay pipes, one might install meters, somebody else connects the meter to the pipes and yet another person will come to test and commission the connections. It's crazy, and the companies probably only get away with such preposterously poor structure and inordinately high costs because they have a monopoly and therefore don't need to compete.

The liaison with utility companies is one of the very first tasks to outsource once you have some developments in hand. Dealing with them personally will be a poor use of your time and will drive you mad. It is well worth £15 an hour on PeoplePerHour to do your admin for you.

In cost terms, we allow £1500 per unit per utility. So for instance, for electricity and water in a development of 10 units, you will need (£1500 x 2) x 10 = £30,000. The risks involved in this 'rule of thumb' are at both ends of the spectrum. With small developments of just a few apartments, you may be unlucky and require a significant upgrade, which could easily cost more than a few thousand pounds if they have to bring services over some distance or under roads filled with other services. If you have a large number of units, you may be required to fit sub-stations, for example, and they can easily run to £100,000 which could blow any assumption based on our rule of thumb! However, until you have firm quotes from the providers, £1500 per utility per apartment will generally work well.

Considering this rule further, you may also appreciate very quickly why we tend to remove gas from our developments. We cannot manage without water or electricity, but by removing gas we remove an additional cost with no real downside. There are perfectly good electric boilers that can run the 'wet' central heating systems that are preferred by most end users, so why go to the extra expense and technical difficulties of running gas into a building?

Building Guarantees

This is one of those items that you think you might need to do at the end of the project, or maybe you think you need to do it at the beginning of the construction phase, but our recommendation to you is that as soon as you have completed the purchase of the building you intend to convert, appoint your building guarantee company immediately. Get them involved early because you need to know what their requirements are. They will require an existing building assessment (EBA) and that will inform you what you are going to need to do to get your contract warranty. By carrying out this assessment early, you can ensure the work is costed and programmed into the ERs. If the building warranty guarantee provider is going to come on site at the beginning of the project, see if you can meet them as they tend to be a bit more 'human' when they meet an individual, and may take a more pragmatic view on some aspects of their recommendations for further work.

The building guarantee company is not a charity, it is an insurance company. The people there are going to provide a 10-year guarantee on your apartments and will require you to carry our any works that they believe mitigate their risk of having that guarantee called upon. The warranty is for the major structural elements of a development to do with the integrity of the apartment, such as windows, roof, walls, insulations, etc. They will not be concerned with dripping taps and leaking pipes that appear in year three or so. They are there to ensure that the property is safe and of adequate construction and accordingly, they will require the apartments to comply with building regulations, and sometimes require you to go even beyond that standard.

On a side note, if you are holding your units you don't necessarily need a building guarantee, but bear in mind that if you don't get a guarantee sorted and you change your mind and decide to sell some or all of the units, you may not then have that option. It is very difficult to sell what are considered new build units by the lenders without a building guarantee, so unless you are absolutely sure that no matter what happens, come hell or high water, you are going to hold those units, our recommendation is that you get a building guarantee company in.

When we have a building guarantee company appointed, they will appoint a surveyor to carry out the EBA. That surveyor will come to your building (the perfect time is just after strip-out because they will see the bare bones of the building), they will say "for you to achieve our warranty, you need to do x, y and z". It could be you need to change all the windows because the existing windows do not have a FENSA guarantee. It could be you need to rebuild the roof, it could be that the insulation needs replacing, it could be anything. Anything that gives them discomfort about their ability to provide a warranty at minimal risk to them will be identified as needing replacement, removal or refurbishment. So you get them in early because if there is a chance you have got to replace any of those items, wouldn't it be a good idea to have them in the building contract? Be on site for their visit. It is just about turning up, being friendly and asking intelligent questions about any of the larger items they identify need doing: "Is there another way round that? Could we possibly refurbish rather than replace? If I can get hold of the existing warranty can we avoid the need to replace?" etc.

The warranty providers will require retention funds probably paid into escrow. It can be £1000 to £1500 per unit, which shouldn't hurt you too much as long as it is included in your deal analyser and you have funds set aside for it. Be careful to look at the small print when you are starting out, as much of the detail about when you will need to pay out funds for the warranty are not immediately apparent. There are plenty of building guarantee companies out there, so shop around for the best quote and the best deal with regard to extra funds that need to be set aside.

The retention will go into an escrow account to be held until the defects liability period has passed, ensuring that if the contractor doesn't return to sort out final issues and the developer has disappeared, that funds exist for the warranty company to solve the problems. An escrow account is simply a bank account which is effectively held to order. Nobody is allowed to touch it, and the money is quite safe and should eventually be returned to you. But of course while it's sat in the bank it can't 'work' for you elsewhere, so it is worthwhile trying to minimise the amount.

Another key consideration is the size and type of warranty company you decide to use. On early office conversions, Glenn decided to use a large, well-known warranty company to provide cover that was acceptable to purchasers' mortgage lenders so that he could sell the flats afterwards. In choosing the warranty company, he naively thought if the building regulations inspector had signed something off that it would be accepted by the warranty company's surveyor. Unfortunately, nothing could have been further from the truth – the warranty company's surveyor spent the next few weeks digging (literally) into everything on site to try to find potential problems that might mean that the warranty company would have to pay out later. This resulted in an unnecessary linings, lintels and other upgrades, which the building regulations inspector and builder viewed as unnecessary. The total cost of these things was over £80,000, which came straight off the profit on this project.

We also learnt the hard way that these warranties are only there for the benefit of future buyers and that as the developer, you are liable for the cost of repairs anyway; the warranty only really acts as insurance should the developer go bust in the first few years after the development is complete. Pick your warranty company carefully and use one that accepts the building inspector's reports, so if the correct building inspector is used and the building inspector signs the site off as approved, so does the warranty company. Having this joined-up approach saves a lot of time and money.

Insurances

Insurance is harder than you might think to organise for developments, so you need to make sure you have a good broker who knows what they are doing, knows the exclusions, knows the property development sector specifically and also knows how the cover required changes as the project proceeds. As previously mentioned, the cover required for vacant buildings is different from that required for a building being stripped out, which is different again from a building under construction, which is different again from one that is finished but not yet occupied which, once again, is different from the cover required when it becomes occupied. Do not be tempted to try and reduce the premium by not giving full disclosure. Keep in touch with your broker, keep them informed of what you are doing, because you don't want to find out you have a problem, only for that problem to get worse because cover hadn't been arranged for the stage of the project you were at. Get a competitive quote from your broker, but the quote is the quote. Whatever it costs to get the right insurance, pay it – you'll have the comfort of knowing that if something does go wrong, your insurance is valid and will pay out.

Snagging

Snagging is the process by which faults, omissions or examples of sloppy workmanship by the contractor are identified for rectification before the contractor leaves the site. Ignore the temptation to think you can personally walk round and snag your own apartments. Even if it was true, the strong recommendation to you is to find a friendly builder, or an experienced project manager, and use them to pick up snags. Even if you can do it and do it well, it will not be a good use of your time. Experienced builders, project managers and QSs look at things very differently, and they will walk round and pick up snags that we would never see because they know what to look for.

Snagging is another task like utilities – it can become an endless list of calls, so we would suggest you try to implement a snagging process similar to the following:

1. The project management company or the architect that is doing your contract administration snags the units for the contractor first. They will go in, look at where the 'finished' product doesn't comply and provide the contractor with a list of items that need improving or fixing. That is the start of your snagging list.

2. The next snagging list is provided by the buyers or occupiers of your flats, but don't let buyers snag the unit until they have exchanged, otherwise you could end up with a whole list of things they want done, and then they may never buy the unit anyway! Further, what they might do is refrain from exchanging until you have done all the work they want, and once they have you over a barrel like that, the list of snags can become an endless list of very minor issues, such as tiny paint splashes, uneven grout or flooring that doesn't quite feel level! Instead, only when the buyer has exchanged and is committed, you then let them do one snagging exercise and that snag list gets added to the main list started by your contract administrator. You must never have more than one snagging list for each apartment, simply add the consumer list to the contract administrator list. The contractor then works through the list until all works are finished.

3. In the home pack (which we will talk about in the chapter on exiting the deal) that you leave, you do not, under any circumstances, give the owner of the flat your company contact details because you will get bombarded with emails and calls, and if give them your address they will come and knock on the door! No matter how much detail you provide in your home pack, and how many instruction manuals you provide, your buyers and tenants will still contact you if they can to ask you the most basic questions with regard to how the appliances in the apartment work! Leave a note in the home pack that says:

    a. If you think your issue is serious and affects the habitability or safety of your apartment, please contact the building warranty company.

b. If the issue is not serious and relates to the communal areas, please contact the management company that has taken over the freehold.

c. If the issue is not serious and relates to your own apartment, then please note it down and when the contractor returns in x months (at the end of the defect liability period), the contractor will resolve your issue.

d. Please note that minor faults that occur after you take occupation, such as broken locks, leaking pipes or appliance failure, are not covered under your building warranty or defect liability period, and as such, they are the homeowner's responsibility to resolve. In the case of appliance failure, please refer to the warranties provided in your home pack and contact the supplier directly.

e. If you consider a minor fault too to be too serious to wait until [xxxx] (the end of the defect liability period), please contact the contractor directly on 01234 000 0000.

This 'waterfall' of contacts for the occupier makes it clear whom they should contact for what, and removes the developer from the call list. If there is a genuine snag, as the developer you don't have to be in the middle of it. The contractor is still on retention; if there is a genuine snag, the contractor has to deal with it, so the list above requires the consumer to liaise directly with the contractor on those faults. This avoids you getting stuck in an endless loop of calls and emails and from becoming the 'bad guy'. Furthermore, the contractor will find it easier to say no to you (the developer) than he will to say no to the consumer directly. So by taking you out of the loop, you are making the process better for the consumer as well.

Project Managers

The use of a project manager in your business will allow you to scale, add much-needed expertise to every stage of the project and help to increase your network of reliable contractors and service providers. Their role in your growing pipeline of projects cannot be over-estimated. If you wish to carry out multiple projects in parallel, then finding a good project manager is essential.

As soon as you find a project big enough to justify a project manager, meet with a mid-range company and discuss your plans for a conversion pipeline of projects. When Glenn did this, he requested that they assign the same project manager to all of his projects so that they would know what he did, how he worked, what finish he required, his specifications, his funding parameters and his timelines. In short, they needed to understand Glenn's business and know it well. Glenn and Justine didn't want to have to work with different people every time, teaching them on each occasion what they did. They met a director of the local Gleeds office and they agreed to their request to work with the same PM on every project. It has been a hugely successful arrangement thus far and is certainly part of the reason Ocea can run up to six or seven projects at once.

The selected project manager, backed by in-house QSs, has become an expert in commercial conversions and knows Ocea's product well. He has worked on every project they have undertaken and runs the project from the moment they start the conveyancing on the purchase of the building, arranging for surveys, soft demolition, project coordination and early liaison with would-be contractors. He coordinates design meetings, oversees communication, chases quotes and reports, and pulls together the design process. Once into the detailed design phase of the project, he prepares the tender and lines up possible contractors with good reputations that are interested in further opportunities, then he runs the tender and contractor selection process. Once on site, he coordinates the project review meetings, on-site meetings, QS reports and contractor payment valuations, along with the monitoring surveyor. At the end of the project, he and his team run the snagging process and agree the final contract sum payable to the contractor. He is an essential part of the team.

There are many project management firms in the UK, varying hugely in size and experience. Choosing a project manager is best done by blending referrals with a good interview process to identify someone who you believe has the requisite experience and who you can work with.

Simply put, if you want to scale, add experience and lighten your workload, find a good project manager as soon as you can.

Summary – Getting it Built

Now you can see why we believe you can make much more money with less work using this strategy. There is a plethora of experts out there that can be found and leveraged to help you on your journey. With expertise, experience, time and networks, they can bring your dreams to fruition, as long as you can provide them with clarity of vision. Larger construction projects are probably less scary than smaller ones given the higher calibre of professionals you will be dealing with; the days of dealing with small, unreliable builders, chasing sub-contractors and dealing with disputed fees and costs should now be behind you.

Chapter 12: Exiting the Deal

This is where we almost go right back to the beginning, because you can't think about exit when you are exiting – you should have thought about exit when you were starting. You have to begin with the end in mind.

By the way, did you know that this is what business is about? What most people do is start a business with no idea how they are going to get out of it, but actually entrepreneurs who are really successful, and usually serially so, get into a business to get out of it. They know how they are going to exit when they start, and everything they do is taking the business to that end. You can do that with your commercial conversion business. To what end do you want a commercial conversion business? What do you want to change in your life and how do you want your life to look? How long do you want it to serve you? How do you want it to serve you? Do you want cash pots or do you want cash flow, or perhaps both? How long do you want to be in this business, and how many hours a week do you want to work? You should build the business you want and that works for you by beginning with the end in mind. Later in this chapter, Mark and Glenn will be sharing their own, very different, approaches to exiting deals, and it is largely led by what they each want from life. They are both operating with the end in mind.

Do you remember the conductor analogy? Many of the instruments in the orchestra are playing at the same time, rather than one after the other. In an easy world, you would only do one thing at a time. You would go and find a deal, then do the redesign, then get a builder, then find an estate agent, etc. This strategy doesn't work like that (although it would be easier if it did). Not all the instruments are playing at the same time because that would sound chaotic, like white noise; instead, they are all coming in and out, blending to create a musical score that moves in sync. There are times where the score is really busy building to a crescendo, and other times where there is a lull and you almost can't hear any music playing at all. That is a fantastic analogy for commercial conversions because that's exactly how it goes. What you need to remember about exiting the deal is that it starts at the beginning and then weaves its way through the process. At the point of exit, you are building up to the final crescendo of this particular movement (deal) in the symphony that is your commercial conversion business.

Are you creating cash flow or cash pots? Create as many exit options as you can; you need at least two and preferably three. Whatever exit you choose, one of the key considerations for you is taxation.

Taxation

Purchasing commercial buildings for conversion to residential requires an understanding of the taxation system, unless you want to hand most of the spoils over to the exchequer.

VAT

The first important area of taxation to understand is VAT. The best way to deal with VAT on the purchase is by using a VAT1614D form, which you complete and serve on the seller solicitor of the building prior to exchange of contracts. You are required to also let the vendor know that you intent to issue the VAT1614D at the time of making the offer. It effectively states that you are going to convert the building into a residential building and that you should therefore not pay the VAT on the purchase. This has two benefits. Firstly, you don't need to register the entity purchasing the building for VAT and opt the building for tax prior to the purchase of the building, which can be time consuming. You also don't need to pay the VAT and wait three months (or longer when HMRC is being inefficient) to claim it back. In addition (and this is the most unjust bit), you don't need to pay stamp duty on the VAT which can't be recovered. Yes, you read that right, the government will charge you SDLT on VAT (tax on tax) and even if the VAT is recoverable, the additional SDLT isn't! You will often find that sellers or solicitors push back on the form saying they can't accept it or asking for further details. This is usually because they don't understand it or are concerned that they will be left out of pocket later if HMRC decides that the transaction wasn't processed correctly. In this scenario, it's definitely worth getting your accountant to contact the seller's solicitor to explain how the form works, why it is valid and how they therefore won't be hit with a big VAT liability.

You also need to consider VAT on the cost of converting the building. Generally, builders can charge you only 5% VAT on the conversion costs rather than the normal 20%, which is a big benefit. Some may not be used to doing this, but refer them (or write a letter to them and ask them to give it to their accountant) to VAT708, which can be found on HMRC's website via Google. This document explains what buildings and projects qualify for reduced-rate VAT. If you are selling the apartments you create from the building then you can generally claim this last 5% element of VAT back, as long as the entity that owns the building is registered for VAT.

If the purchase has a tenant in part or all of the building (which you may be looking to obtain vacant possession from later), it is usually the case that you can purchase the building under transfer of a business as a going concern (TOGC) rules. This means that you don't need to pay VAT on the purchase price of the building, improving cash flow as it will be in your bank for the three months or more that it would otherwise to take to claim back. In addition, you don't have to pay stamp duty on the VAT that you can't claim back. In this instance, if the purchase has been opted to tax by the current owner, you will also need to register your purchasing company for VAT and opt to tax to avoid the VAT charge.

VOA and Rates

Empty property rates are a big reason why many commercial buildings are not worth what it seems they should be. Being such a large part of the cost of running commercial buildings, they are often 50% of the rent the building generates. When the building sits empty, not only does the landlord lose the rent, but they then become liable for the empty property rates, creating a much reduced or often negative cash flow situation for the landlord. One way to mitigate this liability is to apply to the VOA to have the building removed from the rates list, so that empty property rates are not charged because the building is undergoing conversion to residential. This can be an elongated process, with the VOA often taking a long time to respond to requests for inspection. Once they do come around, it is important that they see that major building works are underway and that the internals have been stripped, meaning the building can no longer be used for the previous use, for which the VOA have been charging.

As there has been a court case on this issue recently, the matter should be settled and most VOA offices should now accept the principle that developers don't pay rates when a building is undergoing conversion, and council tax becomes due once the apartments reach practical completion. Unfortunately, the rules can be applied very differently across the country, and some VOA offices don't follow what most would regard as the rules. If you end up in this situation, it's often worth instructing a rates specialist to negotiate with the VOA to reduce or remove your liability. The council will not stop charging you rates until the VOA tells them not to.

For some projects in which you are waiting a while to obtain planning permission before the project starts and can't strip the property out, you might want to put a rates mitigation programme in place. It's usually worth getting a rates specialist to do this for you, which will often involve them moving in to the building for six weeks and occupying it with a number of storage boxes. Once this period of beneficial occupation has been proven with a licence or lease, and sometimes invoices to show the delivery of boxes or items that will be stored in the building, the local council should then award a three-month rates-free period. With this issue also having gone to court recently, most councils should accept this position, as long as the procedure has been correctly followed. Often there is a period where rates are due, as you can't always strip the building out for a variety of reasons. The rates liability may also have been assessed on a historical or outdated use.

A building that Mark purchased recently was assessed for retail but clearly had no retail demand, so a visit was required from the local VOA office to rerate the space. This visit took months to arrange and actually get an officer out, but once they came it was clear that the rates payable needed to be reduced, as a rating specialist had created a strong case. Thankfully the rates payable will usually be backdated to the date when the appeal was first lodged. Big landlords and funds may be unaware of these strategies and are often not close enough to the coalface to implement them, so they end up paying huge rates on buildings when they are empty, which can be a strong motivation for them to offload them on the cheap – this can be your opportunity.

Ironically, the VOA website can also be a good source of information for developers wanting to find out what the current use of a building is registered as and what the gross internal area (GIA – gross floor space/size) of the building is.

VOA data on the type of use a building has been classified under for council rates purposes (which is also useful to prove the planning use class) can be found at the following link:

https://www.tax.service.gov.uk/business-rates-find/search

Mark has picked up a number of buildings that on paper look smaller than they are, but after adding a floor in, using storage space by adding Velux windows or going up into eaves, a deal that didn't work suddenly becomes profitable. Going into loft spaces in buildings with pitched roofs can be an easy win. We frequently find spaces that didn't look like they existed at first glance, or on the agent's details. Good builders spot these, as the best ones know how buildings are engineered and can see when walls in certain positions mean that there is something behind that's not obvious.

Another good source of floor area is the non-domestic EPC register. As we covered earlier in the book, all properties need to be assessed by an energy performance specialist if they are to be let or sold, the register has a large number of properties on it. The most useful information in the document is the floor area, which is shown in square metres. This can be compared with the VOA data above and any other details you get from the agent. Working out a value per square foot of floorspace for properties you purchase, and also a price per square foot on converted residential buildings, should be at the top of your list. Knowing these metrics allows you to make quick decisions and see when a property is a great deal or is a long way from working as a development. Here is the website:

https://www.ndepcregister.com

Stamp Duty

Stamp duty is relatively simple on purchases of this type. You usually end up paying the non-residential rate of stamp duty, which at the time of writing is 0% on the portion up to £150k, 2% on the portion between £100k-£250k and 5% on the portion above £250k. We don't know any way (that ultimately works) of reducing this. There are lots of stamp duty schemes around that will claim to be able to reduce this. We have seen countless people use these and eventually find they end up with a big bill from HMRC with penalties, and a big loss when the company providing the service goes bust and you lose the money you paid them. Many will tell you that they are insured if they go wrong, but plenty of people have found that this insurance has significant exclusions, which means it won't pay out. Also, it is often based in a jurisdiction that means it won't be forced to pay out when the company providing the service isn't around any more to face the music. As mentioned previously, you really want to avoid paying VAT on purchases of this type, even if vendors push back, and you should use the methods we have outlined in the VAT section to help you do this. If you end up paying VAT on the purchase price ,you will end up paying stamp duty on the VAT. On a £1m purchase, the VAT bill would be £200k, meaning that you would pay additional unnecessary stamp duty of 5% on this £200k, which would be £10k.

Generally, accountants will advise that you use a Limited (Ltd) company to purchase commercial conversions. If you plan to sell the apartments post-conversion, you are effectively trading, so you might find it difficult to qualify for capital gains tax rates. Corporation tax within the company is 20% on profit (going down to 17% shortly), allowing you to build up a cash pile, which then allows you to make further acquisitions or loan capital to other Ltd companies you have that are making further purchases. It isn't until you draw this cash out for personal use, in simple terms and subject to some small allowances, that you then pay tax on dividends at a rate of 32.5% to 38.1%. Some developers have liquidated their company and subsequently claimed entrepreneur's relief, which is currently 10%, instead of drawing the cash out and paying tax dividends of 32.5% to 38.1%. The rules have changed on this recently and the process is now subject to further controls that your accountant will need to navigate. This is a moving and complicated feast, so it's really important that you discuss the project with your account before the building is purchased. But don't expect the taxation treatment to be the same when you have completed the building – such is the speed and number of tax changes at the moment!

Capital Allowances

The power of capital allowances on the purchase of commercial buildings can be immense. If compound interest is the eighth wonder of the world, then capital allowances are the ninth in a taxation sense. In simple terms, a capital allowances accountant can usually identify somewhere in excess of 20% of the purchase price of a building to be plant and machinery items, which are claimable as long as a previous owner hasn't claimed them already. These include (to name a few) wiring, heating systems, signage and air conditioning. On a £1m purchase, this could mean that £200k is available in capital allowances, which offset at a nominal rate of tax of 40% is an £80k saving in hard tax terms. Further allowances are available on plant and machinery items installed as part of the conversion in landlord areas outside of the apartments, such as corridors, communal lobbies, communal heating systems, communal fire alarms, wiring and pipes etc., which might add up to another £50k or £60k hard tax saving. It is important to establish that a previous owner hasn't claimed these allowances already (as they won't be available on the purchase cost if they have). If you plan to develop the building and sell the whole lot including the freehold – perhaps to a ground rent purchaser – you usually also can't claim these allowances.

Holding Investments

As Mark is an accumulator and believes that compound interest is the eighth wonder of the world, he is also firmly of the view that any conversion opportunity that ends up with you being able to hold the building at the end of the process has to be a better idea than selling, as long as the income yield it produces is high enough. Let's assume that you have a £10m portfolio of which 60% is subject to a mortgage (sometimes known as leverage) and the remaining 40% is equity that has been created through the conversion process, meaning you have around £4m in equity. If for the purposes of this example we assume that the capital value of UK residential property increases at around 5% per annum (it has increased on average at a greater rate than this historically over the long term), ignoring the returns from rent (income), you could assume that at the end of year one the net worth of your portfolio would increase by £500,000 (£10m x 5% = £500k). At the start of year two, your equity would therefore be £4.5m and the value of your portfolio £10.5m, upon which it is reasonable to assume that you may again enjoy 5% capital growth or £525,000, making your new equity £5,025,000 and portfolio value £11,025,000 (£10,500,000 x 5% = £11,025,000).

Notice that the growth you received this year is £25,000 more than the growth last year; this is because you are now receiving capital growth generated from the capital growth generated in the year before. This works in the same way that over time you receive interest on interest in a bank, or credit card companies make such a lot from charging interest on the interest that charged in the month before. The portfolio value becomes £16.3m after 10 years and £26m after 20 years at a 5% annual growth rate. This means that your equity would be £22m at year 20, which is a 550% increase on your £4m. The effect of compounded (and leveraged) returns is vastly greater in later years, as can be seen above. You are also receiving capital growth on the full value of the portfolio (£10m), which is a lot more than the £4m equity in the portfolio, and which includes the amount that the bank lent (£6m). As the bank's charge for lending this £6m (interest) is covered by the tenant, you aren't therefore paying for it from your own pocket.

Many of you (including Mark) will believe that the year one 5% £500k return on capital employed on your £4m equity is an infinite percentage return on investment because the equity was created from developing buildings rather than it having come about from cash you injected. However, some may say that this is actually a 12.5% return on capital invested (£500k / £4m x 100 = 12.5%) as it is still cash you have tied up. This is in addition to the income return, which could easily be £300k after all costs, and bank interest, which is also an infinite return using Mark's method of calculating return on capital employed (ROCE) or 7.5% (£300k / £4m x 100 = 7.5%) using the traditional method; added to the capital return of 12.5%, that is a ROCE of 20% (12.5% + 7.5% = 20% ROCE). The reality is that capital growth has been higher in the past, making returns better. Irrespective of this, most people would still believe that an overall 20% return on capital is unrealistic in wider investment circles. With the right type of investment property, it is commonplace once you take account of leverage.

The key to holding and getting a good return on investment is to create strong relationships with banks that like what you do. They will end up trusting you more and more over the years, and the rules and/or terms their new customers get, especially when dealing with the bank through a broker, are almost always inferior in terms of higher rates, lower loan to values and more rules that are likely to stop deals taking place. Typically, the refinance model on a block of conventional flats will be based on the capital value of similar flats in the local area. This may be knocked down because of what is often coined by surveyors as "concentration risk", as many apartments exist in the same block. Typically, with blocks of cluster flats where there are up to six bedrooms sharing a communal lounge/kitchen/diner, these have to be valued on a yield basis. These yields can vary a lot and you can frequently see the gap between the meanest and kindest surveyors being in excess of 30% difference in the capital value they attach to buildings.

Clearly, it's important to understand the methodology that these surveyors are using to ascertain what likely value they may put on your building. A call to them before a valuation is instructed on a no-commitment basis can really help guide you on what value you are likely to obtain in your area. Mark has seen yields on buildings like this range anywhere from 6% to 15% gross, depending on the surveyor and where in the country the surveyor is based. If you take the annual gross rent and divide it by these numbers, it won't take too long to realise that the difference between them can be vast, so it's an area worth concentrating on.

The aim is usually to try to get as much money back from the purchase and development costs as possible without ever letting the new mortgage go above the amount of money that is originally put into the property, including refurbishment works, professional fees, legals and any loan interest incurred on the project. It's ok to leave some money in these deals; the reality is that you will be achieving a much higher return on capital invested compared to anyone else investing in residential property using these methods anyway, so don't get hung up on getting every penny back on the refinance of every commercial conversion.

Selling Developments

On the other hand, Ocea currently sell everything they develop. In part, this is because Glenn has come from a background of debt and never having any money. To him, the idea of a big cash pot is appealing and flexible. Whilst he agrees with Mark about the eighth wonder of the world being compound interest, he prefers to see his wealth accumulating through the continued reinvestment of the realised profits and the level of returns generated by this amazing strategy. Even if you were to apply a conservative 20% annualised ROI to the reinvested profits, not only would his wealth accumulate at an astonishing rate, he would also generally have 'liquid' funds available in the event of an economic shock. The more cash that is released, the more Glenn will invest in the next project, thereby becoming not only the developer of the schemes they undertake, but also the investor, hence rapidly increasing his returns from each project.

Let's assume a deal that Glenn runs that is funded by £1.2m from investors and makes a total profit after all other costs of £1m. Assume the investment was made for a 50% share of the profits, the investor is paid £500k and so is Glenn. Assuming the deal took 18 months, the annualised return to the investor was (500/1200000)/(18/12) = 27.8%, typical of the returns available to some of his investors. In the next such deal, Glenn decides to reinvest £300k of his profits as an investor representing 25% of the investor investment return. This means that at the end of this deal, Glenn is entitled to two parts of the pie. First, he still gets the £500k as the developer, but then he also gets 25% of the £500k paid to the investors, namely £125k. If Glenn adds that additional £125k to his next development, he becomes 50% of the investor pool as well as the developer, increasing his return to £750k. Indeed, it is exactly this type of approach that Glenn and his business partner intend to follow, to the inevitable conclusion that ultimately, they can be the investor in all of their own deals.

Instead of growing their workload, Ocea has agreed to target doing just six deals per year, gradually investing some of their profits and thereby increasing their returns without increasing their time in the office. The current preferred 'exit' for Ocea is not to exit at all, but rather to pick a time when their role is simply that of an investor in other developers' deals, thereby making returns of circa 25% on a big cash pot with other people doing 90% of the work. The advantage of this strategy is that by retaining some profits to build up an emergency cash pot, and reinvesting some of the profits to increase the rate of growth of their wealth base, Ocea should be in a good position to ride out any economic storms and still have enough cash kicking around to enjoy the journey!

Selling and Holding

Of course, the reality is that whilst Glenn (through Ocea) will sell most of his developments, and Mark (through Progressive) may retain most of his, both Ocea and Progressive will employ a mixture of sales and holds, enjoying the very best of both worlds but biased towards their own views of what they each want life to look like. And that is the point. Whilst Ocea and Progressive operate in similar sectors utilising the same strategy, both want slightly different outcomes, and that drives their business. The same should be true for you if you are starting with the end in mind.

Geography also plays a part. If you are living and working in the south of England, then your primary option would be to sell the units. That is where the most money is, because there is a big gap between the cost of developing and the capital value of the units at the end. Your secondary exit, might be to sell with planning, because again in the south you have created so much value by getting the planning that even if you don't do the construction there is probably a high enough gap to make it worthwhile just flipping it back onto the market. Probably your last option in the south would be to hold in some way, whether that is through buy-to-let, HMO, multi-let or even serviced accommodation (SA). Each of these hold strategies works and can give you a huge amount of flexibility. Look at your local market, look at your requirements, consider your investor requirements and at what lending is available to you, and then come up with the best solution with all those things combined. But you should be doing this on day one, not on day 391 when you are panicking!

If you are in the north, it tends to flip almost the other way around, because your primary exit might be multi-let, HMO or serviced accommodation. There is a reason that people travel from the south to the north to invest in property: because the purchase price and the capital values are lower, so it is easier to generate significant rental yields further north. In this case, your secondary exit may be selling the units or holding for buy-to-let.

You know buy-to-let as a strategy is very long-term, gradual wealth building, but it is still a strategy. It's not as sexy as some of the other stuff, but you know it is still an exit for you. Your tertiary exit might be to sell with planning.

Of course, there is no absolute rule here. There are clearly areas in the north where the capital values are reasonable enough that you can develop to sell and make a significant profit. Just as there are areas in the south that are pretty run down where you might struggle to make a profit, but you would get some good rental yields. So please don't take this generalisation as absolute. Be very conscious about your area and what you are going to do in it with regard to both the most profitable exit and what you want out of the business.

See how it all comes together? If you don't know what you want, then you can't decide what area you are going to work in, what type of conversions you are going to do and what exit you are going to target because you are not clear about what you are trying to achieve. So bring the whole lot together, look at the area, the prior approval type if that's what you are using and how you intend to exit. This will drive the kind of investors you are going to look for and work with, which in turn will drive the kind of debt you can get because this is what you are going to need to know if you are planning to hold. Which lender are you going to use to refinance out, and what is their attitude to SA (as an example)? Are they going to wait for you to demonstrate the cash flow or are they going to give you a big amount up front? You need all this information before you start.

But location does not have to dictate the strategy if you are prepared to JV and travel. If you live in the south but you want huge cash flow and would prefer to hold, then maybe JV with people in the north. Conversely, if you prefer the idea of generating large pots of cash but live in the north, you may consider working with people in the south. But once again, whilst each area may be 'biased' towards one exit or another, a blend is usually available within an hour or two.

The Geography of Mark's Strategy

As Mark tends to want to keep the properties he sources, this usually involves letting to tenants, which then involves a management operation to look after them. Mark tends to purchase all of his developments in a relatively tight geographical area. For a management team to be able to visit, inspect and maintain properties, it became clear that trying to manage properties that are miles away or scattered across a wide area is difficult and time consuming. This is another reason why Mark's projects are often not offices but might be pubs, retail or other commercial buildings that do require planning permission. Trying to obtain planning permission for commercial conversion projects across a wide geographical area can become very difficult whilst dealing with multiple councils operating from different local plans and that have differing S106, CIL and affordable housing contributions thresholds and application methods. If you are buying buildings on an unconditional basis upon which the purchase is not subject to planning permission, it becomes very important to understand the local authority and the way in which they deal with planning applications. This game is about trying to create as certain an outcome as possible, and Mark finds that keeping these projects within a tight geographical area is a good way to achieve this.

The key to making money in Mark's mind is searching for something that works – testing it and then rinsing and repeating it many times over and over until it becomes boring. Once it becomes boring, it is clear that it works. You can then introduce people into the process, such as staff to help you continue with the model and roll it out on a large scale, keeping the interesting bits that you like doing (or that staff can't do as they are commercially critical, such as signing off the purchase of new buildings) to do yourself. Trying to look for new strategies just because the old one that worked became boring is a sure-fire way to become a busy fool – and leave huge amounts of money on the table from something that works. Getting into good habits like this is key to making business work, and it applies to development and conversion in equal measure.

Some years ago, Mark remembers a chap who was sourcing properties below market value on the internet. He had grown quickly, expanding much faster than those around him without gaining many of the lessons you inevitably pick up along the way. After a while, he realised that because he was running a strategy that meant that he had leads coming in from all over the UK, he was purchasing properties in a scattergun fashion across the country. By not grouping them together, he wasn't able to find a good letting agent, builders, surveyors, etc. in an area in a reasonable timeframe (you have to kiss some frogs and go through a few bad ones until you find the good ones). He effectively had to follow this process in every town where he had properties across the country and manage a huge number of relationships.

But it was worse than this. He didn't even have a letting agent and had decided that he could manage the properties out of his rucksack! Hooked on cashbacks that could be obtained from buying properties cheap from vendors for less than they are worth and getting the bank to lend more than the purchase price, he seemed to be focussing on using these cashbacks to pay the mortgages and live on them, rather than making sure the properties were well managed and using the resulting rent to fund personal consumption.

Some of the best deals that Mark has done have been pubs or drinking establishments that he has converted into apartments. One such project in the centre of Peterborough was a 13,000 sq. ft. drinking establishment. Operating as a rather average bar and restaurant, it was purchased from a national brewery that had let it to a local operator who seemed more interested in upsetting punters than providing a nice place to eat and drink. Advertised on an obscure commercial property agent's website, it had no board outside, an indifferent agent who required six months' notice for a viewing and who would only show people round at 3:45 on Thursdays. Ok, this is an exaggeration, but lots of commercial agents are pretty rubbish when it comes to marketing, viewings and generally getting you to a position where you make an offer. For this game that's

t – you should try and hunt these ones out! Initially putting in an offer
£550k, the sale ended up progressing at £450k due to further issues
ound with the building.

Extra care needs to be taken when conducting viewings of buildings like this,
especially when they are operating as a business. Many tenants won't take
kindly to you purchasing the building they lease and effectively pushing them
out of their business premises. This lady was no different. As the frequency
at which Mark went into the building "for a pint!" increased (which was, in
reality, to survey the available space), Mark would get stares that culminated
in abuse and finger pointing. "That's the arsehole that's kicking us out,
innit... wat a smug nob ed, bet he finks he will be able to make a go of this
place... well it ain't that easy mate". It looked like they hadn't realised that
Mark wanted it for residential conversion, and as he was careful not to let
on to them or the pub chain that owned the building for fear of competition
from other developers, they didn't find out until later.

Around the same time, a planning pre-application went to the council
to convert the building to apartments. As this is a confidential process,
the meetings were conducted and the confidence necessary to exchange
contracts to purchase the building was obtained without anyone knowing,
but with a good level of certainty that the council would support the plans.

He ended up creating over £1.5m in equity on this building, which showed
the capital value of the building as the gross rental income divided by
9%. Part of the reason for this was the cluster flat arrangement, which
helped to drive the capital value much higher than it would have been as
a block of flats.

By adding another floor into the building, thus creating another three
apartments, he added significant value out of what was effectively
free space. He took down the conservatory that was at the back of the
building and replaced it with a brick-built extension, which formed a new
flat. He also went down into the basement by unblocking windows and

creating innovative solutions to introduce light, such as high-level windows operated by motor.

The delivery of this project by the builder was quite late because he hadn't got enough men on site. This is why it is so important to have a contract in place with the builder that has time penalties in it so that the price of the job is reduced when it isn't delivered on time. This project was also progressed on a fixed price design and build contract, meaning that when issues were found with the building and extra work was needed. this was at the liability of the builder (to some extent, as variations can still cause the price to rise). Mark hadn't contracted him to repair the roof, as it had been assumed this would be ok. Unfortunately, it wasn't. The project incurred significant extra expense from re-felting and relaying tiles on the roof, as water started to come into the building. No matter how many surveys and people you have round to look at buildings, you will find things like this that catch you out. Always add 10% contingency onto the estimate build cost, often plus some extra on top of this. It's important to be careful not to tell the builder what you have done though, as the overall price will usually always rise to the level of the contingency.

This building also came with the benefit of a 20-year lease on the building opposite at a peppercorn rent, which had to be further negotiated as a purchase of the freehold with the landed trust that owned it. Wedded to demanding a high price per square foot, they made life difficult on the sale, which was only resolved because we were able to design the new scheme with a new floor, thus doubling the amount of accommodation we could squeeze in. Extras like this can make or break projects, so it's important to look for buildings that you can put extras in like this but that your competition don't necessarily understand.

Mark has also learnt over the years that choosing solicitors, builders and most professionals is certainly a case of horses for courses. For example, if buying a property which we inherently understand and is a simple purchase that needs to be done very quickly without fuss or unnecessary question- he will use a solicitor who practices a "legal light approach! " He certainly wouldn't use this solicitor if entering into a complicated option to purchase with a large developer where there was concern that they may wriggle out of the deal or try to chip the price down later. Likewise, a cheap local project manager may be ok for a small site where there is no lender involved, but larger sites may require a PM who is more adept at dealing with large issues and will charge commensurately larger fees.

Builders are no different. The larger ones with offices and lots of staff may be able to handle large jobs, but they can often be 20%+ more expensive that a smaller local operator. Even more so, Mark has found that the tier one builders that lots of the institutions and private rented sector funds like to use can cost as much as 40% more. Likewise, it is important to use refurb or conversion specialist builders on jobs like that and new build specialists or commercial specialists on larger jobs. Mark has learnt this the hard way, paying over the odds for small jobs or getting a cheap but very delayed and problematic large-scale conversion done by a builder that can't manage the job. Clearly choosing these guys comes with experience, but if you can get an idea of what work they do without necessarily telling them what type of project you have (so they don't just modify their answers to tell you what you want to hear), you are more likely to find out from them what their true specialism is.

It's also a good idea to become close to your professionals. That's especially the case for solicitors and accountants – you will find that they open up and help you a lot more in areas that present risk to them if they trust you. Between-the-lines conversations on issues happen a lot more often over a beer with a solicitor who you have got to know socially, when they don't feel that you may try to sue them if what they are telling you doesn't work for you. Often by taking sensible, calculated risks that a solicitor couldn't advise a normal punter to take in fear that they would mess up, you can increase your profits. Get close to these people if they are good, and treat them well.

Wormholes of opportunity appear all the time. As time goes on, and the law changes or banks decide to do something else or the government decides to change the planning system, an opportunity can disappear only for another to open. Those who don't network and don't employ an attitude of constant improvement and learning get left behind and don't make abnormal profits before competition increases and the market becomes normalised with normal lower levels of profit. Always have one eye on these new opportunities and have a fund you use to test and measure them in the discovery phase before you jump in.

Investing in yourself is probably the best investment you will ever make. Ironically, many people see value as spending money on objects rather than educating themselves or having new experiences that provide food for the brain. Grasp the opportunity here and understand that feeding your brain with good material or surrounding yourself with good people is probably the single most powerful thing that will help you grow. After all, you become the five closest people to you.

Time vs. Profit Quandary

The time vs. profit quandary is also one that should be at the front of your mind when assessing deals. Developments that involve a lot of hassle and time may not be worth it if there isn't a good chance of a healthy profit at the end. Many people don't assess the amount of time they need to invest in a deal to make it work, and they don't effectively cost this time in the form a notional salary that needs to be paid from the deal. A little like a percentage interest rate that needs to be applied to any cash you inject, you must cost this time to get a real understanding of what the overall all-things-considered return is from a deal.

It is also important not to be too swayed by what others are doing. Ironically, the worst time to invest or develop buildings is often when the most people are interested in doing it, as it indicates that you may be nearing the end of the cycle. Conversely, when things are really bad during a recession or downturn, people look at you strangely when you say you want to develop or invest in buildings. Mark has often found that these are the best times to invest. It's therefore important to ignore most people and focus on the few who have been around for a long time, investing at all points of the cycle, and preferably focus on ones that have seen at least one dirty recession.

Critics, or conversely lots of competition, don't make something necessarily bad. In the end, you need to rely on your own testing and measuring as it's the only way you will work out what works for you, with your skill set and with the resources that are specific and unique to you. Once you have found something that works, keep doing it. But make sure you also have other types of business in other sectors, or if something is particularly capital-focussed like developing, make sure you have other income-based streams that won't be affected at the same time as a development or building project may be, for whatever reason. Sometimes people are just jealous – this can manifest itself in multiple ways, and they may knock what you are doing. It's important to insulate yourself from this, and these people, as the toxicity that they can inject into you may be very costly to you over the long run. If you must have them around, perhaps it may be easier not to explain the new journey you are on.

Starting Out

Mark has found over the years that there is always an entrance fee to pay when entering a new market. He found this and paid dearly when he tried to invest in markets he didn't understand abroad. Clearly, each time you start something new, your costs will be higher and income lower, as you are still making mistakes which you will learn from over time. It's important not to go too big too soon before you have worked out what mistakes you are making and how to rectify them, so that future projects are free of these issues, increasing profitability. Even better, if you can watch other people go into markets and make errors that they share with you, your path to riches is likely to be shorter. Just be careful whom you take advise from; it's important that the person you are listening to has actually done what it is you're looking to do, as there are too many people down the pub who will offer opinions on things they know nothing about without being honest about this. It's also important to watch what people do in equal measure as what they say they are doing or what they are telling you is the best way to run a development or investment. Unfortunately, many are liberal with the truth and have ulterior motives in leading down a path that may not work or serve you, for their own means. So be careful.

Remember that it's also easy to do nothing, therefore taking no perceived risk. Taking no risk often results in actually taking more risk, as your money is getting eroded and the market is probably evolving, which is eating away at your business, income and capital. As much as it is a clichéd saying, change is inevitable and it's much better to be on the right side of it. There are too many naysayers who wrap themselves in cotton wool by taking what they view as no risk and encouraging others to do the same. Some, unfortunately, used to be developers and have seen many things go wrong or had extreme negative experiences that they haven't turned into positives by carrying on. Without being ageist, some of the ones Mark has come across tend to be older men. He has also noticed that he has become more resistant to change, and perhaps more cynical, as he has got older, and this hasn't always served him.

Your radar should be on the lookout for these people. Sometimes they may be overly negative about development or investment even if they have masses of experience, as they have made their money and it wouldn't improve their life if they took more risk to earn more money that wouldn't really make a difference to their circumstances. Some want to pull the ladder up now they have got to the top, as they don't want others to make them feel uncomfortable. It's important to see these people for who they are and to have a strong enough conviction to listen to them but verify what they say. If what they are saying is filtered through their overly-negative or glass-half-empty lens, then ignore. Trust but verify is a good way to deal with people: trust what they say but don't let it stop you checking up on their information to make sure it is true for the circumstances that you are faced with.

Building your knowledge, learning a strategy until it is 'boringly safe', then outsourcing it to your team is a hugely efficient way to build your wealth. It doesn't sound that exciting, but commercial conversions are a great way of increasing your portfolio at incredible speed. We don't know of many ways in which you can go and buy one building and turn it into, say, eight units that then get added to your portfolio. You can maybe have three or four of these projects on the go at the same time, so actually in a year and a half, even over the two years at the beginning of your journey, you could quite realistically add 20 or 30 units to your portfolio.

For example, Ocea is working with partners to develop a building in Southampton of 24 apartments that is in area suitable for SA. If Ocea retained those units as SA, they would probably make £1200 a month profit PER APARTMENT after all costs. 24 x £1200 comes to £345,600 a year in net passive income. Now it is only really passive if Ocea aren't at all involved, but do you think if they had £350k a year from one building that they might actually spend £30k a year to get someone to run it for them? So darn, now they are down to only £320k p.a. of almost entirely passive income... from one project! Commercial conversions can be a great holding strategy with great passive income.

Lenders currently offer refurbishment to rent funding and will then calculate how much you will get on the final re-mortgage even before you have started. So speak to them at the outset and be clear about your strategy upfront. Use your broker, as there are so many lenders out there all competing for your business. It is not a good use of your time to phone four, five or six different lenders, answering all their queries. Not only will you miss the people you have never heard of but it would be much simpler to provide all the information once to your broker, and let them liaise with all the different lenders and their queries.

Another benefit of using corporate finance brokers is that they know whose appetite is high. They know who has just come off of another big funding round and are flush with cash that they need to get it into the live market. They know which lenders like the north or when they prefer the south, they know which lenders require a good track record and which lenders are more prepared to work with people starting out that might not have much of a track record. Corporate finance brokers will save you a whole world of pain, and if you explain your strategy to them, pointing out that you would like to hold, they can set that up.

Some lenders perceive the risks associated with SA to be higher. They don't yet understand the model and they fear transient tenants means transient cash flow. Whilst we know that is not necessarily the case, some lenders haven't yet got their head round it. Most of them are traditional, and you may first have to refinance on the brick and mortar value of your finished development, and then go back maybe one to three years later to show them the evidence of your cash flow for a further refinance.

Sales Process

Selling your developments is a great way to generate large pots of cash. We discussed how you might use this earlier in the chapter, but in the end, it is for you to decide what you want your life to look like. If that needs pots of cash, then this strategy is one of the best out there. As ever, you will need to have started with the end in mind. And again, you should use your experts to advise you, and when you decide to sell, that drives you into the arms of the estate agents.

The estate agents local to your development are your experts, although that statement comes with a health warning! If they are a Saturday employee who sits at the front desk by the door, or the young person who has just come from selling used cars and hasn't got any experience yet, then they are not the kind of experts you want to be dealing with. Make sure you are dealing with the right person, the real expert that typically sits at the back of the office or possibly in a side room. The older, more experienced agents are essential to you as a developer, and if you are dealing with the land and new homes department you are probably going to get even better advice.

We recommend that if you are selling up to 10 units, try to find a well-established local agent of some years' standing to work with. If they have been around for many years, they will have a great 'black book' of investors and will really have their finger on the pulse when it comes to pricing. Ensure, of course, that they typically sell the type of units that you will be producing. Working with people that generally sell £1m houses is unlikely to help you move one-bed apartments of £100k or so very quickly. With developments of more than 10 apartments, try to find a good land and new homes department in the area. These departments are set up to help developers move multiple units, and the quality of their information and understanding tends to be more geared towards developments. They will be able to answer the sorts of questions you should be asking, such as "What is going to sell in that area?", "who is going to be buying?" and "what are they prepared to pay?"

Now if you are selling, you are likely to have two main types of buyers. Contrary to all the articles you read about the death of buy-to-let, investors are still investing. There is no doubt that we have recently seen a slowdown in investor activity as a result of the changes to tax rules and the more recent tightening on stress testing of BTL lending, but investors are still investing because they still know that the combination of cash flow and capital growth in property is the best, bar none. Real investors will adapt to the market place and continue to buy, particularly given the increase in BTL demand and growing rents. The property market is moving all the time – the rules change, the conditions change, the taxes change – the people who sustainably make money in property just adapt. Keep an eye on it, keep plugged in, know what is going on and adapt.

The other buyers are likely to be first-time buyers. Given the recent support of the government help to buy (HTB) policy and the units we produce being at the lower end of the market, first-time buyers are likely to remain one of our main markets for some time to come. We cover HTB later in the chapter, but while it remains available, it will continue to fuel and fill demand for buyers of the apartments we develop.

Once you are clear on your target market and their aspirations and pricing, share this information with your designers and architects so that they can design accordingly. Share the resultant floorplans with your selected agents and ask them to provide feedback. Remember, when you are dealing with people you need to get their buy in. They need to feel that they helped you and that they have contributed, because they love being the expert. They will be more 'plugged in' with you if they feel you have asked for and valued their advice, and when they come to sell your apartments they will feel a duty of care to you to sell your units because you listened to them and did what they said. The agents will tell you what the new build premium is in your area, because there is always a new build premium.

Most of the apartment stock on the market will be second hand. Just as a second-hand car is not worth as much the moment you drive the car off the forecourt and drive it 100 yards down the road, it is exactly the same with housing. You are creating new-build flats in your conversions, but the moment you have had a tenant in it for a month, it is not new and it will have lost that new build premium. This is inarguable and is also why the lenders have started reducing their loan to value on new build units, because they know as soon as someone moves in, it is worth less and their security is reduced.

Selling Agents

As mentioned already, for less than 10 units use a good local agent. Make sure they have been in the area for years, because if they have, they will have investor lists and loads of contacts. They will know who is looking, they will be able to pick up the phone and get people to your open day very, very quickly. Don't simply go for people who sound enthusiastic but can't give you masses of data on the lists they are going to call, the people they have been dealing with and all the people they have dealt with in 20 years.

In one of Glenn's developments of nine units, called Prospect House, he didn't even have a show flat. On the advice of the agent, all he did was hold an open day. The viewing public were stepping over building rubble, around scaffolding, looking at unfinished units but sold eight out of nine units in a weekend. That estate agent had also given Glenn the highest values of any agent in the area, so he wasn't simply selling them under value. But he was a local independent agent who had been in that area for 25 years and he knew everybody. He showed Glenn other developments that he had sold for other developers, and he was chosen by the developers on small developments because he knew everybody.

That is who you want if you are selling less than 10units. If you are selling more, then you really do need a land and new homes department, because you are going to need backup and good admin support. Typically agent's fees will be about 1.25% to 1.5%. We advise that you don't tend to try and push that fee any lower because the agents need to make money, and if you go lower than that, they are unlikely to provide you with the service you are hoping for.

EPC

You are going to have to supply EPCs for all your finished flats, but you are buying wholesale now and it should cost a lot less. If you want an EPC done on a one-off basis, it might cost £150, but for multiple units, you shouldn't be paying more than £60 at most, because one assessor will come round and do all the flats together and provide all of the reports. Often you will get a contact for the EPC assessor through the estate agent.

Open Weekend Sales Events

Make sure you are using your open weekends to sell off-plan. Use 'available soon' signage, dress the units, arrange professional photography with lots of lifestyle type shots and put together a sales brochure. If you want to know what to do about a sales brochure just go down to the local Bellway Homes, Barratt Homes or Taylor Wimpey Development and ask for their brochure. Do you think the big housebuilders might know something about selling houses? So we don't need to reinvent the wheel, we just copy them. Get their brochure and see if you find out on the back who produced it and approach them as a starting point.

The photographs shown above are the kind of lifestyle shots you want; Ocea has used these in a lot of their brochures. You want something that shows how the end product looks, without being apartment-specific. The bathroom could be any bathroom Ocea develop – they have used that image in almost every brochure they have produced, because it shows the right tile finish and appropriate white goods, taps and overall finish. Ocea has also used the kitchen picture a number of times, simply to show the specification, colours and flooring that we used.

Dressing Units

Once again, there is no need to reinvent the wheel. There is a reason that housebuilders bring their developments to market with the aid of show homes and marketing suites with glossy brochures – because they help sell their units faster and at higher prices. In most circumstances, on any development of four units or more, you should generate more profit from the uplifted sales values than you will have spent on getting a show furniture pack installed, and you can often recoup your funds by selling your show furniture to one of your purchasers, in any event. There are many suppliers that serve this market, but one you can rely on in your early days is Fusion Furniture. Fusion are very good for basic show home furniture and they work with a lot of housebuilders. They have different quality levels for you to choose from, and whilst they won't feature in Tatler or Country Living, they are more than adequate for our types of buyers. After all, we don't use a hammer to crack a nut.

Help to Buy (HTB)

Help to buy (HTB) is a government scheme that helps first-time buyers with the 25% deposit most lenders require for a new build development. As lenders will only go 75% loan to value, the government has offered buyers the option of borrowing 20% of the 25% deposit at low long-term rates, as long as the buyer can find the other 5%. The 20% loan needs repaying, but over the first 5 number of years the buyers don't have to pay any loan fees. Thereafter, the buyers have to start paying interest, and that interest will gradually start to go up. It is a potent mechanism that really is helping some buyers get out of rented accommodation and into their first property. However, its critics have described HTB as the 'crack cocaine' of the property market, artificially fuelling prices and being taken up by buyers who have not considered the long-term consequences. The bottom line to developers, though, is that it helps sell more units – more quickly, and arguably at higher prices. It is quite admin-heavy and is another reason you will want an administrator early on in your journey.

Indeed, this is a good point to remind ourselves of all the tasks we have now highlighted as better undertaken by an administrator. You can hire someone to do your snagging, utilities liaison and organisation, building warranties administration, estate agent liaison and research, as well as help to buy – and we haven't finished yet. Later in this chapter, we will be adding plot sales and early liaison with block management companies. Given that list, it should be clear to see how someone costing just £16k to £20k a year will save you a whole world of pain.

At the beginning, you don't even need to employ them either. Set up a process document by recording yourself saying what you do and what you need them to do. Then find suitable help on PeoplePerHour, My VA, Upwork, and many other sites out there and send them your process document. Test them and your own process by getting a number of different people to use and test your process, to see which people would work out well. Note the people that give you good feedback, find out how to deliver what you want, and work to improve the process and deliver against it reliably. Whilst you don't necessarily need to employ someone at the beginning, as soon as you get two or three developments, we would recommend you hire an administrator full-time; they will be busy, but you will be free to concentrate on the more important matters such as further deals or money.

HTB not only helps you to sell your apartments more quickly, it also helps you to get a higher value because the buyers are less sensitive to the price, given that they are only coming up with 5% of the deposit, not 25%. If they find a property that meets their needs in an area they want to be in and it happens to be your flat, they are less likely to be concerned about paying £2,000, £3000, £5000 more for the flat, because they are only coming up with a small portion of the uplift in price. 5% of an extra £5000 is just £250 for them to find, and they would rather have the flat they want for an extra £250 than buy another one that doesn't have help to buy on it. It is a big advantage.

The other advantage with HTB is that fewer buyers 'fall out of bed' because they don't want to risk losing the government funding. Not all new developments offer HTB and the buyers can tend to suffer from a fear of missing out. We need to be aware of the risks of our buyers withdrawing from purchases and the impact it can have on the time taken to sell a development. The average sale failure rate for first-time buyers is one in three, so if you have got nine units, how many sales are going to fall over? Most people will answer three (9/3=3) but the answer is four because if three fall over, you have then got to resell those three, and one of those is going to fall over! Consider the implications of those sale failures if they occur late in the sales process. If they each fall over after 12 weeks and then you have to sell them again, and then the second one falls over after another 12 weeks, you have just spent the best part of six months not selling a flat. So, you want to do everything you can to make sure that people don't fall over, and help to buy is a great way of reducing that risk.

Reservation Fees

Another method of reducing the risk of sale failures is to increase the amount of your reservation fees. If you are on a HTB scheme, you are limited to £500 for the reservation and you can't make it non-refundable, as they are the guidelines stipulated by the government for anyone offering the HTB scheme. However, for anyone not using HTB, you may want to increase the reservation fee up to as much as you dare. Many estate agents discourage this because it can be seen as barrier, but as a developer you do not want tyre kickers. You want people who are serious, have considered their finances, arranged funding and are committed to the purchase. You want a sale that is going to go through. By charging a higher fee of something like £2k and making it non-refundable (or at least refundable only in certain circumstances), you are dis-incentivising any buyer that is not fully committed. Someone is not going to want to put down £2k if they think they might lose it.

Legal Fees

It will cost you a minimum of about £725 a unit to sell through conveyancing. Initially you may have to pay a bit more, but ensure that it is accounted for in your deal analyser. Because on bigger schemes those kinds of fees soon rack up. This may be slightly less expensive further north but much will depend on the volume of your sales.

Exchange Deadlines

Another recommendation copied from the big house builders is to put an exchange deadline into your reservation form. If people are going to withdraw, it is much better for everyone if they fall over early. If they are made aware that if they haven't exchanged within six weeks of signing the reservation form, you are going to offer the flat to someone else, they are likely to chase their solicitor more often, arrange their funding more quickly and generally chase the transaction with more fervour. Therefore, if something does come up that precludes them from buying the purchase property, it is likely to become clearer sooner. You might not choose to carry out your threat, but it should have the effect of at least focusing their minds.

Addresses

An Ocea development in St Mary Street, Southampton had its original entrance off St Mary Street right opposite the well-known music pub The Joiners Arms, where lots of famous people have played. Among others, Adele and Oasis played there when they were new and relatively unknown. It is loud, it is noisy and a great night out, but you probably wouldn't want to live right opposite it! The front door to the development was just 20 yards across the road, so the address and entrance location was not entirely helpful. However, on the other side of the development building is a park, and the address sounded a little nicer: St Mary's Place. So we agreed with the local authority that we could use a new entrance onto St Mary's Place, and we also changed the name of the building from 63-65 St Mary Street to Hampton House, St Mary's Place. This made everyone think of Hoglands Park instead of the Joiners pub and gave an altogether different impression! It's impossible to know just how much difference it made or how much extra revenue was banked as a result of this change, but it definitely made a difference, and we would rather have that positive difference in my pocket. It is always worth considering what you can do about addresses and whether new entrances can help the aspect of a development.

Welcome Packs (Home Packs)

Put a welcome pack into flats, otherwise you are going to get a raft of phone calls asking how the oven works, how the heating works, how the door entry system works, etc. In any event, as a developer you want to say welcome and make it all easy for the new owners to move in and enjoy their new property. The good news is that you don't put the welcome pack in there, the contractor does! You simply put the requirement for a pack in the contract, tell them what it has to look like and what has to go in it and they are required to produce it as part of their building contract, leaving it in the flat when they leave. Job done. Another example of leveraging professionals to do the work for you.

Title Splitting

When you pop into a high street coffee shop and buy a slice of cake for £2.95, you are the victim of title splitting! That cake probably had about 10 slices, making the whole cake's value about £29.50, based on coffee shop pricing. However, you can go to a wholesaler and buy virtually the same cake for about £9.50; that, in essence, is title splitting! When you buy a big building and divide it into smaller units, you are benefitting from the same principle. Some property investors specialise in buying freehold blocks of flats, doing virtually nothing with them other than splitting the building into lots of smaller leasehold units, selling the units off piece by piece and reaping the uplift in profits. By the way, that is also how many people make money when they break up failing companies; they buy companies that are close to bankruptcy or running out of money, and just sell the various bits off piece by piece, generating more revenue than they paid for the whole.

There is a difference between us as developers and the coffee shop cake though. When we buy the cake, we throw away the wrapper. But with property, the wrapper is worth a lot of money! If the leases are drafted correctly, being fair to both the leaseholder and the management company, there are many buyers out there interested in purchasing the freehold 'wrapper'. This a complicated and technical area, though, so you won't be surprised that our number one tip is to find an expert. We use a chap called Bernie Wales, who until recently spoke extensively on the subject and now focuses solely on providing an end-to-end service from drafting the leases, calculating service charges, splitting the title, liaising with the conveyancers, taking on interim management of the block and then finally selling the freehold to the end buyer.

When we sell a flat, we are simply selling the right to rent or occupy that flat, typically for 125 years. Let's just be clear, that's what a lease is – it gives that person the right to occupy that flat in return for paying a monthly fee, or in return for paying a one-off fee upfront if they are buying. The lease for a rental is actually very similar to the lease for a purchase, but with the purchase you are just paying all the rent upfront. What happens when you split a building up into apartments is that you create a lease for all those apartments, and the leases are sold off if you are selling. What you are left with is the wrapper (the freehold) that holds all those little boxes called flats. You still have a big box (the building freehold) that holds all the little boxes. Now, each of those little boxes has to pay what is called a ground rent for the right to occupy its space in the big box; what you can do is sell the big box full of little boxes. The value of the wrapper (the building freehold) is calculated by multiplying the number of apartments you have created (the number of little boxes) by the ground rent – i.e. what is being paid by the little box holder for the right to be in the big box – by a multiplying number, which will typically be somewhere between 20 and 35.

Let's put that a different way. Ground rent times the number of units (the total of all the ground rents added together, if that's an easier way of remembering it), times a multiplying number, which will be between 20 and 35. So let's say a block of 10 apartments each has ground rent of £200. That is £2000, times a multiple of let's say 30 = £60k. That is your freehold value, and you can sell the freehold to management companies that specialise in holding these wrappers for many years, making money from the management and lease renewals.

There is a challenge in the market at the moment: some unscrupulous developers were drafting leases wherein the ground rent doubled every five years. This was ridiculous and unfair and has seen a market backlash. The market response to these unfair leases is still working its way through, but it may be that we see ground rents limited to a percentage of the property value. Nationwide, one of the biggest lenders has indicated that they may not lend on any property where the annual ground rent is greater than 1% of the property value. Typically, ground rents have been nearer to 2% of property value, which in our area means a flat might sell for £150k but we have ground rent of £250 or £300. Hitherto, this has not been an issue to our buyers, or indeed their lenders, but we may see some downward pressure on ground rents soon.

PART 3: THE WAY FORWARD

Chapter 13: The Future of Commercial Conversions

The current government has promised further permitted development rights, including air rights for buildings, potentially allowing you to build up to the level of the two buildings either side. This would create some form of air rights for existing commercial buildings, which means that planning permission would not be required for extending these buildings upwards. Clearly there will need to be some checks around light and the usual B1(a) office to residential checks around environmental, traffic safety and noise issues, but nonetheless this will be an exciting progression.

B1c Light Industrial units can also now be converted under permitted development to residential or C3 without planning permission up to 500 m². This may be enough space for around 10 or 11 flats once you take account of circulation space in the building. Many of these buildings are on industrial estates, so works are likely to be required to the externals of the building, which will require planning consent. It's also important to understand how much demand there may be for the apartments to rent or sell if the building actually is on an industrial estate. Mark has been surprised at how these apartments do still rent and sell, just for lower values than better locations. As conversions like this can also establish the site as a residential site once complete, if there is land that comes with the building, you could then look to develop this into housing subject to planning, which may be easier to obtain next to an already converted apartment building, even when originally zoned for industrial.

Mark has heard many say that this is a moment in time, and that when these buildings are converted, developers will go back to developing new build sites. This may be the case to an extent, and specifically with office conversions we can see that the supply of offices will reduce over time as more and more get converted. Indeed, in Peterborough this has largely happened. The reality, however, is that industries will die and the buildings that have been developed to house them will therefore have no use. As we go through further cycles, this is likely to continue to take place on new and differing types of buildings, the value of these buildings will drop and they may become ripe for conversion.

The key to getting buildings that work for permitted development is to jump on new buildings with which you can use the new rights as they are confirmed by your planning consultant or architect.

Glenn's view on the poor state of most planning departments putting a brake on development, alongside the generally accepted view of the success of prior approval, means he believes we may see further prior approval legislation in the future. However, prior approval is not universally popular and may well be a hugely political game of football. There is an opportunity now, though, and one that is unlikely to be unravelled in the next five years or so. Beyond that, adapt, survive and thrive is always an evergreen strategy.

Chapter 14: Conclusion

Commercial conversions are not new. Adaptations of buildings between uses has been going on since buildings were first erected. The popularity of the strategy at present is probably down to just two main factors: market conditions and the introduction of prior approval legislation.

Wherever you are based, whether north or south, whether you are in England and can use prior approval or are outside England and relying on full planning consents, whether you want cash flow or to generate cash pots, whether you like holding assets or selling them, this is a strategy that can work for you. Whatever your experience level, there are experts out there that you can leverage, JV partners you can work with and commercial conversions that can generate life changing sums of money for you.

Whether you choose to use prior approval or become an expert in a particular planning strategy in a given area, there are opportunities to be secured. Just one or two deals can generate enough funds for you to become a full-time property developer/investor, and from there on, exactly what your business looks like is simply down to what you want to achieve and what you want your life to look like.

By employing our proven system, you can be sure that GOing LARGE is going to work for you, should you work hard enough for long enough. Get Outsourcing, Locate deals, Arrange funds, Redesign, Get it built and Exit the deal is a system that Glenn and Mark have now taught to hundreds of people and is being used to change lives. As with all strategies, it only works when you do. But with that initial dedicated impetus, and a determination not to quit until the first deal has been secured, life can be changed by this strategy in a way few other strategies can rival.

Go out and find the deals. Tell everybody what you do. Be excited and share the excitement at every opportunity you get. Consistently applied action generates momentum, and momentum generates results, and results can be a lot of fun! 100% of people who give up, fail. But to those who determine that they will not stop: your life is about to change! Re-read this book again and again until you have the system down pat. It can be truly transformative and we want nothing less for you.

If you feel like you want to know more, get in touch with Progressive Property or Ocea group at the contact details below. This book has given you the bones of a proven system to true property wealth and we wish you every success as you seek to deploy it in your own life. GO LARGE!

If you would like to learn more, contact Progressive Property at hello@ progressiveproperty.co.uk or on 01733 898557 and ask about our commercial conversion training opportunities, or follow Mark and Glenn on Facebook and Twitter.

Appendix 1: Prior Approval Types

Class O Prior Approval Office (B1a) to Residential (C3)

This is a change of use of an office building and any land in its curtilage subject to restrictions, qualifications and conditions. In May 2016, this prior approval was made permanent.

Main qualifications and conditions (summary only):

- Class B1a is now a permanent prior approval.

- Building's lawful use as an office on or before 29th March 2013 has to be established.

- Class B1a only covers the change of use of the building, not the building operations or external work you might have to do to make the scheme work. All of the externals will require separate planning permission unless very minor and that won't constitute material change to the externals of the building. It is safe to assume that most external changes would need separate planning permission. Although you can submit your planning application at the same time as prior approval, it is recommended that you establish the change of use first by obtaining prior approval and then apply for planning for the elevation changes. Once the change of use is established, the council is limited in what they can look at in terms of changes.

- The whole building and any land in its immediate curtilage can be developed, but not parking areas without planning permission.

- No new exempt regional areas are to be created. Existing exemptions may remain in place for a further three years until 30th May 2019, after which councils will have to impose Article 4 directions.

- Be aware – more councils are now imposing Article 4 directions around prior approval. Check the council's website to check whether they have done this as some areas are now effectively removed from this prior approval class (e.g. Bracknell).

- New prior approvals will now have three years for completion from date of decision. Completion is a grey area, but it is currently thought that, whilst all units may not yet be occupied, they will be complete and ready for sale or very close to it.

- Excludes safety hazard areas, listed building or curtilage and Article 2(5) land (certain local authorities applied for parts of boroughs to be excluded from the 2015 PD rights – a lot of London Boroughs, East Hants, Vale of White Horse, Stevenage, Ashford and parts of Manchester).

- Exclusions do not include conservation areas (CAs), areas of outstanding natural beauty (AONB), national parks or sites of special scientific interest (SSSI).

Class M Prior Approval Retail (Class A1 and A2) to Residential (C3)

Class A1 and A2 uses cover retail services, where the general public walk in and out of the premises and can utilise the services at any time, such as a bank or building society. Solicitors' offices can be confusing, because use class may include solicitors or accountants, but it is easy to argue that as people do not walk in off the street and use the services without an appointment, the main part of the business is office and should therefore be classified as B1a.

There may be mixed use in this case, so be aware and check the use class.

Laundrettes, betting shops and pay day load shops are 'sui generis' and have a use class of their own, but for the purposes of permitted development they are treated as shops.

Under this class, unlike B1a for office to residential, the PD rights exist that allow the change use of building, but also building operations necessary to convert parts of the external fabric of the building like doors, windows, cladding and other external changes necessary to implement the Change of Use.

Developers can include any external changes in their prior approval application and, as long as they are reasonable, the planning officer should approve them. This does not include extensions to the building, which would require a planning application.

Main qualifications and conditions (summary only):

- Retail use must be lawful and the building must have been in use on 20th March 2013 or in use for retail as the last lawful use, so the PD rights can apply to vacant properties.

- Be careful retail use must not have been granted under other PD rights.

- A1 and A2 prior approval allows you to develop 150 m² of the cumulative floor space. There are ways to maximise this.

- Unlike offices, you cannot use these PD rights in conservation areas, national parks, SSSIs, areas of outstanding natural beauty or listed buildings.

- There are no Article 2(5) exceptions with A1 and A2 permitted development rights.

- In addition to the conditions of Class B1a (offices), councils can also look at all the impact of the proposed development on the shopping area.

  There is a very vague description of what this means: "prior approval will be reviewed as to whether it is undesirable for the building to change because of impact of change of adequate provision of services as a shop but only where there is a reasonable prospect the building could be used to provide that provision…"

For example, in a defined village centre where the council has a black line around the area in the local plan and a policy that applies to that area regarding the percentage of non-retail uses for properties in the village, there might be a concern that if the shop isn't vacant, prior approval would not be granted. If the shop was a charity shop or other non-essential service, then it could be argued that the development will not affect the functioning of the village in the same way that a post office, chemist or only provision shop would.

This will very much depend whether there is a key shopping area defined in the local plan or any policy related to shopping. You will need to know your council's local plan.

- With Class A1 and A2, the council cannot look at the internal layout. Their review and approval only relates to external changes. Application includes conversion and how the building has been split into units and elevational changes. Councils can only look at the external windows and doors to decide if they are essential and they like them.

- Completion has to occur within three years of prior approval date.

Class P Prior Approval Storage and Distribution (Class B8) to Residential (C3)

Permits the change of use of a building and its curtilage from distribution and storage uses (B8) to residential use, subject to restrictions, exclusions and conditions.

- The curtilage has to be very tight and will not include any land around the building, which can affect your plans to put in cycle and bin stores and other services.

- This is a temporary permitted development right and will expire in 2018, so residential use has to have begun before 15th April 2018.

- In this class the building must have been used solely for that purpose for at least four years prior to residential use starting. Developers have to provide evidence of that, which can be quite testing. Historically there must have been a chunk of four years for that use, not necessarily just prior.

- Gross floor area developed cannot exceed 500 m². If the floor area exceeds this limit, then you cannot convert the whole building under permitted development rights.

- This right does not apply in areas of outstanding national beauty, national parks, SSSIs or listed buildings/buildings in the curtilage of a listed building BUT can apply in conservation areas.

- This permitted development covers the use only, so, like Class O (B1a) approvals, any changes to externals have to have a separate planning application.

Class PA Prior Approval Light Industrial (B1c) to Residential (C3)

Permitted development applications cannot be made before 30th September 2017.

Main qualifications and conditions (summary only):

- Must be solely in light industrial use prior to 19th March 2014. Developers will need to provide evidence of this.

  Light industrial is quite vague. It is defined as industrial use that can take place adjacent to residential use so is quite loosely interpreted but some examples could be an artisan workshop or photographic studio. Check with a planning consultant if you are unsure as some uses are described as light industrial but are more akin to general industrial in their defined class use.

- This is a temporary PD right and expires 1st October 2020. To be on the safe side, to engage in a conversion of a light industrial unit, submit the application any time after 30th September 2017 but no later than 30th June 2020.

  When the government comes to review this right it may well be extended, but this is unknown until they see what the uptake is.

- Restriction on floor space 500 m^2.

- Again, three years to complete from date of being granted prior approval.

- PD Issues that can be considered are as per other use classes – flood, highways, contamination and noise. In addition, sustainability of provision of services is also considered. The schedule states, "where the authority considers the building to which the development relates is within an area that is important for providing industrial services or storage or distribution services or a mix of those services (which includes, where the development relates to part of a building, services provided from any other part of the building), whether the introduction of, or an increase in, a residential use of premises in the area would have an adverse impact on the sustainability of the provision of those services."

Class Q – Agricultural to Residential

Permits the change of use of a building and land in the curtilage to residential and allows limited building operations reasonably necessary to convert the building to residential use (external alterations). There is a very restrictive definition of curtilage, for example, access cannot be included in the permitted development. Basically, the curtilage is not really bigger than the footprint of the existing building.

Main qualifications and conditions:

- Has to have been in agricultural use on or before 20th March 2013, excluding hobby farming and mixed use such as holiday lets, horse breeding and possibly farm shops. If occupied after 20th March 2013 it will only qualify for permitted development after 10 years.

- Exclusions – agricultural tenants, listed buildings (but modern buildings in the curtilage of a listed building may benefit from permitted development), national parks, areas of outstanding national beauty, conservation areas, SSSIs, safety hazard/military explosives areas.

- Can't convert more than 450 m² of existing floor space within the same agricultural unit.

- Three dwelling unit restriction.

- Limited building operations (external alterations) – only allows installation of windows, doors, roof and partial demolition. Government guidance in planning states that no new structural elements are allowed under PD. However, planning permission is not required for internal alterations, so if you are reinforcing structural elements, this can be done without planning permission.

- PA matters are all the normal ones plus whether locational siting makes it impractical or undesirable to change the use. There is a very wide interpretation of this, but in practice it is meant to limit the conversion of the equivalent of a barn on a hill with no access and no services.

- The council can only look at those issues in the design or external appearance when you have proposed external changes to the windows, doors and new roofs, etc.

- Once again, three years for completion from date of prior approval

Appendix 2: Website Addresses for Site Finding

https://www.fleurets.com

https://propertylink.estatesgazette.com

https://www.christie.com

http://www.rightmove.co.uk/commercial-property-for-sale.html

https://www.morningadvertiser.co.uk

https://www.daltonsbusiness.com

https://www.eigpropertyauctions.co.uk